A HISTORY OF
CHRISTIAN EDUCATION
PROTESTANT, CATHOLIC, AND
ORTHODOX PERSPECTIVES

John L. Elias
Professor of Religion and Education
Fordham University

KRIEGER PUBLISHING COMPANY
Malabar, Florida
2002

Original Edition 2002

Printed and Published by
KRIEGER PUBLISHING COMPANY
KRIEGER DRIVE
MALABAR, FLORIDA 32950

Library of Congress Cataloging-in-Publication Data

Elias, John L., 1933–
    A history of Christian education : Protestant, Catholic, and Orthodox perspectives / John L. Elias.
        p. cm.
    Includes bibliographical references and index.
    ISBN 1-57524-150-1 (alk. paper)
    1. Christian education—History.   I. Title

BV1465 .E45 2001
268'.09—dc21
                                                                    2001037654

        10 9 8 7 6 5 4 3 2

Contents

FAITH IN WRITING

Faith is a farm in Canastota, New York:
    Jumping into the stack, flying with the birds
    Sleeping in the smell of freshly-cut grass fields.
    The scarecrow loses his stuffing and so do I
        I'm afraid of fire sometimes
        and the all-too-early frosts
        rains that flood the fields
        clouds that might not come.
    Dust in the balance and soil for the seed.
    Straw on the scale may not seem that much
        unless
            you're a cow
            or a scarecrow, or Rumpelstiltzkin, or
            a newborn child with nowhere to go.

Faith is writing a book:
    Adding to the volumes of wisdom to the stacks of centuries
    Caressing each paragraph and smooth page.
    Wondering will anyone ever read this labor of love
        critics are carnivores
        scholars are cynics
        wide acclaim is always too thin
        polite silence is a huge, dark, empty cavern.
    The death and life of ideas depend on the desire of a writer.
    Farming a good book isn't really important
        except if
            you're hungry
            you have students
            you are writing the Republic or John's Gospel or
            whatever someone may read two thousand years
from now.

What did you mean, Angelic Doctor, "It's all straw"?
Did you lose your faith?
Was this a plate piled high with piety
    when your palate for life had gone sour;
Or a manger of softest humility
    welcoming our finest hour?

David Coppola, September 1998

Preface

In introducing this book I have good reason for taking the liberty of making my own St. Bonaventure's admonition to readers of his *The Journey of the Mind to God* (1956): "I entreat the reader to consider the intention of the writer more than the work, the sense of the words more than the uncultivated style, the truth more than the adornment . . . " (p. 3).

In the many years in which I have lectured at Fordham University and other institutions no topic has so engaged my mind and heart as the history of Christian education. Introducing students to what the best minds of Christianity have written on the education of Christians has afforded me, and hopefully many of my students, a greater appreciation for the ministry of teaching in the church.

It is with some hesitation that I offer these lectures to a larger audience. Not being trained as a historian, I have not delved extensively into the rich social, cultural, and political contexts of the various persons and movements which I attempt to describe. What I attempt to do in this work, with a philosopher's perspective, is focus primarily on the history of the idea of Christian education.

This book details major developments in the history of Christian education. It offers a context for understanding present efforts among Protestants, Roman Catholics, and Orthodox Christians. The history explores major thinkers and practitioners who have influenced how Christians transmit their faith both to their young and to other adults. It also shows how Christian education has been influenced by major historical events.

The origins of Christian education are in Jewish practice as well as in the educational ideas of the Greeks and Romans. The Gospels present Jesus as an effective teacher or rabbi who used many ways to present his message. His teaching ministry was continued in the early Church through the preaching and teaching of his apostles and disciples. Christian education developed fully in this period when the Christian community, notably in the Alexandria of Clement and Origen, attempted to appropriate elements of the classical paideia into Christian education.

Medieval Christianity witnessed the emergence of more fully developed approaches to Christian education. The educational writings of Augustine of Hippo are authoritative. A lifelong learner and teacher, he wrote many treatises on education. Other key contributors to the concept of Christian education from this rich period include John Chrysostom, Gregory of Nyssa, Gregory of Nazianzan, Alcuin, Bernard of Clairvaux, Abelard, Thomas Aquinas, and Bonaventure. Institutions for promoting Christian learning also appeared in the form of monasteries, dioceses, parishes, and universities. By the end of this period one can distinguish a rational and intellectual approach to Christian education from a spiritual and affective approach.

Christian education was a principal component of the Renaissance humanism that shaped education in Europe and in those parts of the world where Europe colonized—the Americas, Africa, and Asia. The Italian Renaissance reintroduced Greek and Latin classical models that shaped literature and the arts. The Northern Renaissance in England and Holland, so ably fostered by the writings of Erasmus of Rotterdam, Thomas More, and John Colet, made a learned piety, *pietas literata,* an integral part of Renaissance education. The Protestant Reformers Martin Luther, Philip Melanchthon, John Calvin, and Urich Zwingli integrated elements of this humanism into their many proposals for reforming the Christian Church and its education.

After the Protestant Reformation two separate and competing strains of Christian education developed in the West. Roman Catholic education received its primary inspiration from the decrees of the Council of Trent. Its educational efforts were carried out mainly by religious orders of men and women, especially by the Jesuits, Brothers of the Christian Schools, and the Ursuline Sisters. Protestant education took root in the countries of Europe and later in the United States. Different emphases emerged among Lutherans, Pietists, Reformed Calvinists, Anglicans, Puritans, Quakers, and Methodists. Early education in the United States had all the marks of Protestant European developments transported to the new nation. Approaches to Christian education during this period included dogmatic or doctrinal instruction, Bible-centered instruction, and spiritual or affective expressions.

The greatest challenge to Christian education in the West came from the ideas on religion and education proposed by Enlightenment thinkers. Enlightenment ideas on religion included atheism and the rational piety of deism. Many of the chief figures of the Enlightenment wrote treatises on education in which they addressed the role of religious education: John Locke, Jean Jacques Rousseau, Claude Adrien Helvetius, Mary Wollstonecraft, and Immanuel Kant. Prominent educators included Johann Pestalozzi and Friedrich Froebel. Enlightenment ideas were essential factors in the establishment of national systems of education in Europe and the United States. In these countries there often flared up bitter conflicts among competing religious groups as well as between religious groups and the state. Christian education often became defensive against the efforts of competing church groups and the attempts of states to secularize it.

Protestant religious education in the past two centuries has undergone a number of significant shifts. During the Great Awakenings evangelists such as Jonathan Edwards taught by using highly emotional preaching. Horace Bushnell in the middle of the nineteenth century pointed out the dangers in this approach and advocated a slower process of Christian nurture. With the advent of Liberal Protestantism, the religious education movement under the leadership of George Coe and the newly founded Religious Education Association made significant use of the social sciences and educational theory in promoting a more disciplined approach to education. The rise of neoorthodoxy gave rise to a distinctive form of Christian education where theology was considered the clue to religious education. The present situation is marked by a richness of theological and educational pluralism. This period has also witnessed what many call the secularization of Protestant higher education.

Catholic education in the nineteenth and twentieth centuries has accepted the challenge of dealing with Enlightenment thought and liberalism. In the context of European liberalism John Cardinal Newman's *Idea of a University* is a classic work that has influenced education both within and outside Catholicism with its well-reasoned and passionate defense of a liberal arts education and the role of theology in it. The charter for Catholic education is undoubtedly Pius XI's encyclical letter on Christian Education. This letter espoused the neo-Thomistic or neo-Scholastic educational theory, which received its classic expression in the writings of Jacques Maritain and others. A significant turning point in Catholic education revolved around the decrees of the Second Vatican Council, which espoused openness to new forms of thought in theology and education. Creative thinking about religious education has entered Catholicism through the catechetical or religious education movement that began in Europe and flourished in the United States. The past two decades have seen a spirited debate on the mission and identity of Catholic educational institutions, especially those of higher education.

Closure is brought to this work by an exploration of Orthodox Christian education. This chapter affords an opportunity to revisit earlier forms of Christian education from an Eastern perspective. Orthodox education considers normative the conciliar decrees and patristic writings of the first five centuries. Education in the Byzantine Empire developed its own modes of inner or mystical and outer or classical learning. While Western captivity of orthodoxy snuffed out much of the richness of the Orthodox tradition in theology and education, the renewal of Orthodoxy in Russian Orthodoxy has led to a widespread revival of theology, spirituality, and education. The past two decades have witnessed notable attempts by North American scholars to formulate distinctive approaches to Orthodox education.

The history of Christian education is such a vast enterprise that even a work of much greater length could not do justice to what might be treated. This history is necessarily selective. I have been guided in my selectivity by the writers that have shaped my views and whom I have freely utilized: James Bowen, Mary Boys, E. B. Castle, Lawrence Cremin, Werner Jaeger, Jacques LeClerq, George Mardsen, Henri Marrou, Pierre Riche, and Marianne Sawicki.

My indebtedness in writing this book is principally to doctoral students in the Church Leadership program in Fordham University's Graduate School of Education. Their enthusiastic participation in my classes has been my main inspiration. The work would not have been completed except for the gentle goading of David Coppola whose poetic words urged me to take up the writing of the book after I had abandoned it. James Morgan and Mary Roberts provided many helpful insights in making the writing smoother. As always my loving family, Eleanor Flanigan, Rachel, and Rebecca, offered the encouragement and support needed for such an endeavor.

The Author

John L. Elias, Ed.D., is Professor of Religion and Education in Fordham University's Graduate School of Religion and Religious Education. He is also a member of the faculty of the Graduate School of Education in the same university. Dr. Elias has been active for many decades in religious education as a teacher, administrator, consultant, and author. Among his publications are *Philosophy of Education: Classical and Contemporary, The Foundations and Practice of Adult Religious Education, Philosophical Foundations of Adult Education, Paulo Freire: Pedagogue of Liberation, Studies in Theology and Education, Psychology and Religious Education,* and *Moral Education: Secular and Religious*—all with Krieger Publishing Company. Dr. Elias lives in Madison, New Jersey.

Chapter 1

Foundations of Christian Education

> Let our children share in the education which is in Christ, let them
> learn the strength of humility before God, the power of pure love
> before God, how beautiful and great is his fear and how it gives
> salvation to all who live holily in it with a pure mind. (Clement of
> Rome, *Apostolic Fathers,* 1952, pp. 47–49)

Christian education has its foundations in the educational practices of
the early church. It developed in relationship to the education prevalent among Hebrews, Greeks, and Romans. While Christian education
acquired something from these peoples, it also reacted against certain
objectionable elements in their education. From the Hebrews Christians learned respect for the study of the Scriptures as the way to a life
pleasing to God. From the Greeks and Romans they learned the value
of philosophical thought and literature as preparation for understanding religious truths. To these truths early Christians gradually added
their own distinctive ideas and practices. Christians, however, found
elements in Greek and Roman literature that they did not want their
members to read and study. Eventually Christian leaders came to recognize the value of the classics and preserved this literature and philosophy for succeeding generations. While some Christians, notably
Marcion, saw little value in what is called the Old Testament or Jewish Scriptures, the majority in the Church prevailed and Jewish Scriptures became a valuable source for sound teaching.

In these early years Christian education was largely a matter of
educating new adults into the faith, adults who had already been educated in the classical literature. As to the education of the young, they
continued to study in the classical schools. It was only in a much later

period that Christians established their own schools for the education of the young.

The Classical Heritage of Greece and Rome

Early Christian education was steeped in the heritage of the ancient world. The Latin and Greek classics were important mainstays alongside the Hebrew Scriptures. Christians developed their education in dialogue with the educational systems of ancient Greece and Rome. In fact the ancient classical ideals of education have prevailed as almost normative educational ideals at least until the twenty-first century.

The Greek philosopher who has had the greatest influence on Christian education was Plato (427–346 B.C.). He presented an educational ideal based on a philosophy of life which Christians have found consonant with Christian life and paideia (instruction or discipline). Plato's Academy, where people gathered for dialogue and the pursuit of such intellectual and spiritual realities as beauty, truth, and goodness, was a model for Augustine, monastic education, and Renaissance education.

Plato's *Republic,* which details his educational ideals, is one of the most influential books in Western culture. Plato argued in this work that the ultimate aim of education is to help individuals go beyond opinions and beliefs in order to arrive at knowledge that is certain and true. For him, besides the ordinary realities of life there exists a realm where pure forms of goodness, justice, and love dwell. Through education learners arrive at knowledge of eternal truths, which gives perfection, permanence, security, and certainty to human life. What gives greatest value to human life for Plato is the ascent of the soul from attachment to earthly things to the eternal contemplation of and union with the Good.

Christian educators from Augustine on adopted Plato's educational ideals and theory. They have found in the *Republic* lofty educational ideals and aims, a liberal arts curriculum, and sound suggestions on method. They prized his emphasis on dialectic, philosophy, and mystical experience. While one can point to questionable aspects of Plato's influence on Christian education, such as his advocacy of censorship of ancient writings and his body and soul dualism, his overall influence has been positive. A study of Augustine's educational theory concludes that:

It was from Platonism that Augustine understood both the aim and
the method of education: the aim is a knowledge of the ultimate,
transcendent cause of all existence, which Plato called the idea of
the Good; the method is the Socratic method of question and answer,
which must begin with self-examination, for it is within the soul and
not in the external physical environment that dependable knowledge
is to be found. (Howie, 1969, p. 47)

Aristotle's influence on Christian thought and education did not
begin until the twelfth century when Arab scholars introduced his complete writings into the West. Aristotle's school was known as the
Lyceum and his followers were called peripatetic (walking around). Although Aristotle's writings do not have the charm and beauty of Plato's
works, it can be stated that what Plato was to Augustine, Aristotle was
to Thomas Aquinas and the scholastics in medieval universities.

While Plato's philosophy has been characterized as idealistic because of its emphasis on eternal ideals, Aristotle possessed a more
realistic or scientific mentality, due to his penchant for gathering
data, collecting information, and making generalizations. Scholastic
philosophers made use of many of the ideas from his logic, metaphysics, and ethics to expound the deeper meaning of Christian teachings. Aristotle's logic was a powerful ally in the hands of scholastic
philosophers who ascribed great power to human reason in understanding, propounding, and defending Christian teachings. His metaphysics mapped out a basic approach and language for understanding
Christian truths and realities, such as the existence and nature of God,
the existence and nature of the human soul, and the sacramental rites
of the Church. Aristotle's ethical teachings on the value of habits and
virtues in moral education have had a lasting influence in Christian
teaching.

While many have judged Aristotle's writings abstract, dry, and
theoretical, especially in comparison with Plato's writings, there is no
denying his influence on Christian thought and education at specific
periods of Church history. His prescription for education as the effort
to shape minds in logical thinking and good habits may seem to lack
the emotional appeal of Plato's educational goal as the discovery of ultimate and eternal truth. Yet Aristotle did set contemplation as the ultimate goal of education and saw this accomplished through the liberal
arts. For many centuries Christian theology and education have been
enriched by his wisdom.

The third great influence on Christianity from the Greek and Roman world was the philosophy of Stoicism, found in the writings of Greek and Roman authors such as Zeno, Marcus Aurelius, Seneca, and Epictetus. Stoicism was fundamentally an ethical stance in which individuals attempted to remain in harmony with the universe and not to become overly attached to material things. Christians found many things to admire in Stoicism: a focus on control of feelings, an emphasis on the private person, as well as a devotion to family, beauty, and the arts.

The influence of Stoicism is found in the writings of the New Testament and the early Christian literature. The concept of the natural law in Christian ethics owes much to Stoic thought. According to the Stoics the educational ideal is to teach people to live according to the laws of nature and submit to the divinely established order in the world. From the Stoics Christians learned that they should appeal to the power of reason that enables individuals to know what is according to nature and what is not. Education should aid people to use logic and reasoning to determine what is in their power to do and not to do.

Many early Christian writers found much to value in Stoic ethics and used its thought to formulate an approach to moral education. The Stoics emphasized duty, the will of God, living the rational life in accordance with nature, and the presence of the divine in humans. Christian writers pressed these concepts into service in their efforts to educate Christians to live the moral life. Christian educators, while rejecting the materialistic and deterministic aspects of this philosophy, accepted the Stoic focus on human kinship with the divine, human purification through self-control, and the concept of the unity of all creation as foundational elements in their educational approach. They found much wisdom in the Stoics' maxims and suggestions for moral guidance.

Another important classical influence on Christian education was the writings of Greek and Roman orators and rhetoricians. Isocrates (436–338 B.C.), an orator and rhetorician, was skeptical of the dialectic approach to education favored by Plato. In contrast, he championed an educational ideal that emphasized speaking well and thinking right. Isocrates' approach to education was practical: teach people the skills needed for participation in public life and political activity. He even established a school in which students paid for a course of study that lasted three or four years. Of his education it has been noted that:

He educated his students for life, particularly political life, preferring
to teach them to be able to form sensible opinions about things that
were useful rather then spend their time in hair-splitting about points
that were utterly useless. (Marrou, 1956, p. 133)

For Isocrates it seemed useless to ascend to the heaven of ideas as Plato
attempted with his students or to play about with paradoxes, as was the
practice of the Stoic philosophers. Isocrates declared that: "for the purpose of living properly what we need is not new and surprising ideas
but established good sense, traditional wisdom" (Marrou, 1956, p. 133).

The rhetorical and oratorical tradition begun by Isocrates and
continued by the Romans Cicero and Quintilian has been influential
among many Christian educators from the time of Augustine and
Jerome to Christian humanists like Erasmus, Martin Luther, and Ignatius of Loyola. Since the heart of Christian education concerns the
reading and understanding of biblical writings and the effective teaching of them to others, many Christian educators have stressed grammar, rhetoric, and oratory.

Christian education was also indebted to two Roman writers who
wrote extensively on education, Cicero (d. 43 B.C.) and Quintilian (d.
ca. A.D. 90). Roman education in turn was in large part influenced by
the ideals and forms of Greek education. In their writings Cicero and
Quintilian continue the rhetorical tradition of the Greek rhetor Isocrates.
Cicero is the first and foremost Roman writer on education. Cicero's
views on education are found in his *De Oratore,* a work that shows the
influence of Stoic philosophy. For him the goal of education was *humanitas,* a term parallel to the Greek *paideia. Humanitas* refers to the
lifelong striving for both erudition and ethical character that are to be
achieved through the traditional liberal arts with special emphasis on
rhetoric. This education for public life consisted in extensive reading
and discussion of history and literature, the writing of model speeches,
and participation in mock trials. Cicero's approach to education did not
give a high priority to philosophical contemplation.

Quintilian followed in the tradition of the Greek Isocrates and the
Roman Cicero. For him, as for Cicero, education should produce intelligent and ethical persons and orators active in public life. Accordingly, they should be able to discourse on any subject and take up leadership roles in the state. For Qunitilian only the good man can be a
good orator. His *Institutio Oratoria,* which is considered perhaps the
first important systematic manual in the theory and practice of educa-

tion, dealt extensively with rhetoric and oratory. This work, echoing
Cicero's *De Oratore,* describes how teachers should go about teaching
reading as well as all the subjects of the liberal arts. It also gives attention to adapting learning to the developing child. He placed great
stress on the character of the teacher.

The classical heritage of the Greeks as well as the Romans provided the basis of the liberal education that many Christians have trea-
sured throughout history. The tensions between Greco-Roman ideals
and Judeo-Christian ideals will be discussed later in this chapter. Some
church leaders were so smitten by the grandeur of classical thought that
they even invented myths and stories to support their contention that
classical learning and the liberal arts were derived from Scripture or
from scholars in Egypt who learned it from the Hebrews (Kimball,
1995, p.40).

Cicero and Quintilian influenced the educational writings of Augustine and Jerome in the early church. In the ninth century Alcuin accepted Cicero's notion that rhetoric is the means of acquiring truth.
The medieval scholastics wanted their students to be educated according to the ideals of Quintilian. Renaissance writers such as Petrarch
and Vergerio imitated the literary models of the two great Roman
teachers. The discovery of the full text of Quintilian's *Institutio Oratoria* galvanized the cause of Renaissance humanism. The concept of
humanism propounded by Renaissance writers as well as the Renaissance ideal of the *uomo universale* is indebted to the Roman notion of
humanitas. Jesuit education gave a prominent role to the study of Cicero both for his language and his oratorical skills.

The Jewish Heritage

While Greece and Rome influenced early Christian education, it was
the Hebrew writings that had the greatest impact on Christian life and
education. Early Christian education was rooted in the Bible, including both Jewish and Christian. The Jewish Scriptures were an essential part of the curriculum of early Christian education. Much of Christian education consisted in the reading, interpretation, and application
of biblical history, myth, stories, laws, and counsels for ordinary life.

The early Christians adapted for their own purposes the modes of
teaching and instruction that were utilized in Judaism. As a nascent
community Christians wanted to perpetuate themselves and promote
their vision and way of life to the next generation. From the Jews

Christians adapted modes of education that not only ensured their community's continuity but also its regeneration and development.

Education in Judaism was not only a socializing and nurturing agency but also a challenging and criticizing force. This dual focus was accomplished through three modes of education: the teaching of the Torah by the priests; the preaching of the word of God by the prophets; and the offering of counsel by the wise persons or sages. While some persons are more prone to accept the teaching of one or other of these groups, a complete education in the community entails listening to all three groups: priests, prophets, and sages (Brueggemann, 1982, p. 10).

The first mode of instruction in Judaism was the authoritative teaching of the Torah, the books which defined the origins and nature of the community. This form of instruction is thus described:

> And these words which I command you this day shall be upon your heart; and you shall teach them diligently to your children, and shall talk of them when you sit in your house, and when you walk by the way, and when you lie down and when you rise. (Deut: 6:6–7)

This form of education took place informally in homes and formally in rituals such as the Passover. Torah teaching was authoritative and consisted in precise stories and testimonies of faith. Adults gave answers to the questions of children:

> When your son asks you in time to come, "What is the meaning of the testimonies and the statutes and the ordinances which the Lord our God has commanded you?" Then you shall say to your son. . . . (Deut: 6:20–21)

Very often the answers to these questions were in the form of concrete stories that recounted significant events in the history of Israel. The stories tell of God's powerful and saving actions in behalf of the people. At other times the answers were in the form of laws which were given to the people through Moses.

Teaching in the early church took the form of teaching the New Torah or the law of love and the Beatitudes. This form of teaching is found predominately in Jesus' presentation of the New Torah in the fifth chapter of Matthew's Gospel. The Christian teaching permeated the homes and the weekly gatherings of followers of Jesus. Being a Christian meant being in covenant with God and agreeing to live in a certain way, and showing others that one is a believer. Teachers within the community taught authoritatively when they recounted significant events in the life of the community.

Authoritative teaching has had a place within all religious traditions. In the Christian churches such teaching comes from synods, councils, bishops, and pastors. There are many occasions when decisions must be made about just what is the teaching of the religious body. Authoritative teaching, however, is not all weighted the same way. Christian history reveals many disputes around authoritative teaching.

In Judaism a second form of education emerged from the speeches and writings of the prophets. While the teaching of the prophets was rooted in the Torah, it often challenged or criticized the convenient consensus that the Torah held together. Thus a creative tension often existed between the priests and kings who taught the Torah and the prophets who spoke a new word from the Lord. The teaching and activities of the prophets were characteristically unconventional. The existence of prophetic teaching proposed new truths to the people. Often prophets uttered radical and disruptive words, for example when Jeremiah announced the destruction of Jerusalem and the taking of the people into captivity. The Hebrew prophet Jeremiah uttered a pithy statement describing the unenviable vocation of the prophet:

See, I have set you this day over nations and over kingdoms,
To pluck up and to break down,
To destroy and to overthrow,
And build and to plant. (Jer 1: 10)

Among the prophets there was openness to new truths from God that were not found in the official Torah. Accepting the message of the prophets entailed believing that knowledge does not always come from formal and official channels. To be receptive to accept this message listeners had to be open to hearing God's word through the mouths of unexpected sources. Prophets appealed to God's authority in making their statements and defended the poor and oppressed members of the community. To understand prophetic teaching it is essential to recognize that the prophets were poets who imaginatively spoke about what was befalling God's people. Acting almost as subversives within the community they often uttered words that shattered and disrupted ordinary ways of understanding things. Often prophets dolefully proclaimed the end of the Old World and in the next breath announced in a hopeful manner a New World to come. The utterances of the prophets, however, needed to be scrutinized by the community for there were false prophets in Israel.

In the early Christian churches there was a similar openness to prophetic teachings that existed alongside the normative and traditional teaching. The Christian Scriptures show Jesus himself as a prophet who was in tension with the official teachers of Judaism. The followers of Jesus challenged the teachers of Judaism as well as the Greek and Roman authorities. Prophetic voices emerged within the community, even though there arose early a powerful impulse to root out heresies and false teachings. One can see elements of prophetic teachings in the letters and activities of the apostle Paul. Throughout Christian history prophetic voices have initiated great changes in the lives of communities of faith. The community has not always welcomed such dissonant voices; but it is a weak and flabby form of Christian education that does not allow the voices of questioners, critics, challengers, and dissenters. It has been noted that:

> The educational task of the community is to nurture some to prophetic speech. But for many others, it is to nurture an awareness that we must permit and welcome and evoke that prophetic tongue among us. Otherwise we will be diminished into the prose world of the king, and, finally, without hope. Where there is no tongue for new truth, we are consigned to the coldness of the old truth. (Brueggmann, 1982, p. 54)

The third part of the Jewish Scriptures that influenced education in the early Church and in later periods was the Writings. The most important of these writings were the Psalms, the Book of Job, and Proverbs. While the Torah and the prophets were directed to the concerns of the community, the Writings aimed at the moral or ethical growth of individual persons. The Writings did not have the same authority as the Law and the Prophets. These pointed sayings reflected the community's experience in the world more than the great saving actions of God in its history.

Of the three parts of the Jewish canon it is in the Writings that the task of education looms the largest. Pointedly, this literature is also referred to as the Wisdom Literature. A considerable part of this literature deals with rules for the socialization of the young into the community, a task accomplished by pointing out which paths are in conformity with the community's ethos and which run counter to it. The Wisdom Literature proposed to train the young in the wisdom that the community has gathered in its historical development. Following these charted paths the young could avoid the mistakes made by others in their attempts to live a decent and good life.

The method of instruction that the Writings imply is that of observation, generalization, and exploration (Brueggeman, 1982, p. 73). In this tradition learning begins with an observation of one's own experience. This observation is then put to the test vis-à-vis a generalized norm applicable to the situation of other individuals. Generalization is considered possible because of a fundamental belief in an ordered and regulated world that flows from the action of God. Finally, there is an exploration to determine how a new experience would fit into the bounds of the generalization, challenge it, or reject it. What lies at the heart of this method is an implied dialogue between teachers and learners as well as between learners and their own experience. Further, what gives religious value to this ordinary human wisdom and this manner of instruction is the Hebrew belief that ultimately all wisdom comes from God.

The Book of Job brings out this truth dramatically. It explains that there is a limit to what Job can know through his ordinary human experience in the world. Brought to his knees Job recognized that there is much about the world and about God's activity in it that is beyond his understanding.

> Whence then comes wisdom,
>   And where is the place of understanding . . .
> God only knows the way to it;
>   It is he who is familiar with its place.
> For he holds the ends of the earth
>   And sees all that is under the heaven . . .
> And to man he said:
>   Behold the fear of the Lord is wisdom;
>   And avoiding evil is understanding. (Job 28, 20–28)

With regard to method, the educational values of the Wisdom Literature have been tersely catalogued. Wisdom teaching is based on the experience of daily life, whose shape must be respected, honored, and discerned. The activity of teaching is connected with the building up and maintenance of a community. A community must know certain things if it is to remain a community. Wisdom thrives in an open atmosphere of dialogue in which all parties are stakeholders, thus affording more opportunity for new understandings and insights. This teaching needs an element of playfulness, humor, and delight. Finally, the pragmatic teaching of the sages, different from that of the Torah and the prophets, has a provisional nature, being open to new experiences and insights.

> The wisdom teacher is neither a pliable heir who agrees to everything, . . . nor is he a rebellious cynic who rejects everything. Rather the wisdom teacher is a faithful product of the tradition, for it is the fullness of the wisdom tradition not just to repeat and trust and parrot old judgments, but to make new judgments on the basis of new data. (Brueggeman 1982, p. 87)

The ultimate message of the Wisdom Literature, however, is an ironical one. The rather worldly Wisdom Literature teaches that wisdom is a gift of God:

> But where can wisdom be found?
> Where can we learn to understand?
> Wisdom is not to be found among men;
> No one knows its true value.
> The depths of the oceans and seas
> Say that wisdom is not found there.
> It cannot be bought with silver or gold.
> . . . .
> No living creature can see it,
> Not even a bird in flight.
> Even death and destruction
> Admit they have heard only rumors
> God alone knows the way.
> Knows the place where wisdom is found. (Job 28: 12–23)

The educational values of this rich literature have made their mark on the pastoral and educational ministries of the church. Through care, counseling, and instruction wisdom is brought to the community, particular problems are dealt with, and individuals are prepared to cope with the pains and suffering of life. These ministries of the church still explore human experience, but they do so today with the help of the human sciences of psychology, sociology, anthropology, and pedagogy. Dialogue is often used as the method of preference since this mode of instruction engages all persons in processes of instruction and counseling. Advocates of play, humor, and delight often make the case for less heavy-handed modes of instruction. In an age of pluralism and relativism we are more attuned to the limited dimension of all knowledge and solutions.

In the years after the Babylonian Captivity schools were established in Judaism to supplement education given in the home. The Talmud, a compilation of Jewish knowledge during the early centuries of Christian history, contains much anecdotal wisdom about the practice of education. The Talmud recognized different types of students:

> There are four types of students; swift to hear and swift to lose—his gain is canceled by his loss; slow to hear and slow to lose—his loss is canceled by his gain; swift to hear and slow to lose—this is a happy lot; slow to hear and swift to lose—this is an evil lot. (In Ulich, 1968, pp. 14–15)

The Talmud offers another interesting classification of students: some are sponges since they absorb everything; others are funnels that take in at one end and let out at the other; still others are strainers which let out the wine and collect the dregs; finally, there are sieves which eliminate the coarse material and collect the fine flour (In Ulich, 1968, p. 15).

Although there were major conflicts between Christians and Jews in the Middle Ages, this did not stop the influence of Jewish teachers and philosophers on Christian theology and education. Thomas Aquinas and other scholastics often cited the great philosopher Moses Maimonides and the eminent Scripture commentator Rashi.

Jesus as Teacher

Christian education finds its primary foundation in the ministry of Jesus' teaching as described in the Gospels. To his disciples and others who heard him Jesus was the master or teacher. This title is used fifty times in the Gospel of John alone. Even when Jesus performs one of his works of wonder or miracles, it is always accompanied with teaching and explanation. When most of us visualize Jesus, we most readily picture him as teaching. He instructed the Twelve and larger groups of disciples. After instructing these disciples he sent them out to teach others. Jesus taught individuals: Nicodemus, the Samaritan woman, the disciples on the way to Emmaus; groups of individuals, such as the disciples and other small gatherings; and large groups that listened to his Sermon on the Mount. In the singular incident where children are mentioned as part of his audience, they appear as interrupting his teaching of adults. Jesus then uses children as an example for openness that every seeker of the Kingdom of God should possess.

The Gospel traditions show clearly that in his mission Jesus utilized the three forms of teaching found in the Jewish Scriptures. Jesus is cast as the teacher of the Torah, the New Law. The Sermon on the Mount describes Jesus as the New Moses giving the New Law and New Commandments to his followers. Jesus takes on the role of a prophetic teacher when he castigated the religious leaders of the people for their failings. Jesus used the words of the Hebrew prophet Isaiah to announce his mission of preaching the Gospel and performing miracles. Like Jeremiah he warned that the coming catastrophe of the destruction of Jerusalem is a punishment for sin. In his use of parables to challenge his listeners Jesus is a sage, a storyteller, and teacher of the wisdom that leads to eternal life.

Christian educators can benefit from reflection on the mode and style of Jesus' teaching, for it is clear that Jesus was an effective teacher. He attracted many types of persons into his audience. His message challenged them to change their ways and to make radical commitments. He chose a close circle of disciples around him and motivated many of them to follow him. The Gospels also revealed that Jesus angered many by his teachings since he challenged their usual perceptions and the traditional wisdom. His teachings were often misunderstood either because of the studied depth of his message or because of a lack of receptiveness on the part of the listeners. He once told a parable in which he compared teaching to the sowing of seed. One of the telling points of this parable is that for teaching to bear fruit it needs certain conditions in learners.

Jesus' teaching played out in many forms. His parables provoked persons to think differently about their lives and the roles that God played in their lives. He taught about Jewish law revealing a knowledge of the many interpretations of this law. At times Jesus actually interpreted Jewish law, especially when he commented on the Ten Commandments. His style of teaching reached into the realities of daily life to make his meaning clear, dramatic, and at times even inspiring. Fisherman, farmers, married couples, shepherds, tax collectors, religious leaders, foreigners, physicians, and lawyers make cameo appearances in Jesus' talks. These images made his religious teachings clearer.

From the many examples of the teaching of Jesus in the Scriptures, one particular incident stands out to show how his disciples got involved in the learning process. This example affords us the earliest bit of theory and practice about Christian teaching and learning. It is the ironic story recounted in Luke 22 about Jesus instructing disciples on the road to Emmaus.

Jesus appears as the stranger. The disciples in the story did not recognize him, even though they appeared to have been disciples of his. This surprising lack of recognition is also found in a number of the resurrection narratives.

Jesus begins his teaching by drawing on the experience of the disciples. As a good teacher he asks them questions, what is it that you were discussing? They respond to his questioning with an edge to it, but this does not put off Jesus. Jesus follows with another question in order to lead them to greater understanding. After they had spoken and expressed their disappointment at the disappearance of Jesus, he chided them for their failure to understand.

Jesus instructs them about the true meaning of the Messiah. He breaks open the Scriptures to them, explaining Moses and the prophets. As observant Jews his disciples no doubt knew the Scriptures. Alone and without their teacher, however, they were unable to perceive the deeper meaning of these Scriptures, the application of these Scriptures to Jesus. Jesus opened their eyes and made their hearts burn with excitement.

Religious teaching in the Christian tradition entails dealing with the texts and companion messages. Since the meaning of the texts is not always clear, the texts beg for interpretation. This is precisely what Jesus provided. While many things can be learned without benefit of a teacher, there are still many other times when a teacher is an indispensable guide. While exaggerated claims are at times made for self-directed learning, experienced teachers recognize the need for and pursue a line of direct instruction. Teaching, however, should not be reduced to direct instruction. But instruction that is related to life experience and offered in an interesting and challenging form, as was the teaching of Jesus, remains a powerful form of teaching in Christian as well as in other communities.

Jesus deeply cared for his students. The disciples on the road to Emmaus were moved by his care and exclaimed how their hearts burned when he talked to them and expounded the meaning of the Scriptures. This expression of emotion by the disciples stands out as a rare passage in the often matter-of-fact way in which the Gospels are written.

What Jesus taught was not fully understood until the learners saw him involved in an action, the breaking of the bread. Thus the effectiveness of the teaching of Jesus cannot be disconnected from the deeds of his life. The simplicity and beauty of his life drew many persons to him. It was both his deeds and his words that brought him into conflict with the authorities of his time. Perhaps many a sage or scribe could have interpreted the Scriptures for the disciples on the way to Emmaus. But when interpretation was connected with actions that the disciples readily recognized as characteristic of Jesus, the disciples clearly knew him.

What this incident tells us about all teaching is that words are not enough; teaching needs actions, meaningful or symbolic actions, if it is to be understood. There is a danger in an excess of words that are not steeped in life and action. Words and actions must go together. Actions by themselves can often be instructive, but they often need words to express their deeper meaning. The ultimate proof of learning is that people will do something. Once the disciples learned that the Lord had broken bread and spoken to them they felt compelled to carry the message to others. Learning is something contagious that needs to be shared with others.

The Gospel tradition makes it clear that the disciples or students of Jesus were themselves to become teachers and healers announcing the Reign of God. Eventually, almost inevitably, the twelve apostles became traveling gospel teachers (Lk 9:1–6). The Gospel tradition also recounts Jesus sending seventy-two additional teachers to preach the gospel (Lk 10:1). Jesus warned his followers that they could expect conflict and confrontation, similar to what he had experienced. The Acts of the Apostles and the Epistles recount their experiences in teaching.

Education in the Apostolic Church

Christian education has its foundations in the efforts, described in the canonical literature, of the early Christians to preach the good news to potential members and to provide for continuing education in the community. Jesus was best remembered as a rabbi or teacher who gathered around himself disciples or students whom he commissioned to be teachers of others, to teach all persons all that he had commanded, guaranteeing his presence for all days. From the beginning this teaching mission was carried out in the Christian community. The Gospels not only describe the content and manner of his teaching but also record the varied responses people made to this teaching. In addition, the letters of Paul and others reflect teachings about what the community should believe and how members of the community should live.

The Acts of the Apostles depicts teaching and learning as important dimensions of the growing community. Early on these two activities were institutionalized into a ministry of the word:

> Christians of the first century preached, prophesied, taught, exhorted, debated, testified, catechized, evangelized, corresponded, and, finally, composed the oral tradition of the Jesus movement into written narratives, the Gospels. (Sawicki, 1988, p. 89)

Thus teaching in the apostolic church took shape in a number of specific forms, borrowed but adapted from the Jewish methods of teaching: proclamation, instruction, exhortation, and prophetic discourse. The early Christians proclaimed its good news (*kerygma*), attempted to build community (*koininia*), witnessed (*marturion*) to their faith in Jesus, and served (*diakonia*) the needy of the community. Many of these activities evolved in and from the worship (*liturgia*) of the church. As time went on the community developed its own particular teaching or doctrine (*didache*). From the very beginning, however, it was clear that there were certain tensions among these different forms of education: namely, between the teaching of the law and the prophetic criticism of the law; between the social criticism of prophetic teachers and the practical advice given to individuals. Nevertheless the Christian community engaged in all forms of education, attempting to deal conscientiously with these intrinsic tensions.

Paul has described the fundamental ideal of Christian education as the imitation of and assimilation to Christ, actions that perhaps mirrored the mystery cults prevalent in his times. In the letter to the Ephesians Paul presented the ultimate goal of all Christian education:

> You certainly heard about him, and as his followers you were taught the truth that is in Jesus. So get rid of your old self, which made you live as you used to—the old self that was being destroyed by its deceitful desires. Your hearts and minds must be made completely new, and you must put on the new self, which is created in God's likeness and reveals itself in the true life that is upright and holy. (Eph 4:21–24)

Communities of Christians and their leaders grappled with the complexities of determining how the imitation of Christ was to be accomplished in the Greco-Roman world.

The early disciples engaged in teaching and proclamation. Spirited teaching in the apostolic church took many forms. After the first Pentecost Peter was filled with the holy spirit and preached a sermon which is considered the basic proclamation of the good news of the life, death, resurrection, and ascension of Jesus (Acts 2). The response of those who listened was that "they were cut to the heart, and said to Peter and the rest of the disciples, "Brethren what shall we do?" (Acts 2: 37). Peter urged them to repent of their sins in the name of Jesus. Those who received the word were baptized, "and they devoted themselves to the apostles' teaching and fellowship, to the breaking of the bread and the prayers" (Acts 2: 42).

On another occasion when Peter preached the same message in the Jewish temple the response was "many of those who heard the word and believed" (Acts 4:4). Peter was caught up in what is now called Gospel or evangelical preaching or simply evangelization. He proclaimed the basic message of the Christian faith, the good news about the redeeming and saving life, death, and resurrection of Jesus Christ. Proclamation is thus the public presentation of the Christian message to prospective believers. Many in the audience were prepared for this message since they had either known or known of Jesus. No doubt, there was something for people to build on. Patently Peter's preaching was effective since many became converted, baptized, and joined the Christian community. Once again, we note that devotion to learning accompanied devotion to fellowship, prayer, and worship. Within the early Christian communities teaching and learning went hand in hand. Teachers within these churches included not only the original apostles but also many others whose special gifts of prophecy, tongues, healing, and teaching were recognized by the community.

Besides proclamation there were other forms of Christian preaching and teaching. The early church employed the exhortation or homily in the activity of the worshipping community as a form of teaching. Its main objective was to revive or keep the faith of believers alive. Another form of teaching that developed within the community was the sermon or instruction whose purpose was to give explanations, guidance, and lessons for believers.

The Acts gives us a revealing glimpse of the small community in Jerusalem. This description presents us with the essentials of Christian faith and life:

> Now the company of those who believed was of one heart and soul,
> and no one said that any of the things that he possessed was his own,

> but they had everything in common. And with great power the
> apostles gave their testimony to the resurrection of the Lord Jesus,
> and great grace was upon them. There was not a needy person among
> them, for as many as were possessors of lands or houses sold them,
> and laid it at the apostles feet; and distribution was made to each as
> any had need. (Acts 4: 32–35)

This idealized passage shows clearly the connection between teaching
and action. People were drawn into the early Christian communities
because the group's teachings were confirmed by a way of life that
showed in action toward the needy. This combination—word and
deed—meant the life of Jesus radically changed relationships among
people. Thus teaching connected with fellowship and charity characterized the community of believers in Jesus. Christian preaching and
teaching were incessant: "And every day they did not cease teaching
and preaching Jesus as the Christ" (Acts 5:42).

The need for teaching in order to understand Jesus' message is
demonstrated in Philip's encounter with the Ethiopian eunuch. This
man was reading Isaiah but admitted he did not understand what he
was reading "How can I, unless someone guides me?" (Acts 8:31).
Philip jumped at the chance and instructed him in the meaning of the
passage. The man believed and was baptized.

Besides the terms already explained above, the New Testament
also uses the word *catechesis* to refer to the teaching of the early apostles. This term, derived from the Greek verb *to echo,* is still used by
many in the Christian church to describe Christian teaching and education. The words *catechize, catechesis, catechism, catechumenate,*
and *catechetics* come from this word. The Apostle Paul used the term
when referring to the oral instruction in the contents of the faith. The
earliest Christian catecheses, as presented in the Acts of the Apostles,
were given to converts from Judaism. In the second and third centuries
we have evidences of catechesis given to Greeks and Romans.

Needless to say, the charism of teaching was important in the
early church. When we move from the Gospels and Acts to the Epistles we see a development of a distinct office of teaching in the early
Christian communities. The followers of Jesus sanctioned many ministries, gifts, and charisms in the community. Teaching is prized and
finds special mention in the letters of Paul, Peter, and John. Paul included teaching among the gifts of the Holy Spirit (1 Cor 12). Some
teachers were known for their wisdom and others for their knowledge.
Paul alludes to the gift of speaking God's message (v. 10). Paul's or-

dering of the communities' gifts shows the priority given to teaching. Apostles, prophets, and teachers hold the first three places in the community (v. 27). Although Paul's point is to stress to the Corinthians that all members of the body of Christ have value, he does rate some gifts as more important within the community. Furthermore, he declared that all of these gifts are as nothing compared to the gift of love that should characterize the lives of all followers of Jesus.

Evidently some among the Corinthians thought that speaking in tongues was the greatest gift in the community (I Cor 14). Paul thinks otherwise:

> Set your heart on spiritual gifts, especially the gift of proclaiming God's message. The one who speaks in strange tongues does not speak to others but to God, because no one understands him. He is speaking secret truths by the power of the Spirit. But the one who proclaims God's message speaks to people and gives them help, encouragement, and comfort. The one who speaks in strange tongues helps only himself, but the one who proclaims God's message helps the whole church. (1 Cor 14: 1–4)

Paul repeated this teaching on the unity of the body of Christ to the Ephesians (ch. 4). In the one body of the Church are many gifts bestowed by Jesus:

> It was he who gave gifts to mankind; he appointed some to be apostles, others to be prophets, others to be evangelists, others to be pastors and teachers. He did this to prepare all God's people for the work of Christian service, in order to build up the body of Christ. (Eph 4: 11–12)

Teachers are lynchpins in the church's growth because it is only through correct teaching that persons can reach full adult maturity and are able to distinguish between true and false teachings (v. 13–14).

Paul defended his ministry of preaching not only against those who considered speaking in tongues a greater gift than the others but also against those who considered preaching a weak form of Christian ministry that he exercised for unworthy motives (2 Cor 10). He vigorously argued that he used God's weapons in destroying false arguments and in removing obstacles raised against the knowledge of God. With no holds barred, he boasted about the authority given to him to preach about Christ. Paul recounted his sufferings and his visions as well as the power of his preaching.

The early Christian communities eventually faced the problem of false teachers and preachers (Gal 1). Paul was sure that the Gospel he preached was from Jesus himself who revealed it to him (v. 12). He felt impelled to reach out and preach the Gospel message to the Gentiles, a difficult task since it was to be done in places where there were many who expressed views contrary to the Gospel. Paul takes on the matter of false teachers in Colossians, chapter two.

The insidious presence of false teachers and dealing with them are also an important issue in the Epistles. Paul entrusted Timothy with the charge of using words as weapons in order to fight well (1 Tim 1:8). Timothy was urged to feed himself on the words of faith and on the true teachings that he has long followed (1 Tim 4: 6–6). He was also exhorted to give time and effort to "the public reading of the Scriptures and to preaching and teaching" (v. 13). Furthermore, Timothy was warned against looking at preaching as a way to become rich, as false teachers have done (Ch. 6). A strong condemnation of false teachers also appears in 2 Peter and the Letter of Jude. Such renegade teachers are called immoral, greedy, arrogant, boastful, and damnable.

These warnings against false teachers reflect the ambivalent situation in which the small Christian communities existed. Jews who became Christians were asked to separate themselves from their former communities and from the teachings and practices of these communities. Also, Gentiles who became Christians still lived in societies that fostered ideas and practices that went contrary to the beliefs of Christians. Both neophyte groups experienced a real separation.

While the canonical literature is our main source for how various forms of education were conducted in the early years of the Christian church, there soon appeared other documents and writings which were used in the education of members. One of the oldest surviving documents is the *Didache*, subtitled *Teaching of the Twelve Apostles* or *Teaching of the Lord Through the Twelve Apostles to the Gentiles* (*Apostolic Fathers*, 1952). This document, dating from the late first or early second century, contrasts the way of life (the Christian life) and the way of death (the non-Christian life):

> Two Ways there are, one of Life and one of Death, and there is a great difference between the two ways. Now the way of life is this: first, love the God who made you; secondly, your neighbor as yourself; do not do to another what you do not wish done to yourself. . . . But the way of death is this: first of all it is wicked and altogether accursed: murders, adulteries, lustful desires. . . . (*Apostolic Fathers*, 309, 317)

In addition, the *Didache* also touches upon the rites of baptism and Eucharist, the role of prayer and fasting, and matters relating to bishops and deacons. The *Didache,* probably the first Christian catechism, is largely a manual for the moral life of Christians and is closely related to the Gospel of Matthew with its Christian commandments and the Sermon on the Mount. From the *Didache* we learn that the first teachers in the Christian communities were itinerant prophets who moved from community to community. In time communities appointed their own resident teachers who gave instruction and guidance to Christians. Within the early church, teachers took on functions similar to those of the Jewish rabbis:

> To instruct children and other new members of the community; to conserve, interpret, and apply the tradition to new circumstances; to inculcate a distinctive religious identity over against that of the dominant culture; and to answer the attacks of learned nonbelievers. (Sawicki in Cully and Cully, 1990, p. 295)

In summary, what the apostolic period contributed to Christian education were the fundamental modes for education in the Christian faith: education for community building, education as proclamation of a message, education as a prophetic witnessing to the truth, education as moral instruction, and education in service of the material and spiritual needs of the community. Apostolic Christian education was not restricted to any social institution or to any age group.

The social forms of Christian education at this time were the informally organized small group or the large audience. Education took place in homes, synagogues, and open spaces. The fact that no lasting institution emerged in this period highlights the principle that education in the Christian church is not limited to any social institution such as a parish or school. The ideal of Christian education as the imitation of Jesus and assimilation to him realized itself in the many social institutions that developed and flourished in later years: catechetical schools, monasteries, universities, and loosely organized groups of people. Furthermore, the fact that the canonical literature recounts only the education of adults should warn against narrowing the concept of Christian education to the education of children.

It should be noted that the Christian Scriptures have practically nothing to say about the education of children. They do speak about the obligation of children to obey their parents (Eph 6:1) and the obligation of parents to provide for their children (2 Cor 12:14). Paul warns fathers not to provoke their children (Eph 6:4). The presumption is that parents are to take care to educate their children. With the introduction of infant baptism in later years the education of children became of greater concern to the Christian communities. With increased concern for this education arose the issue of what attitude to take toward the classical Greek and Roman education.

Christianity and the Classical Paideia

The first use of the expression "Christian education" appears in Clement of Rome's letter to the Corinthians written at the end of the first century:

> Let our children share in the education which is in Christ, let them learn the strength of humility before God, the power of pure love before God, how beautiful and great is his fear and how it gives salvation to all who live holily in it with a pure mind. (*Apostolic Fathers,* 1952, pp. 47–49)

Clement speaks of the paideia of Christ or the paideia (instruction or discipline) of God as providing a protective force for Christians. In his letters Clement utilized the language and concepts of Greek philosophy, especially Stoicism, to urge the Christians in Corinth to maintain unity among themselves. He based his moral argument on the harmony and laws of nature that guide the heavens and the earth as well as the rest of creation (Jaeger, 1961, pp. 25–26).

As the community of Christians increased in numbers it faced the issue of dealing with prospective converts to the Christian faith, who had been educated in the classical schools. The Acts of the Apostles described how the community grew as individuals began to respond to the preaching of the good news about Jesus. By the second century there emerged the catechumenate, a ritual and form of Christian formation or education whose purpose was the initiation of prospective converts to the faith. A rather developed form of the catechumenate is described by Hippolytus of Rome in his *The Apostolic Tradition* (ca. 215). The catechumenate offered a group experience for those who wished to become Christians. It borrowed elements from Jewish practice: a period of instruction and testing of new members, a reading of the Scriptures, a rabbinical application of the Scriptures, a communal reading and interpretation of the texts, and an exhortation to translate the Christian message into daily living.

Prospective converts to the Christian community went through a two or three-year probationary period in which they received a special course of instruction which prepared them for entrance into the church. The purpose of the catechumenate was both instructional and liturgical. The instruction afforded an understanding of the principal teachings of the community and aimed at moral and spiritual formation. The course of instruction also included a time of evangelization, a general introduction to the Christian faith, a fuller explanation of the history of salvation from creation to the last judgment, and then, after reception into the church, a deeper instruction (mystagogy) in central mysteries of the faith found in the Gospels, the Apostles Creed, and the Lord's Prayer. The process included rituals for the renouncing of evil and the acceptance of the central truths of the faith. The concluding ritual, which took place on Easter, marked formal acceptance into the community by participation in the rites of initiation: baptism, confirmation, and Eucharist.

Instruction in the faith was conveyed chiefly through homilies and lectures. Some of these courses of instruction have been preserved: those given by Cyril of Jerusalem, Gregory of Nyssa, John Chrysostom, and Augustine. The catechesis also included scrutinies, that is, questioning of the catechumens about their knowledge and commitment to the faith.

The catechumenate was one way in which the community dealt with the critical conflict between Christian teaching and classical paideia. As educated persons desired to become members of the community, they needed help to reconcile their secular lifestyle with the new faith that they now wished to embrace. The catechumenate also helped new Christians to deal with surrounding culture by ensuring that they did not cling to elements that were inimical to Christian life. By attempting to bring its message to bear on contemporary life and by appealing to intellectual classes, the Christian church attracted potential members. All in all, the catechumenate included the various components of education developed up to the time: community or fellowship to support learning, proclamation of the word of God, learning by active participation in the liturgy, and educative witness of a serving community. Since all members of the community participated in the initiation of new members, this form of liturgy and education became a way in which all members continued their education in the faith.

By the fourth century with the spread of Christianity and the wide acceptance of infant baptism the catechumenate for adults disap-

peared. The revival in our time of the catechumenate in Roman
Catholicism and in other Christian churches such as Episcopal and
Lutheran acknowledges a significant institution had been lost from the
liturgical and catechetical heritage of the Church. This mode of initiation and education stresses some values that are important in contemporary culture. Contemporary Christian educational theory needs to
draw on the two decades' experience with the restored catechumenate.

From the earliest years of its existence the Christian church experienced the problem of how to incorporate within its milieu the classical culture and educational ideals of the Greeks and Romans. The
emphasis on teaching and learning found in the time of the apostles
was continued in the efforts of Christians in the first five centuries of
the Christian era to come to grips with the content and form of classical Greek and Roman education. Though there was much opposition
to this education, a large part of the Christian church did eventually accept the classical school and the customs and culture that surrounded
it as valuable parts of the education of Christians. By accepting the
classical school Christians did not follow the example of the Jews who
organized their own schools around the study of the Bible, the Mishna,
and the Talmud. Except in a few cases, Christians in this period:

> Simply added their own specifically religious kind of training—which
> came from the Church and the family—on to the classical teaching
> that they received along with their non-Christian fellows in
> established schools. (Marrou, 1956, p. 424)

In dealing with classical culture church leaders drew different
lessons from the canonical writings. Jesus seemed to have defined his
mission as one primarily directed to the Jewish people. Paul devoted a
great deal of his attention to preaching the Gospel to the Gentiles. He
even addressed Epicurean and Stoic philosophers in Athens. According to many biblical scholars the Gospel of John utilized the Platonic-
Stoic concept of logos to explain the fundamental mystery of Jesus as
the Word of God.

Early Christians seemed to be of two minds with regard to their
life and activity in the world. Some spoke of Christians being only so-
journers in this world, eagerly awaiting the world to come. Other
Church writers expressed the view that Christians have no concern in
this life except to pass from it into the next life. In this vein there were
many statements urging Christian to shun such activities as politics,
education, and the military (Barclay, 1959, pp. 192–195). On the other

hand there were also sentiments expressing the view that, while aliens in the world, Christians did not withdraw from it but participated in its life. The remarkable *Letter to Diognetus* written in the second century has this to say:

> For Christians are distinguished from the rest of men neither by country, nor by language, nor by custom. For nowhere do they dwell in cities of their own; they do not use any strange forms of speech or practice a singular mode of life. . . . But while they dwell both in Greek and barbarian cities, each as his lot was cast, and follow the customs of the land in dress and food and other matters of living, they show the remarkable and admitted strange order of their own citizenship. They live in fatherlands of their own, but as aliens. They suffer all things. They share all things as citizens, and suffer all things as strangers. Every foreign land is their fatherland, and every fatherland a foreign land. They pass their days on earth, but they have their citizenship in heaven. (*The Apostolic Fathers,* 1948, p. 359)

Ambivalent attitudes toward Christian life in the world led to a difference of opinion about the value of classical Greek and Roman culture. Two early teachers and apologists for the Christian faith who grappled with the relationship between Christianity and classical culture came to different conclusions. Justin Martyr (b. 114), a Christian apologist in the second century, considered the Greek philosophic tradition to be a valuable asset in the ascent to truth. In his *Dialogue with Trypho* he showed himself at home with the various Greek schools of philosophy: the Stoics, Aristotle, Plato, and Pythagoras. Speaking of the Greek philosophers he explained:

> For each man spoke well in proportion to the share he had of the spermatic word, seeing what was related to it. But they who contradict themselves on the more important points appear not to have possessed the heavenly wisdom, and the knowledge that cannot be spoken against. Whatever things were rightly said among all men, is the property of us Christians. For next to God, we worship and love the Word. . . . For whatever either lawgivers or philosophers spoke well, they elaborated by finding and contemplating some part of the Logos. (In Quasten, 1992 [1950]. p. 210)

According to Justin, since the divine principle spread like a seed through all persons, all could utter the truth. Therefore in his view there existed an incarnational basis for reconciling the faith of the Scriptures with the philosophy of the Greeks. Justin found in classical literature support for the Christian doctrines on creation, life after death, eternal rewards and punishments, and prohibitions against the worship of idols. In Justin's opinion the wisdom of the Greeks came from Moses through the Egyptians. Justin initiated in his teaching and writing the process of thought that viewed Christianity as a philosophy comparable to the philosophies of the Greeks. He considered it a philosophy since it dealt with God, the world, and ethics (Jaeger, 1961, 29–31).

Tatian, (120–173), an Assyrian disciple of Justin, found this approach of Justin's too compromising for Christianity and wrote attacks on the study of Greek philosophy. In his *Address against the Greeks,* often characterized as an intemperate polemical treatise, he condemned all aspects of Greek culture, especially philosophy and literature. He admonished members of the church to avoid the meetings of philosophers whom he chastised for deceit, casuistry, and evil morals. He addressed the Greeks:

> What noble thing have you produced by your pursuit of philosophy? Who of your most eminent men has been free from vain boasting?. . . . The reading of your books is like walking through a labyrinth. . . . While you arrogate to yourselves the sole right of discussion, you discourse like the blind man with the deaf. (In Ulich, 1968, p. 36)

For Tatian Christianity's future did not lie in the assimilation of Greek thought but in maintaining itself pure and detached.

Tertullian (155–220), the African apologist for the faith, argued strenuously against the gods and superstitions of the Greeks. Although his attitude toward the classical literature was inconsistent, he allowed such study with qualifications. Tertullian opposed the classical education in his famous questions:

> What indeed does Athens have to do with Jerusalem? What concord is there between the Academy and the Church?. . . . With our faith, we desire no further belief. For this is our palmary faith, that there is nothing which we ought to believe besides. (In Fuller, 1957, p. 228)

Yet when he dealt concretely with occupations for Christian in the world, Tertullian softened his position:

> If the servants of God are not permitted to teach the letters, they also cannot be permitted to learn them. But since the knowledge of

literature is requisite to any lasting occupation, how without it can one acquire secular wisdom, common sense and efficiency in action? Thus how can we reject worldly studies, since without them the sacred studies could not exist? Hence we must admit the necessity of literary pursuits. Nevertheless, we must be aware that a part of them cannot be allowed but must be shunned, and that the faithful should be versed in literature, but not teach it. (In Ulich, 1968, pp. 36–37)

An influential third century document, *Didascalia Apostolorum* warned in strong terms against reading the classical literature. It argued that since Christians had the word of God they did not need secular works that contained so many errors. This work went so far as to contend that the Bible, besides giving a spiritual meaning, satisfied all the cultural needs of Christians since it contained history, poetry, eloquence, laws, lyrics, and cosmology. The treatise concluded that the works by pagans could be thrown away without any great loss (Marrou, 1956, p. 427).

Despite the admonitions of Tatian and others, classical culture could not be ignored if the Christian church was to gain converts from the educated classes of the time. Even those who railed against the so-called pagan culture were deeply influenced by it in their writings since they were trained in that culture. Despite the warnings of those who opposed classical culture, practical-minded Christians still sent their children to the classical schools. As mentioned above, even the rigorist Tertullian recognized the necessity for Christian children to attend the secular schools to gain knowledge of basic literacy necessary to read the Scriptures. However, he did not want Christian adults teaching there. The viewpoint prevailed in early church that

A Christian upbringing was something superimposed on a humanistic education that had taken place without it, something that had not previously been subjected to the requirements of the Christian religion. (Marrou, 1956, p. 427)

At the intellectual level it became clear that Christians needed the best of both worlds. A creative synthesis that combined Christian teachings with the best of classical learning had to be forged. It was in the city of Alexandria in the second and third century that Christians shaped such a powerful synthesis between Christianity and classical paideia. This intellectual alliance took place in the catechetical school established for the study of theology. The primary function of this school was to develop a description of Christian faith that would be intellectually acceptable for prospective converts from the educated classes. Thus began a tradition in which the arguments for Christian faith were made by an appeal to the powers of human reason. The classic expression of Christian education from this period is found in Clement of Alexandria's *Paedagogus.*

Clement (ca. 150–ca. 220), who received an extensive philosophical education before his conversion, succeeded his teacher Pantaenus as head of the catechetical school in Alexandria in the second century. His foremost student was Origen. This was a school where studies in biblical interpretation and apologetics prevailed. The *Paedagogus* described this Christian learning and analyzed the relationship between teacher and learner. Clement offered an analysis of the term *education* in general and then a description of Christian education:

> Education is a word used in many different senses. There is education in the sense of the one who is being led and instructed; there is that of the one who leads and gives instruction; and thirdly there is education in the sense of the guidance itself; finally, the things that are taught, such as precepts. The education that God gives is the imparting of the truth that will guide us correctly to the contemplation of God, and a description of holy deeds that endure forever. (In Cully, 1960, p. 22)

In *Paedagogus* Clement presented Christ as the teacher of humanity, as a model in which all can find example, precept, exhortation, reproof, and love. It is Christ who can lead souls to improvement, conversion, and final redemption. Clement ascribed value to the traditional liberal arts in that they enabled people to arrive at the first stage of wisdom. The higher stage of wisdom, however, was achieved only through special divine illumination. Clement gauged the two levels of Christian education: a simple way for the masses and a sophisticated way for intellectuals. What reason or philosophy added to faith, in his view, was a demonstration of the truths of faith.

For simple Christians the pedagogue was an attendant, a guide, and a master of instruction. What the simple Christian needed was faith in God and persistence in following the precepts of Jesus. For intellectuals Clement upheld education as the acquiring of a special knowledge or *gnosis,* of which God is the foundation. This gnosis was built upon the classical philosophy of the Greeks which was "a slender spark, capable of being fanned into flame, a trace of wisdom and an impulse from God" (In Bowen, 1975, p. 243). For Clement one's en-

tire life unfolded as an educational process in which a person grew
spiritually in knowledge.

Clement's ideas on Christian theology and education found their
continuation in the work of Origen, (d. ca. 254) the greatest theologian
of the Alexandrian school. Origen was thoroughly schooled in Greek
philosophy, especially that of Plato. He established a full-fledged
school at Alexandria, with both classical studies and studies in the
Scriptures. He instructed youth in the subjects of the classical school—
grammar, rhetoric and logic, arithmetic, astronomy, and music. After
their instruction in these subjects Origen directed the students in the
study and understanding of the Scriptures. Not only did Origen not
consider classical studies harmful for Christian life; he actually viewed
them as necessary for educating intelligent Christians (Murray, 1957,
pp. 155–157). In a letter he had this to say about the relationship of
Christianity to classical studies:

> I am anxious that you should devote all the strength of your natural
> good parts to Christianity for your end; and in order to [achieve] this,
> I wish to ask you to extract from the philosophy of the Greeks what
> may serve as a course of study or a preparation for Christianity, and
> from geometry and astronomy what will serve to explain the sacred
> Scriptures, in order that all that the sons of the philosophers are wont
> to say about geometry, and music, grammar, rhetoric and astronomy,
> as fellow helpers to philosophy, we may say about philosophy itself,
> in relation to Christianity. (In Bowen, 1972, p. 247)

The thoroughness of the education given at Origen's school is attested to in the praise that Gregory Thaumaturgos of Neocaesarea (ca.
210–ca. 270), a lawyer and later a bishop, gave to Origen and to the
education he received at the school in Alexandria. In his autobiography Gregory viewed Jesus as his primary teacher, but praised Origen
as the person through whom Jesus had taught him. He recalled that
while Origen taught through dialogue with warmth and love, there was
also some pain associated with the educational process. He recalled
that Origen:

> At times attacked us in the manner typically used by Socrates and
> tripped us up with his arguments when he saw us becoming restless
> with him, like unbroken horses that ran away from the road and
> galloped about randomly until with a bridle, he persuaded us. And this
> process was at first unpleasant and painful to us, when he drove and
> cleansed us with his own learned discourse, we who were

inexperienced and unprepared for reason. (Gregory in Olson, 1995, pp. 29–30)

From Origen Gregory learned all the liberal arts. Gregory then proceeded to the study of physics and ethics and then to the study of philosophy. About his education in philosophy at the feet of Origin he recalled:

> He introduced us to all schools of thought and was determined that we should be ignorant of no type of Greek doctrine. Nothing was forbidden us, nothing hidden from us, nothing inaccessible to us. We were to learn all manner of doctrine—barbarian, Greek, mystical or political, divine and human. We went into and examined with entire freedom all sorts of ideas, in order to satisfy ourselves and enjoy to the full these goods of the mind. When an ancient thought was true it belonged to us and was at our disposition with all its marvelous possibilities of delightful contemplation. (In Murray, 1957, p. 157)

Gregory went on to depict how Origen directed the entire educational process. This openness to all learning manifested in this school has unfortunately not been the case with all teachers of Christianity. Far from being a hindrance to the Christian life as Tatian and others thought, Origen saw education in the classics as a good thing and as a way to virtue. He stated that "in fact, to have been educated, and to have studied the best doctrines, and to be intelligent, does not hinder us from knowing God, but helps us" (In Bowen, 1975, p. 247).

In order to reconcile Christian faith with classical philosophy Origen fashioned a form of biblical interpretation that recognized three levels of meaning for the texts of Scripture—literal, historical, and spiritual. Origen made extensive use of allegorical interpretations of scriptural texts for purposes of reconciling them with the teachings of Greek philosophers.

Origen imagined the spiritual life of Christians as a journey of the soul from the purgation of sin to illumination by God. For him "life is itself a process of education, the church a school for the soul, the world a vast educational setting, and God himself the supreme teacher" (In Bowen, 1972, p. 248). Jesus as the incarnation of God provides the example that others should follow on their way to virtue. By imitating him Christians become sharers in the divine nature.

The important advancement in this period in the development of Christian education is the balanced realization that Christian education should include a serious dealing with contemporary culture. One does not deal in extremes with a culture, however, by either totally embracing it or totally accepting it. The Christian normally strikes a balance by finding the proper relationship between religion and culture. Various ways of reconciling Christ and culture have been developed within the Christian church: the forging of syntheses drawing on Christianity and culture, holding Christianity culture in a paradoxical or dialectical relationship, and utilizing Christianity to transform a particular culture (H. R. Niebuhr, 1951).

The educational ideas of Clement and Origen, though impressive, were not a complete theory of Christian education that led to a distinctive practice. Their chief intent rather was to explain the world in Christian concepts. Their writings on education were focused on establishing a place for Christian concepts in the ideas and institutions of the time. But two basic ideals embraced by the Alexandrian school have become essential for the development of a Christian theory of education. The Alexandrians believed that the powers of reason and intelligence had an important role to play in Christian education. Secondly, they propounded the intellectually satisfying view that there was a unity of truth which embraced both classical culture and Christian doctrines.

The principles involved in the educational efforts at Alexandria have been aptly described (Olson, 1995, pp. 32–40). Education for the Alexandrians was depicted as a journey to Wisdom and a journey to Christ who is the author of all knowledge and of all creation. First, education must sometimes involve redemptive pain and suffering if it is to be effective. Second, this pain should lead students from grappling with their studies to a struggle with real life problems. Third, students should study the conventional academic disciplines of their culture, moving from basic studies to the higher disciplines of ethics and physics and then to contemplation or theology. Fourth, education should lead students to an appreciation of the beauty and sublimity of creation. Fifth, the teacher is the vehicle that mediates between the wisdom of God, the true teacher, and the learning of students. For the Alexandrians "Learning thus becomes the result of a collaboration between the teacher, the Logos that structures the universe, and a Logos that comes to dwell within the individual to drive him to learn" (Olson, 1995, p. 35). Sixth, Jesus himself is the ultimate Wisdom which students should believe in and study. These educational ideals became warp and woof of the first Christian educational theory, namely, that of Augustine of Hippo.

Earlier it was pointed out that the Christian Scriptures make little mention of the education of children. Gradually over the years children received more mention in early church writings. Clement of Rome spoke of the training of children in his letter to the church at Corinth:

> Let our children share in the instruction which is in Christ, let them learn the strength of humility before God, the power of pure love before God, how beautiful and great is his fear and how it gives salvation to all who live holily in it with a pure mind. (*Apostolic Fathers,* 1952, pp. 48–49)

Church writers speak of the necessity for family training and discipline. As mentioned earlier, the early church set up no separate schools for the education of children. In his speculation about reasons for this decision Barclay pointed to the poverty of the early Christians, their belief in the imminent coming of Jesus, and the illegality of setting up such schools (1959, p. 239).

Summary

This chapter has explained how the foundations of Christian education were established in the classical heritage of Greeks and Romans, the Jewish Scriptures, the instructive example of Jesus' teaching, the teaching ministry of the early church, and the efforts of early church fathers to deal with conflicts between the classical heritage and the Christian tradition. These elements come into play and punctuate each period of Christian history. Every reform movement in Christian education has echoed back to these basic principles. Many of the disputes that have raged over the years are implicated in the interpretation and interrelationship of these principles.

The next chapter will make the case for the first distinctive theory of Christian education found in three developments: the writings of Eastern Fathers such as Basil of Caesarea, education within the newly established monastic communities, and the writings of Augustine of Hippo. These notable developments are treated within the context of medieval Christian education. At the end of the medieval period another approach to education emerged to challenge the ideas of the early period, synthesized in the work of Augustine. A scholastic theory of education, formulated by great university teachers, began to dominate Christian educational thought.

Chapter 2

Medieval Christian Education

> It has seemed to us and our faithful counselors that it would be of
> great profit and sovereign utility that the bishoprics and monasteries
> of which Christ has deigned to entrust unto us the government should
> not be content with leading a regular and devout life, but should
> undertake the task of teaching those who have received from God the
> capacity to learn, each according to his own abilities. (Charlemagne in
> Knowles, 1962, p. 71).

For most historians medieval history embraces the period from 300 to
1500 in Europe. European civilization began when the countries of
Western Europe accepted "the ways of life, ideas and religious attitudes
that had prevailed for many centuries in the Mediterranean world (Cantor, 1993, p. 1). The Christian Church was the principal institution in the
transition between the ancient world and the medieval world. Understanding the modern world entails an appreciation of the ideals that medieval civilization has bequeathed to it through its extensive literature.

Within medieval Europe there developed a particular theory and
approach to education that dominated the curriculum of schools and
colleges the world over at least to the beginning of the twentieth century. This humanistic curriculum is still a powerful force in education
today. Greek and Latin classical literature, which makes up the heart
of this education, portrays examples of what constitutes the good person and the good society. What medieval education added to the classical education was a distinctive Christian approach to the teaching of
the liberal arts.

Medieval Christian education was dominated by the ideas of Augustine, bishop of Hippo. It took another genius, the Dominican friar
Thomas Aquinas, and his fellow scholastics at the University of Paris

to challenge and modify the Augustinian worldview. Besides examining the overarching influence of these two great thinkers, this chapter
also explores other writings on education that appeared between the
fourth and fifteenth centuries. This chapter treats Christian education in
the West. Medieval developments in the East are treated in chapter 8.

Christian Education in the Fourth and Fifth Centuries

By the fourth century there existed no clearly expressed theory of
Christian education and no truly Christian schools besides the catechumenate. Steps towards developing a distinctive theory of education
began with writings in the fourth century, the beginning of the medieval period. The genesis of a distinctive approach to Christian education emerged in the writings of church fathers in both the eastern and
western parts of the Roman Empire. While it was within the monasteries that this approach to Christian education began, this avenue to
education soon spread to royal courts and schools. These paths developed at the same time that the Roman Empire as well as its educational
institutions began to decline.

The monasteries that dotted the landscape east and west between
the third and fifth centuries quickly became agencies of education in
the Christian faith. Early monasteries promoted literacy at least to the
extent that their members were able to participate in the daily worship.
These monasteries crackled with the tension between Christian teaching and classical paideia. Earlier monasteries or houses downplayed
profane learning. However, by the end of the seventh century monasteries entertained profane learning along with sacred learning.

Some significant works relating to monastic Christian education
and learning were written in the fourth and fifth centuries. While the
church father Basil of Caesarea assigned a prominent place for classical learning in Christian education, other fathers like Jerome and John
Chrysostom railed against moral and intellectual dangers in classical
learning. Notwithstanding the opposition of many in the monastic
movement to classical learning, the medieval monasteries conserved
and continued the knowledge of the classics during the so-called Dark
Ages. In a wasteland of barbaric invasions, monasteries stood for sev-
eral centuries as the sole institutions of education in Western Europe.

Prominent among the advocates of classical learning was certainly
Basil of Caesarea (329–379), a fourth century bishop of the Church
whose early education before he became a Christian was in rhetoric and

philosophy. Basil established a monastery, what he called a community or fraternity of men engaged in a common task. In this community he integrated scholarship and contemplation. His rule for monastic life became a model on which later foundations were based. Though Basil became a monk and established a monastery, he still remained convinced of the value of classical learning. He wanted his monks to be educated men. In his attitudes towards learning he was greatly influenced by Origen.

A lifelong concern of Basil was the education of the young, expressed chiefly in his tract, *Address to Young Men on Reading Greek Literature.* This work is basically a homily or oration, similar to Clement's *Pedagogus,* on the dangers of reading Greek literature and the way to avoid these dangers. In this address, which was regarded as the charter of all Christian higher education for many centuries, Basil does not argue for the elimination of Greek authors from the curriculum but rather exhorts students to get the best advantage out of their reading by focusing not on the moral and religious content but on the forms of the literature (Jaeger, 1961, p. 81).

For Basil, the primary purpose of Christian education was to enhance the journey of the soul to its final union with God. In his view while the Christian Scriptures remained an authoritative guide for such a journey, the classics could also be a valuable companion in this journey. He argued that the classics are a prelude and preparation for the study of the Scriptures. True wisdom for Basil consisted in culling from classical literature what is appropriate for the journey of the soul and passing over other parts of the classics. Finding value in both the poets and the philosophers, Basil offered as a test of their true value whether or not they advanced the life of virtue. Unfortunately Basil did not provide enough specific guidance on how to make the choices between what is valuable and what is not in the classical literature. In his monastic rule Basil directed the education of young boys in the monasteries, suggesting the use of stories which, though based on characters in Greek mythology, made use of the names of people in the Bible, verses of Proverbs, and stories from the Bible (Marrou, 1956, p. 440).

Basil's close friend Gregory of Nazianzen shared his attitude toward the values of education in the Greek classics. His great love and respect for the Greek classic literature were expressed in one of his letters to a young man:

> Perfect yourself in studies, in the work of the historians, in the books of the poets, in the smooth-flowing eloquence of orators. Be versed

too in the subtle disquisitions of philosophers. Have a prudent familiarity with all of these, wisely culling from them all that is useful, carefully avoiding what is injurious in each, imitating the practice of the wise bee which alights on every flower, but with infinite wisdom sucks only what is useful from each. . . . Meeting in your reading both their theology and their eloquence, the former ridiculous, the latter charming, despise their pleasure-loving deities, but respect their eloquence. Pluck the rose but shun the thorns, the same tree bears both. These are the best principles with regard to profane learning. (In Barclay, 1959, pp. 222–223)

These positive appraisals of classical learning, however, have to be balanced with the countervailing views of church leaders who continued to see dangers in the classical education. A major Christian opponent of hellenized education was John Chrysostom (c. 345–407), the bishop of Constantinople. This bishop, renown for his eloquence, placed the good of the soul above education in eloquence:

If the soul is prudent, lack of the power to speak will not result in any loss; if it is destroyed, the harm done is most serious, even though the tongue happens to be sharp and polished, and the greater the power of speaking, the greater the harm done. . . . The study of eloquence requires good morals, but good morals do not require eloquence. (In Barclay, 1959, p. 230)

Though strictly speaking not in the monastic tradition, the writings of John Chrysostom offer an insight into the education advocated for boys and to a lesser degree for girls, who did not enter monasteries but lived an ordinary life in the world. In his *Address on Vainglory and the Right Way for Parents to Bring up their Children,* John stressed education in morality in his advice to parents on shaping their children's behavior. Most of the treatise is concerned with the education of boys for life in society. Chrysostom highlighted teaching by positive example, not by punishment. The central focus of education for him was the Scriptures, which supplied valuable examples of how Christians should live. In his view these religious examples should replace the Greek heroes in the imagination of children. Children's experiences are to be censored; the theater is not to be attended. Physical passion is to be channeled into an early marriage. Golden-tongued John tried to dissuade parents from using physical punishment for disciplining their children, for in his view this form of discipline would negate positive learning. The negative tone in his admonitions and in those of other Christian writers attest to the perceived difficulties Christians had in living in a predominantly pagan society. Although Bowen (1972, p. 289) contends that this work of Chrysostom demonstrates the poverty of Christian educational thought at this time, this particular Greek father's warning has influenced a long tradition of a guarded Christian education. Many Christian educators over the years have regarded with suspicion certain aspects of contemporary culture as impediments to the achievement of Christian ideals.

Ideas similar to those of John Chrysostom resonate in the writings of Jerome (342–420). This noted Christian scholar of the Scriptures as well as the pagan classics, ironically voiced strong opposition to an education that included a study of Greek and Roman literature in annunciating an ascetic ideal for Christian education. Jerome was consumed with the study of the Bible and with the translation of the Hebrew Bible into the Latin of the common people. Anything that distracted him from this task was suspect. Jerome recounts that he was scared off from a too great love for the classics by a dream about his own death and judgment:

> Suddenly I was caught up in the spirit and dragged before the judgment seat of the Judge. . . . Asked who and what I was I replied: "I am a Christian." But He who presided said "Thou liest, thou art a follower of Cicero and not of Christ. For where thy treasure is, there will thy heart be also." (In Tierney, 1992, p. 31)

Though Jerome did not totally abandon the classical authors, since his writings after the famous dream are peppered with references to the Roman authors whom he greatly admired, he did dedicate himself even more assiduously to the study of the Bible and to the practice of the ascetic life.

Jerome delineated an ascetic or guarded approach to education, notably in his letter *To Laeta, Concerning the Education of her Daughter*. Since Laeta had been dedicated to God before she was born and was to enter a convent, Jerome's view can be generalized to others only with caution. The heart of the Christian life for Jerome is the fear of the Lord. This fear meant that all potentially harmful influences are to be censored. Inhibitors to spiritual growth should be shunned. For him learning the alphabet and learning to read are to be connected with reading and learning the Scriptures. He counseled that rhetoric, poetry, and music should be avoided. Laeta's daughter Paula should be "deaf to all musical instruments, and never even know why the flute, the lyre

and the harp came into existence" (In Bowen, 1972, p. 270). Moral
training, also of a highly ascetic nature, surpassed in importance intellectual education. For Jerome this education should eventually lead
Paula to enter a convent. Though knowledgeable in the Roman classics himself, Jerome saw no place for this type of learning in the education of Laeta's daughter. Since this is the only educational tract on
education we have from Jerome, we have no way of knowing what his
views were on the education of sons or daughters not destined for the
convent. Jerome's ideas on education have had an influence only
within the monastic movement. Educators have looked elsewhere for
more positive approaches to education.

The children of Christians in the fourth and fifth centuries continued to attend the secular schools, since Christians still did not sense
the need for establishing schools of their own. For a short period of
time under the emperor Julian in the fourth century Christians were
prohibited from attending the state schools. Both Christians and even
non-Christians opposed this prohibition, which was also directed
against Christian teachers. At Julian's death this prohibition was lifted,
with the result that Christian teachers and students returned to the state
schools.

Augustine of Hippo and Christian Education

The paramount intellectual, theological, and educational force of the
medieval period was Augustine of Hippo (354–430). This remarkable
saint and bishop did not have Jerome's fear of classical learning, even
though he warned against certain aspects of classical learning. Steeped
in classical learning, especially the Latin authors, Augustine mined
classical literature and Christian sources to propound what is considered the first full-blown theory of Christian education. Augustine's
views on education weave in and out of works in which he treated
many phases of education. He was able to do this with authority since
for a number of years before his conversion to Christianity he was a
teacher of rhetoric. After his conversion he became bishop of Hippo
and engaged vigorously in many theological disputes about basic
Christian doctrines. Even as bishop he continued to work on his educational treatises.

Augustine's autobiography, the *Confessions,* describes his self-
education and development that lasted throughout his entire life. Educated in classical rhetoric, he initially found the Christian teachings

naïve and distasteful, but later was taken by their spiritual beauty. Accepting Platonic teachings on human life as the journey of the soul to God, he described how he came to religious faith through study, prayer, and exposure to the example of Christians. In this penetrating and faith-filled testimony in praise of God and recounting his journey to God, he combined the many elements of Christian and classical learning that were influential in his self-education.

Augustine wrote a great deal on education, including *De Magistro,* a philosophical treatise on how we learn, *De Catechizandis Rudibus,* an instruction on how catechumens should be educated, and *De Doctrina Christiana,* a discourse on how the Scriptures are to be interpreted and their truth communicated. His principal concerns in these works are theological, philosophical, and educational. In his works Augustine addressed these questions: what is the nature of knowledge and how do we arrive at it? How can human reason attain this knowledge? How can humans acquire ultimate knowledge? How are faith and reason related in human knowing? How best can the truths of faith be communicated?

All of Augustine's fundamental theological concepts are closely aligned with the process of education: faith, understanding, free will, grace, sin, and love. Education for Augustine moves from doubt to understanding and faith. His view of education has a supernatural basis since its ultimate end for the Christian is the possession of eternal happiness. For the attainment of this happiness the intellectual activity of learning is the engine. For Augustine happiness is the intellectual grasp of the eternal. In his *Against the Academics* Augustine pursued these themes arguing against skeptics who scoffed at the possibility of coming to knowledge. Succinctly, he enunciated his fundamental theological and educational principle that faith comes before understanding: "Do not seek to understand in order that you may believe, but believe in order that you may understand, since, unless you believe, you will not understand" (In Howie, 1969, p. 49–50). For him understanding and faith work together in the educational process. According to Augustine the central belief of faith is that God exists and is the lasting hope of human kind. He contended that the love of learning lies deep in the human soul. Yet this love and its aim need direction and focus. Augustine advised that the free will of persons to choose what they will love should be respected in the educational process. For him, educators need to teach with awareness that the reality of sin that weakens human understanding can be overcome only by God's grace.

According to Augustine the purpose of education is to enable individuals to attain complete union with God; thus it was primarily an eschatological education. In his great work *De Civitate Dei* Augustine placed all human life, including education, within an eschatological world-view. He argued that although all human institutions are of the city of man and transitory, nevertheless, the city of God that is constructed as people progress toward God is eternal and ultimate. Education for Augustine is thus not destined for any impossible earthly paradise but rather for the future state of humankind. Consequently, personal salvation is paramount for all individuals in their thoughts, actions, and education. This earthly city has value only insofar as it is the place where people work out their salvation. Augustine, however, did not urge withdrawal from the world as many monks and ascetics did; rather he affirmed the value of the human city and society in which humans are educated for the city of God.

Many scholars have noted the psychological richness found in Augustine's writings, especially the penetrating self-analysis found in the *Confessions.* His analysis of the inner workings of the person earmarked the beginnings of a psychology of learning. For his basic philosophical ideas Augustine was indebted to Plato. According to Plato humans are composed of rational souls that make temporary use of mortal and earthly bodies. In this work Augustine provided piercing analyses of sense perception, sensation, knowledge, volition, memory, and motivation. While he treated the parts of the soul separately, he still emphasized "the unity of the personality and the self-activity of the thinking self as the basis of all effective learning. . . . which is sufficient to form the basis of a consistent and effective theory of education" (Howie, 1969, p. 98).

Augustine also developed an epistemology or theory of knowledge that has implications for learning and education. In his earlier writings he was totally dependent on Plato's theory of knowing, which equated knowledge with remembrance of ideas from a former existence. In later writings Augustine explained that knowing and learning come about through a process of divine illumination in which God brings forth knowledge from within the person. Scholars' explanations abound for this process of illumination, but in this view of human knowing there is a clear emphasis on the role of God in human knowing and learning. Augustine like Plato recognized two forms of knowing: science in which what is known comes from the world of sense; and wisdom in which what one knows comes from a contemplation of absolute truth. Augustine also discussed the role of doubt in learning. Arguing against skeptics he pointed out the positive function of doubt as a starting point for learning. In his *Confessions* he described his own movement from doubt to certitude. People learn by raising doubts and questions and seeking answers from teachers. Augustine's theory of knowing outlined and underscored the orderly steps one must take in order to learn: animation or physical activity; sense perception of pains and pleasures; activity of understanding the natural world; self mastery and control; self purification from pressures and allurements of the environment; progress in learning; and finally contemplation, the highest spiritual activity

Teacher that he was, Augustine wrote extensively on teaching as an art. He had a lofty view of the profession of teaching, considering it a commission from God and a calling through which individuals can express their love of God and their fellow humans. A few of his insights and suggestions for teaching may give a flavor of his thinking in this area: teachers teach eloquently through their style and manner of life; they should teach in calmness and tranquility; the natural curiosity of learners needs to be directed to specific objects; teachers should proceed from what students already know or have doubts about to what they do not know; successful teaching is adapted to the interests and experiences of students. Augustine likewise drew attention to the importance of love and respect in teacher-pupil relationships. He recommended that teachers should try to cultivate a pleasant and attractive style. Augustine emphasized the importance of student activity in learning: "You would learn better by watching us and listening to us when actually engaged in the work itself than by reading what we write" (In Howie, 1969, p. 159). Finally, he placed emphasis on the importance of spontaneity in teaching.

Augustine provided an insightful analysis of teaching and learning in his work *The Teacher*. This delightful piece takes the form of a dialogue between Augustine and his son Adeodatus. Augustine argued against the notion that teachers are the cause of learning through the words that they utter. He contended that:

> We go astray when we talk about teachers, when there are really no teachers at all. The reason why we do talk in this way is that there is often no time lapse between the moment of speaking and the moment of learning. (In Howie, p. 192)

For Augustine, following Plato's ideas, the teacher's words serve only to remind learners of something they already know. What teachers actually do is direct students' attention to objects or ideas to be learned as well as stimulate learners to learn for themselves. In all cases students, however, must learn for themselves. In the learning of spiritual truths, on the other hand, God is the sole teacher and acts through illuminating the minds of learners. Human teachers can only enkindle in the hearts of students a desire for learning spiritual things. Thus for Augustine there was no a clearcut distinction between teaching and learning. Learners become their own teachers and teachers learn as they teach their students. Augustine's discussion of the nature of teaching has been contrasted with Thomas Aquinas' view, to presented later in this chapter, according to which teachers can be real, though secondary, causes of learning.

One of Augustine's most influential educational treatises is *De Doctrina Christiana* [*Teaching Christianity*], a work which describes the education for persons who want to be Christian teachers (Augustine, 1996). In this work Augustine propounded that Christian teachers should be adequately prepared for their tasks through a general education, a specialized study of subject matter, and a study of the principles of teaching. He insisted on the importance of teacher training, artfully arguing that God assists those who assist themselves. Rejecting the view that the Holy Spirit will provide all that teachers need for accomplishing their task, Augustine counseled that the Christian teacher should have an education comparable to the secular teacher. For Augustine the content of Christian teaching resides primarily in the Scriptures. In this work he also presented principles for interpreting the Scriptures and pointed out the many difficulties interpretation presents.

The more down-to-earth Augustine takes a somewhat different view from the ascetical Jerome on the issue of classical learning. His view is that the essential truths of classical literature can be incorporated into the Christian curriculum. For the bishop of Hippo learning about contemporary culture is indispensable if Christians are to be able to communicate with non-Christians. Augustine's ideas in this matter essentially provided the philosophy for the Christian school that was to appear in later years. In this philosophy religious truths occupy the center of the curriculum and the liberal arts are to be taught in relation to them. Augustine especially commended those forms of learning that would promote a person's understanding of the Scriptures and would advance communication with non-Christians. He accepted all subjects of the classical curriculum, save for the fine arts about which he shares the negative opinions of Plato. As for learning the principles of teaching Augustine recommended the study of rhetoric, dialectics, exposition, and method. He wanted teachers to be eloquent but in the service of the truth of the Scriptures. The enduring value of this work for Christian education and the Christian school lies in his statement that "every good and true Christian should understand that, wherever he may find truth, it is his Lord's." This nugget has been judged "the watchword of Christian humanism" (In Howie, 1969, pp. 238–239).

In a number of works Augustine presented his views about education in the liberal arts. He considered the seven liberal arts the first steps that individuals take in progressing towards divine wisdom. He made suggestions about the teacher of the liberal arts of grammar, dialectic, rhetoric, arithmetic, music, geometry, and astronomy. Within the liberal arts education he also included philosophy, which for him is the search for answers to more difficult problems than supplied by the other arts. He stated that:

> Through philosophy the learner discovers the nature of unity but in a deeper and more divine sense. Philosophy asks a double question—on the one hand about the soul and on the other hand about God. (In Howie, 1969, p. 249)

Augustine felt philosophy unifies the study of the liberal arts. His version of the liberal arts, with the inclusion of philosophy, influenced latter developments in medieval education.

As the chief teacher in Hippo Augustine offered guidance for catechists in *De Catechizandis Rudibus,* written in response to deacon Deognates, catechist in Carthage. In this still relevant work he advised catechists to adapt their lessons to the mentality and interests of the catechumens. Urging catechists not to become discouraged when they meet with failure or indifference he drew on his own experience in offering this advice:

> I would not have you be disturbed because you have often seemed to yourself to be delivering a worthless and wearisome discourse. For it may very well be that it was not so regarded by the one whom you were endeavoring to instruct, but because you were earnestly desiring to have something better for your hearers, on this account what you were saying did not seem worthy of others's ears. For my part, I am always dissatisfied with my discourse. (Augustine, 1926, p. 17)

In this work Augustine offered practical ideas for catechizing both those who are well cultured and those who have had little education.

Reflecting on his own journey of faith, Augustine showed awareness
that highly educated catechumens might at first tend to find the Scriptures lacking in elegance.

Augustine's influence on all subsequent theology, philosophy
and education has been immense throughout all periods of Christian
history. His input on educational theory has been felt throughout the
medieval and modern periods. He influenced the educational writings
of Boethius, Cassiodorus, Bede, Alcuin, John the Scot, and Anselm.
Thomas Aquinas accepted many of Augustine's teachings, though differing from him on a number of points. As will be seen, he disagreed
with Augustine on the nature of teaching, giving more influence to human efforts to bring about learning. Furthermore, Augustine was a favorite among Renaissance writers who discoursed on education, including Castiglione and Petrarch. Religious reformers Martin Luther
and John Calvin were deeply affected by Augustinian ideas. Augustine
had a special influence among sixteenth and seventeenth century French
scholars: Michel de Montaigne, Descartes, Bossuet, and Fenelon. His intellectual signature can be seen in the theological and educational ideas
of the Jansenist movement in France. In modern times when the trend in
theology, philosophy, and education has turned to a more relativist and
pragmatic orientation, Augustine has had less influence. However, religious existentialists such as Søren Kierkegaard and Martin Buber drew
on elements of his thought.

Christian Education from the Sixth to the Eighth Century

The first distinctively Christian school was the monastic school in the
fifth century. Until this time Christians had continued to attend the
classical schools. Yet voices critical of the study of classical education
began to be raised again in the fifth century. Rigorists among the Christians stigmatized classical education as a menace to the Christian faith.
Within the monasteries there had emerged a Christian culture that for
a time avoided classical or profane learning and established a separate
Christian culture centered on the Bible and the writings of the fathers
of the church. The attitudes and practices of the monks had an impact
on the practice of bishops with regard to the education of clerics.

In reality the monasteries were schools, centers of ascetic living
and learning. Some children and adolescents were accepted into these
institutions where they received elementary instruction. The most famous monastery in the West was established at Monte Cassino in the

early years of the sixth century by Benedict of Nursia (480–547), the founder of the Benedictine Order. The rule of Benedict speaks of the abbot as a teacher who instructs in Christian doctrine and adapts his methods to the learners. Education in monastic schools consisted in learning to read, memorization of the one hundred and fifty psalms, listening to public reading, and the practice of personal spiritual reading. These activities took on the character of prayer and contemplation.

During the sixth century there also existed episcopal and parish schools, modeled after the monastic schools. While these schools were designed primarily for the education of clerics, they also enrolled children and adolescents. At this time nonclerics continued to receive their education at the classical schools. There was even an attempt by Cassiodorus to establish a Christian university in Rome (Riche, 1976, chapter 3).

While learning was not a major focus in the monasteries of the East, which stressed the contemplative life, classical learning eventually became part of the education provided in monasteries of the West. With the barbarian invasions and the fall of the Roman Empire classical learning drastically declined in the West. Classical learning was preserved especially in Irish monasteries and was brought to the continent by Irish missionaries like St. Columban. By the end of the eighth century within these monasteries a form of Christian education developed that had great influence in the subsequent history of the Church. Monasteries became centers of learning by default. Monastic scholarship evolved an almost exclusively religious character. By the end of the seventh century "monastic learning—centered on grammar, computus, and chant—had as its essential goal the study of the Bible and the celebration of the liturgy, in which the love of learning and the desire for God are reconciled" (Riche, 1976, p. 497). The Christian church gained a monopoly over education and learning, which it maintained until the fifteenth century.

In the period between the sixth and eighth centuries there were a few individuals who were prominent in shaping Christian education. As mentioned earlier, monasteries did not all take the same approach to education. Cassiodorus of Vivarium (d. 575) advocated a scholarly approach to education in the monasteries, viewing these institutions not merely as contemplative places but also as places of learning. Cassiodorus proposed a balance between discipline and leisure, labor and learning, artistic appreciation and spiritual life. His *Introduction to Divine and Human Reading* initiated prospective members into monastic life at Vivarium and introduced them to both classical and religious studies. Cassiodorus encouraged the copying of manuscripts for the purposes of study. He also developed a learned and critical approach to the Scriptures. Cassiordorus was the first writer to refer to the liberal arts as the *trivium* (grammar, rhetoric, and dialectic) and *quadrivium* (mathematics, geometry, astronomy, and music). He also favored direct contact with the classical writings:

> We shall not fail to revere the authors, both Greek and Latin, whose explanations of the matters which we discuss have become famous, in order that those who desire to read zealously may more lucidly understand the words of the ancients after having first been introduced to them in abridged form. (In Bowen, 1972, p. 329)

Cassiodorus's commitment to education was so strong that he even conceived of establishing a Christian university in Rome where both sacred and profane subjects were studied. In his *Institutiones* he wrote:

> When I saw the great longing to study profane letters, so great that many men thought of attaining the wisdom of the world by them, I admit I was quite saddened to see that the Divine Scriptures were not publicly taught, whereas brilliant teaching made the profane authors celebrated. With the blessed Pope Agapitus, imitating what had been done at Alexandria, I tried, after having obtained the necessary funds, to arrange that Christian rather than secular schools would receive professors in Rome so that the souls of the faithful would be assured of eternal salvation and so that their tongues would speak a pure and correct language. (In Riche, 1976, p. 133)

There is no evidence that such an institution was ever established, due no doubt to invasions of Visogoths.

Cassiodorus's ideal of the cultured and highly educated individual who pursued learning with intensity was hard to attain. His high intellectual standards were increasingly impossible to maintain with the passing of the empire. Yet Cassiodorus is credited with adding the importance of learning to the Benedictine tradition, which previously had centered almost exclusively on prayer and manual work.

Cassiodorus's ideal can be contrasted with the limited attention given to education and intellectual activity in profane subjects in Benedict's Rule. Benedict had abandoned profane studies in Rome when he sensed they were dangerous to his faith. Apparently he never returned to them. In the Rule of St. Benedict monks are urged to avoid idleness by engaging in physical labor and the reading of sacred works. The abbot appears as a teacher but of spiritual learning. Some scholars have conjectured that the rule of Benedict does not mention studies because these were presumed to be part of the educational background of the monks. The rule, however, does not appear to have an opinion about the value of the study of letters. The rule cultivates a spiritual program but no *ratio studiorum* as developed by later religious orders. If there were studies and love of secular learning in the early monasteries, they were certainly subordinated to the love of God.

Clearly classical learning and study gained ascendancy and were fostered in monasteries, but always as a handmaiden to sacred learning. In time the Benedictine tradition added love of learning to love of God. Monastic education, however, always paid great attention to biblical sources and less to classical literature. Mystical union with God was the primary focus of this education. Thus these two men, Cassiodorus and Benedict, stand at the beginning of two essential elements in Western monastic education:

> On the one hand, the study of letters; on the other, the exclusive search for God, to love of eternal life, and the consequent detachment from all else, including the study of letters. . . . There is no ideal synthesis that can be expressed in a speculative order; only raising it to the spiritual order can transcend the conflict. (LeClerq, 1958, p. 25)

Though classical learning may or may not have had a prominent place in the creation of monastic schools, what is most significant and enduring about the monastic tradition is the decidedly spiritual nature of the education and the focus on the liturgical life of the community. In particular, the Benedictine tradition in education has been mainly a liturgical and a contemplative one. This educational and spiritual ideal had a powerful influence in the establishment of monasteries, schools, colleges, and universities throughout the world. Unfortunately, with the passage of time the spiritual salient was submerged within the more rational approach to education proposed by the scholastics. The contemporary interest in spiritual and ascetic education is in many ways a recovery of this ancient tradition of education.

While most of the work relating to learning during this period flourished in monasteries, influential works for medieval Europe increased outside monastery walls. Boethius's (ca. 480–524 or 525) *Consolation of Philosophy* (1969), written when the author was in prison, was cast as a dialogue between the author and philosophy, the queen of the sciences. The book summarizes classical ethical theories, with a primary emphasis on Stoicism. In its bittersweet pages are poems of great beauty. The influence of Plato colors Boethius's description of the ascent and illumination of the soul by philosophy. Union with God the creator of the universe, the passing of all human realities, and an emphasis on the priority of the moral life are the principal themes in this work. Besides this work Boethius wrote treatises on the liberal arts which were important for the development of medieval education. Boethius, whether he was a Christian or not (there are no citations of the Bible or mention of Jesus in the book), influenced many church people in succeeding centuries, including Alcuin, Hugh of St. Victor, John of Salisbury, Thomas Aquinas, and Dante.

Another influential work from this period was *Etymologies* or *Origines,* written by Isidore, bishop of Seville (570–636). In this twenty-book encyclopedia the author attempted to arrange in order all existing knowledge, including the liberal arts and languages, as well as Greek and Roman authors. This work was widely used in the medieval period and has survived in many manuscripts. In his copious writings Isidore placed profane studies at the service of sacred learning. At the Council of Toledo, which he presided over, he championed the establishment of episcopal schools. Isidore also wrote a monastic rule for monks in Seville, where they spent three hours a day in reading and meditating on the Bible. While Isidore did not recommend profane learning for younger monks, he did advise this study for more experienced monks. Isidore has been called the most famous pedagogue of the Middle Ages. Although some scholars even speak of an Isidorian renaissance in Spain, his influence in Spain was restricted to the monastic and episcopal schools (Riche, 1976, pp. 296–303).

Isidore's work had influence on Rabanus Maurus's (ca. 776–656) *Education of the Clergy* in which the author presented the study of the Scriptures and the seven liberal arts as the foundation for clerical education. Rabanus recommended that those destined for the ministry of divine service should acquire a fullness of knowledge which includes:

> An acquaintance with Holy Scripture, the unadulterated truth of history, the derivative modes of speech, the mystical sense of words, the advantages growing out of the separate branches of knowledge, the integrity of life that manifests itself in good morals, delicacy and good taste in oral discourse, penetration in the explanation of doctrine. . . . (In Cully, 1960, p. 95)

When it comes to the advancement of learning, however, the most valuable work for the preservation of Western learning took place in monasteries in Ireland, England, Italy, and Gaul where monks made copies of the Christian and classical literature. Irish and English monks established monasteries on the Continent where they utilized the materials that they had copied. By the eighth century virtually all education in the West, including the conduct of the schools, had become centered in the churches and monasteries. Monasteries were the principal centers for the preservation of learning.

Within the monasteries of England the most outstanding scholar of the period was Bede (c. 673–735), a teacher in the monastery at Jarrow. Bede attests to his love of study: "While observing the discipline of the rule and the daily chanting of the offices of the church, my chief pleasure has been to learn, to teach, and to write" (In Riche, 1976, pp. 380–381). While Bede is best known for his *History of the English Church and People,* he also composed textbooks on grammar, science, and poetry for the education of monks. Bede, however, was not a strong supporter of monks studying profane literature. His educational efforts were directed almost exclusively at preparing monks for the reading of the Scriptures. One critical appraisal of Bede's and other monks' work in regard to advancing culture in England seems an apt summary: "An elite of monks and clerics defined the principles of a new Christian culture but were followed by only a few lay princes. The great mass of the regular and secular clergy did not have access to Latin culture and they shared the culture of the majority of laymen" (Riche, 1976, p. 399).

The Carolingian Renaissance:
The Ninth and Tenth Centuries

While the Christian church did not establish its own schools in the early years of its existence, it is evident that from the early Middle Ages on the church established many different types of schools from grammar to university. To chronicle the development of Christian education during this period means to focus on the different kinds of schools and, more importantly, cast a sharper eye on the scholars who wrote and argued about the kind of education these schools should provide. During this particular time there was a reformulation of the seven liberal arts as the basic school curriculum. Education in grammar, rhetoric, and mathematics were accompanied by scriptural learning in both monastic and cathedral schools.

In the early Middle Ages Christians began to establish schools on a wide scale. During the rule of Charlemagne in the ninth century a concerted effort fostered increased literacy in the West. The Carolingian Renaissance began with an all-out effort to improve the education of the clergy and involved scholars from England, Italy, and Spain. It featured a revival in the study of the Latin fathers and classics that had been neglected in previous years. The movement centered around the court and palace of Charlemagne. Charlemagne insisted that each monastery and cathedral establish a school. This Renaissance in learning lasted to the end of the ninth century with the dissolution of the Frankish Empire.

Charlemagne pressured into service the English Benedictine monk Alcuin (735–804) to expand and strengthen the palace school at Aachen. Alcuin set in motion a revival of learning in the Frankish Empire and developed the materials to be used in this educational reform. He introduced the study of grammar, rhetoric, and the classical literature. Alcuin's hand in raising the standard of education for clergy was felt throughout the empire. Through the work of Alcuin Charlemagne commenced the establishment of schools. He announced his policy:

> It has seemed to us and our faithful counselors that it would be of great profit and sovereign utility that the bishoprics and monasteries of which Christ has deigned to entrust unto us the government should not be content with leading a regular and devout life, but should undertake the task of teaching those who have received from God the capacity to learn, each according to his own abilities. (In Knowles, 1962, p. 71)

As would be expected, religion was the hub of the education that the monk Alcuin proposed for the schools of the empire. The chief task of education was to draw students closer to divine truths by inculcating a correct knowledge of religious literature. Alcuin offered this exhortation:

> And let schools be established in which boys learn to read. Correct carefully the Psalms, the signs in writing, the songs, the calendar, the grammar, in each monastery or bishopric and the Catholic books; because often men desire to pray to God properly, but they pray badly because of incorrect books. And do not permit mere boys to corrupt them in reading or writing. If the Gospel, Psalter and Missal have to be copied let men of mature age do the copying, with the greatest care. (In Bowen, 1975, p. 13)

While classical literature was studied, it was carefully censored since Alcuin's goal was clearly religious: to adapt classical culture to education in the Christian faith. Though not an original thinker in theology, Alcuin indirectly raised the level of religious knowledge in the Frankish Empire. His educational work succeeded in increasing the extent and depth of learning. He not only succeeded in the area of literacy but also presided over the recovery of the biblical-patristic tradition of the fourth century (Cantor, 1993, p. 189).

At this time cathedral or collegiate schools were set up for clerics and for those who desired to be clerics. In time the schools also opened their doors to boys who wanted a career in public service. The seven liberal arts were introduced into these schools, as well as the study of dialectic and logic. These latter subjects refer to the art of discussion and verbal reasoning. The four works of Aristotle—*Categories, On Interpretation, Prior Analytics,* and *Posterior Analytics*—were used for this study. These came to be called Aristotle's *Organon* or instrument. Logic and dialectic included a study of the nature of ideas, judgments and terminology, syllogistic reasoning, definition, and demonstration. Moral education or education for virtue received equal time in cathedral schools, under such famous scholars as Gerbert of Aurilac (d. 1003) at Rheims and Bishop Fulbert at Chartres.

The efforts to raise the educational level of the secular clergy eventually resulted in the strengthening of cathedral schools and monastic schools for nonmonks. The Carolingian schools gave birth to the intellectual life of the late Middle Ages. By the eleventh century the values and ideals of the cathedral schools had been shaped. While these schools remained true to their task of imparting religion, philosophy, and ethics, these centers of learning:

> [W]ere humanistic in various senses of the word. They aimed at the
> development of the articulate individual, his integration into society,
> his active role in politics and administration. They aimed at
> humanizing the individual and through the humane individual,
> society. They cultivated poetry, oratory and conduct based on
> classical models. (Jaeger, 1994, p. 194)

While there is evidence of the church mandating such schools as early as the sixth century, it is only in the eleventh century that the cathedral schools became a powerful educational force. After this era it could be said that:

> There is such a thing as European education and thought, and
> though technique and framework change, there is a steady passage
> from one phase to another, and generally speaking, from the
> superficial to the deeper and from the narrow to the broader. . . .
> (Knowles, 1962, p. 78)

While the Carolingian Renaissance as such ended at the end of
the ninth century, its traditions were continued in Germany in the tenth
century. Some historians speak of the Ottonian Renaissance in Germany, because of the influence of the German Emperor Otto the Great
(936–973). During this time cathedral schools shouldered the responsibility for civic education as the church became more integrated into
the activities of the state. There were no significant advances in education during this period for the Ottonian Renaissance's "contribution
to rational thought was minimal, in fact retarding, since it was based
on personal authority and discouraged skeptical, critical thinking"
(Jaeger, 1994, p. 325). Scanty evidence from the eleventh century
shows that the most significant educational developments were in
Italy, fast becoming the center for the study of law and medicine.
Bologna became an international center for the study of law.

The Renaissance of the Twelfth Century

Developments in culture and learning in the twelfth century have led
historians to write of a twelfth century Renaissance, also called the
Medieval Renaissance. This Renaissance witnessed developments in
Italy, France, England, Germany, and Spain. Simultaneously, this century saw the beginning of Gothic architecture, the rise of vernacular
languages, and a renewed interest in Latin classics, Greek science, and
Greek philosophy. Furthermore the shaping of scholastic philosophy
and higher education was hammered out at this time in the important
debates on the nature of education (Haskins, 1955).

The first major figure in the twelfth century Renaissance was
Anselm of Canterbury (d. 1109), considered as the "last of the Fathers
and the first of the scholastics." Anselm was a devoted follower of Augustine and influenced the theology of both Bonaventure and Thomas
Aquinas. He is responsible for enunciating the important theological
and educational principle, *fides quaerens intellectum* [I believe in order that I may understand]. This principle canonized the major role understanding or reason plays in religious education. For Anselm:

> The proper order requires that we should believe with profound faith
> before we presume to discuss by our reason, but after we are
> strengthened in the faith we should not neglect to study to understand
> what we believe. (In Haskins, 1955, p. 350)

Anselm was ceaseless in his discoursing on the existence and nature of
God with his foil Bozo. He developed what is called the ontological argument for God's existence, an argument that deduces the existence of
God from our concept of God as an infinitely perfect Being (Gilson,
1991).

The twelfth century opened the curtain with a major theological
controversy over the power of dialectic or human reasoning as applied
to faith. This century was marked by a battle between teachers in the
cathedral schools and teachers in the monastic tradition. The prominent cathedral schoolteacher Abelard (1079–1142) in his *Sic et Non*
[*Yes and No*] applied human reason to the doctrines of the faith,
proposing arguments from the fathers for and against particular doctrines. He fashioned certain rules by which apparent contradictions
were to be resolved: examine contexts of passages; eliminate corrup-
tion in the text; make comparisons between disputed passages with
others of proven meaning; make sure there were no retractions of opinions; search for the facts that led to the decision of church; if incom-
patibilities still remain then one should conclude that this was a mystery that was to be believed or that a theory was needed to reconcile
the views (Broudy and Palmer, 1965, pp. 62–63). These dialogical
principles can easily be applied to the teaching and learning process.

As a theologian, Abelard approached and addressed all aspects of
Christian faith. His import in educational history lies in the questioning
method by which he proposed to arrive at theological opinions. Abelard's
effort amounted to testing the limits of belief and subjecting faith to criticism within certain parameters. He represents the questioning approach
to all of human experience. He stated that "by doubting we come to questioning, and by questioning we perceive the truth" (In Knowles, 1962, p.
125). While Abelard utilized this method to stimulate discussion among
his students, "his emphasis upon contradictions rather than upon agreement and the failure to furnish any solutions, real or superficial, tended
powerfully to expose the weaknesses in the orthodox position and to undermine authority generally" (Haskins, 1955, p. 355).

While Abelard influenced the scholastic method of teaching with
his presentation of arguments for and against certain propositions, the

canonist Gratian (c. 1140) with his *Decretum* or *Concord of Discordant Canons* had a even greater impact on education since his method consisted of proposition, opposition, and solution. Gratian not only collected opinions but also attempted to explain, reconcile, and harmonize the opinions of the fathers. Peter Lombard (d. 1160), a theologian in Paris, used a similar method in his *Sentences* which, next to the Bible, was the most used book in the teaching of theology in the Middle Ages.

Abelard ran afoul of the mystical Christian leaders such as Bernard of Clairvaux and their Chartrian notables. Because some of his theological opinions challenged the older educators' reliance on personal authority in their teaching, he made enemies. Abelard responded to those critics that judged his methods as disruptive of faith, "I replied that it was not my custom to have recourse to others to teach, but rather to the resources of my mind" (In LeGoff, 1993, p. 37). He advised students to:

> Care not who speaks but what the value of his words are. Things well said give an author his reputation. Neither put your faith in the words of a master out of love for him, nor let a learned man hold you in his influence by his love alone. We are nourished not by the leaves of trees, but by their fruits. The meaning is to be preferred to the mere words. The rhetoric of ornate words may capture minds effectively but true learning prefers plain speech. A wealth of words conceals a poverty of understanding. If you see that a man's teaching is inconsistent in itself you may take it that there is nothing reliable for you in it. (In Jaeger, 1994, p. 230)

Though condemned by many in his time and accused of heresy at two church councils, Abelard is still considered:

> One of the conspicuous examples of the human spirit which is encountered so rarely, that tests the limits of belief and so opposes tradition with criticism, conservation with creativity. His entire life was eloquent testimony to a refusal to compromise with the need for inquiry, wherever it may lead. (Bowen, 1975, p. 55)

Abelard accepted the judgment of the church on his teachings, living his last days in a monastery.

The most sustained reaction to Abelard's rationalism in the faith came from Bernard of Clairvaux (d. 1153), a monastic abbot in the Benedictine tradition. Bernard was committed to two things: the reform of the Benedictine movement toward greater asceticism and the suppression of the newly introduced scholastic style of dialectical inquiry. He achieved the former by establishing a monastery of Cistercian reform; he achieved the latter by having Abelard condemned as unorthodox. Bernard believed that humans gain their salvation not through dialectics or reasoning but through the life of contemplation. He insisted that salvation comes from a prior faith in God, a commitment to contemplation and an ascetical life. This life may be granted through God's grace in the form of a vision of the ultimate, which is the most intense moment in life. Bernard saw some value in classical learning but only as a way to strengthen a faith that came not from dialectics but from union with God. For Bernard true education resides in the ideals of beauty of soul and purity of conscience. His great faith in the traditional theology manifested itself through his often-quoted words:

> We are dwarfs perched on the shoulders of giants. We therefore see more and farther than they, not because we have keener vision or greater height, but because we are lifted up and born aloft on their gigantic shoulders. (In LeGoff, 1993, p. 12)

The contrast between the emerging scholastic approach to education and the older monastic way can be best understood in how each treated Scriptures. Although monastic education presumed some basic literacy, that is, knowledge of grammar and literature, its focus as found in Bernard and other monastic educators was different. In contrast to the rational approach of the scholastics, it did not attempt to deal with knowledge but strove to encourage the monks to focus on the one thing necessary, the love of God. A particular form of learning originated within this mode of education, the *lectio divina,* the slow and meditative reading, often out loud, of the word of God for the purposes of spiritual nourishment. This form of reading or study differed from the *lectio,* which developed in scholastic institutions. The *lectio divina* in monasteries was oriented toward *meditatio* (reflection, reminiscing, and ruminating) and *oratio* (prayerfulness) while the *lectio* in scholastic schools came from *quaestio* (question) proposed to the *pagina* (text) and was oriented toward the *disputatio* (debate). The sermon or spiritual talk also originated within monastic education (LeClerq, 1961, p. 72).

These two different approaches to learning—the dialectical and the mystical—are both contained in the comprehensive and systematic theory of education offered by Hugh of St. Victor (1096–1141). Elements of the Platonic-Augustinian tradition are tailored to elements of Aristotle in his writings, which were directed at the education of the clergy. In his *Didascalion—On the Study of Teaching* (1961) Hugh treats both secular and religious learning. He lines up the order in which books are to be read and studied. His discussion of knowledge includes theoretical knowledge or the apprehension of truth and practical knowledge or the learning of morality. The latter is broken down into solitary, private, and public (subdivided into ethics, economics, and politics). He also treats mechanical knowledge (textiles, armament, and commerce). Hugh's greatest attention was given to logical knowledge, which roughly corresponds to the liberal arts. He offers a pithy summary of logical knowledge:

> Grammar is the knowledge of how to speak without error; dialectic is
> clear-sighted argument which separates the true from the false;
> rhetoric is the discipline of persuading to every suitable thing. (In
> Bowen, 1975, p. 65)

In the latter part of this comprehensive work Hugh describes the study of theology. This largely consists in the study of the Scriptures and the writings of the fathers of the church. He also urged the study of Christian history. These writings are to be examined not to seek fame or in search of wondrous deeds but to strengthen one's faith.

Hugh as a master teacher also focused on the importance of method in teaching and learning. He noted that:

> The students of our day, whether from ignorance or from
> unwillingness, fail to hold to a fit method of study, and therefore we
> find many who study but few who are wise. (In Bowen, 1975, p. 66)

Hugh suggested mnemonic schemes for learning history and other subject matter. He stressed the importance of being organized in one's study. Facts are classified in the mind according to numbers, place, and time. Hugh's work evidenced a systematic manner of teaching that could be utilized by schoolmasters of the time. It was also valuable in maintaining the connection between the two traditions, monastic and scholastic, that competed against each another at that time.

The school of St. Victor of which Hugh was the most prominent member struck a balance between the strictly monastic schools and education at the secular courts. The teachers were canons regular who superimposed "an ethic of gentle, refined, courtly and urbane bearing onto the ideals of the apostolic life: equality of manners and renunciation of possessions." They stressed acquiring virtue through the training of the body, proper poise, and bearing. What they offered young men was education in "letters, beautiful manners, theological illumination, the good—that is the ordained and regulated—life, a life that left open the possibility of advancement in the church" (Jaeger, 1994, p. 267–268).

While Hugh was concerned chiefly with the education of churchmen, John of Salisbury (d. 1181), Bishop of Chartres, shifted his attention to the education of clerics who would be leaders in society. At the time when he was associated with the cathedral and court at Canterbury, he became the central figure of English learning. He considered it the function of the church and not the state to provide the educated leaders for society. This opinion flowed from his theory of church-state relationships according to which the church was the soul of the state. Thus the cathedral school under his direction added the task of civic education to its curriculum.

In his educational work *The Metalogicon* (1162) John asserted that the quality most needed for leadership in society was *civilitas,* the ability to lead in a virtuous manner in social and political life. While the principles for this education are philosophical, they are fundamentally based on the Bible. The ideal of *civilitas* included balancing ethical, moral, intellectual, and aesthetic qualities, a position that can be contrasted with the ascetical and contemplative ideal presented by Bernard and others.

Utmost in John's work was that special quality, namely, the eloquence of the ecclesiastical or political leader. John was broadly educated in and deeply committed to the ideals of classical education. He argued for a rightful place for eloquence in education in contrast to the many who felt it encouraged the demagogic person who practiced deceit. The urbane John posited eloquence as a foundation for the truth about God and the world. While John was critical of many teachers of philosophy, he still insisted on the value of rhetoric and dialectic in establishing Christian truths. He warned that the gift of eloquence had to be applied to real issues if wisdom was to result. He also commented that there were truths of faith that transcended the experience of reason. John's writings prepared the way for the flowering of the Christian humanism in the thirteenth century.

The Thirteenth Century: Scholasticism

From some perspectives the thirteenth century may be considered a golden age for Christian education. This century saw the emergence of the teaching of theology at the first universities. During this century two orders of friars (Franciscans and Dominicans) were established and devoted themselves assiduously to the task of preaching and teaching the Christian faith. The Fourth Lateran Council emphasized the importance of Christian education when it mandated that each cathedral should hire a teacher of grammar while archdioceses should have teachers in philosophy, canon law, and theology. It was also legislated that parishes should establish schools. Bishops were urged to provide suitably trained teachers for their people (Sawicki, 1988, pp. 318ff). On the negative side, it must be noted, however, that it was in this century that the Inquisition was established by the church to root out heretical ideas among ordinary people as well as suspected heretical teachers. The work of the Inquisition was placed in the hands of the two orders of friars. However, of all positive achievements of this century none had greater impact on the direction of Christian theology and education than the study of theology at the universities.

Undoubtedly, the distinctive educational achievement of the thirteenth century was the development of universities, which came into their own and flourished. Within these universities a distinctive approach to education, scholasticism, was fashioned which had great influence on Christian education. Universities emerged around prominent cathedral schools when these added to their curriculum Aristotelian logic, a new mathematics, and a new astronomy. Universities were first established at Paris, Bologna, and Salerno under papal authority. Eventually they cropped up throughout Europe. The degrees offered were bachelors, license to teach, and masters.

Of greatest concern in the history of Christian education is the University of Paris where theological studies were offered. Since in the early years of Paris all the degrees conferred were intended to certify teachers, Paris became "a city of teachers—the first city of teachers the medieval world had known" (Haskins, 1955, p. 379). Theology included the study of the sacred Scriptures and the patristic literature. While the study of theology was long recognized as a valuable activity in the Church, its study at this time became more systematic. A prominent text was the *Sentences* of Peter Lombard, which treated the doctrines of the trinity, creation, salvation, and sacraments. Continuing attention was given to the commentaries written by famous teachers and, at times, these commentaries got even more attention from teachers and students than the Scriptures themselves. Methods of teaching included the *lectio* or lecture, disputations, and debates. Some of the great teachers of theology produced well-organized *summas* or summaries of their lectures. It must also be noted that those studying theology were small in numbers since the standards for admission in theology were high and the course was extremely long. The study of theology became more popular after the Council of Trent in the sixteenth century when theological education became mandatory for clergy (Haskins, 1957).

In the course of time two religious orders came to dominate intellectual life at the University of Paris, the Franciscans and the Dominicans. While in its beginnings the Franciscan order was not committed to the intellectual life, a group within the order known as conventuals early on recognized the need for scholarship. The Dominicans or Order of Preachers were committed from their founding to preaching, teaching, and theological debate. Members of these two orders had received a mandate from the Pope to preach and to teach in parishes and universities. In this work they were also joined by other religious order such as the Augustinians, Premonstratensians, and even the Cistercians, all of whom established schools for novices around university towns (Goff, 1993, p. xv).

Within the medieval universities that emerged around the eleventh century a particular approach to education developed that challenged the prevailing monastic education. This soon came to be known as scholasticism and was based on the philosophy of Aristotle. The main theological and educational debate in the twelfth and thirteenth centuries pitted the scholastic teachers in the cathedral schools and universities against the older monastic tradition in education. The former were the innovators in bringing to bear on Christian theology and education the power of logic and dialectics. The latter remained committed to the more spiritual approach that focused almost exclusively on the Scriptures and the patristic literature. In many ways this monastic education aligned itself with the patristic education, especially with the teachings of Augustine. The scholastic theologians who pushed the power of reason to its limits in philosophy and theology prepared the way for a more rational theology and the separation of philosophy from theology. They were also the precursors of the thinkers of the Enlightenment period in their emphasis on the power of human logic and reasoning.

The chief argument that divided scholars at this time was what role should the philosophy of Aristotle play in the explanations of the Christian faith. Many felt that the Platonic-Augustinian tradition with its emphasis on intuitive knowledge was the best way to express Christian faith. For the most part the Franciscans were associated with this point of view. Others saw the philosophy of Aristotle, with its grounding in human experience of the world, as a preferable way to present Christian teachings. In their view human experience of the world could form the basis for the demonstration of God's existence. Dominicans for the most part were associated with this approach.

The leading intellectual among the Franciscans was Bonaventure (1217–1274), a teacher at the University of Paris. Though he utilized Aristotle in his teaching, he was committed to the Augustinian position that faith is necessary in order to ensure the full functioning of reason. As a spiritual disciple of Augustine Bonaventure made his exclusive concern the human soul and its progress towards union with God. His thought is summed up in the title of his principal book: *The Journey of the Soul to God.* For him knowledge without faith and centered on worldly matters is virtually useless. Bonaventure did not have the full range of intellectual interests that Thomas Aquinas had in law, art, society, and politics. For Bonaventure:

> Philosophy, faith, theology, contemplation, and ecstasy were stages in the journey that the Christian doctor was himself making and teaching others to make. All teaching, all knowledge, therefore was dynamic, progressive, and teleological. All conceptions of philosophy or even theology as a purely intellectual discipline was entirely alien from his mind. (Knowles, 1962, p. 244)

While Bonaventure remained faithful to the basic theological and educational ideals of Augustine, other minds in the universities started to compartimentalize philosophy and other disciplines. Theology seemed headed for an intellectual limbo and eventually became a science. A synthesis of Christian thought that took into account growing human knowledge awaited the work of Thomas Aquinas.

The intellectual leader of the Dominicans and one of the most influential theologians in the Catholic Church was Thomas Aquinas (1224–1274) who built his impressive synthesis chiefly on the philosophy of Aristotle, all the while incorporating elements of the Augustinian-Platonic tradition. Thomas made use of human experience in establishing Christian beliefs. He attempted a synthesis between learning from experience and learning from faith. In 1879 his theology, found principally in the massive *Summa Theologica,* was made the official norm for Catholic theology by Pope Leo XIII.

From the point of view of educational theory Thomas's ideas on education are less important than the use that others made of his entire system of thought in developing the neo-Thomism or neoscholasticism of the nineteenth and twentieth centuries. In a later chapter we will treat this influential theory of Christian education which was dominant among Roman Catholic scholars, notably Jacques Maritain and Etienne Gilson, in the first half of the twentieth century. Thomas Aquinas was also influential in the work of the American educators Mortimer Adler and Robert Hutchins during this same period.

Although Aquinas is credited by some with presenting a new theory of Christian education that challenged the Augustinian-Platonic theory, he did not write extensively on educational theory. Rather than look for a full theory of education it is more realistic to identify themes from Thomas that have relevance for education, as Donohoe has done in *St. Thomas and Education* (1958).

For Aquinas there were two forms of learning. Humans learn by *discovery* when natural reason acquires knowledge by its own operations alone, by coming to clear awareness of what was previously known only implicitly. The second form of learning takes place by *instruction* in which a person transmits knowledge to another. In Thomas's view "the words of the teacher, heard or seen in writing, have the same efficacy in causing knowledge as things outside the soul" (In Bowen, 1975, p. 154). Thus teaching is understood as a dynamic process in which there are two causes: the teacher and the active mind of the student.

Christian scholars before Aquinas, notably Origen and Augustine, were reluctant to give the title of teacher to humans, insisting that God alone is the teacher in that God illuminates human understanding. Thomas assigned an important role to the teacher in his *De Magistro* in which he applied Aristotle's theory of causality to an understanding of teaching and learning. Rather than calling the teacher merely a midwife that assisted in bringing innate knowledge to consciousness, Thomas enhanced the role of the teacher by elevating the teacher to the level of instrumental cause of learning. For Thomas the teacher draws out human potentiality to perfection and activity. The child is the material cause with which the teacher works. The student's activity is the efficient cause of learning. Thus the principle of knowledge is within the learner. The formal cause or aim of learning is the integrated and liberated human person. The final cause is the ideal to which education aspires, the vision of God. The teacher acts as an instrumental cause to stimulate the activity of the learner by presenting ideas. In his theory the teacher acts as a secondary or ministerial cause since the teacher cooperates with God and nature in assisting students to learn. For Thomas the role of the teacher is similar to that of the doctor in the healing of patients. Like the doctor the teacher assists nature by administering to the mind, contributing judgment, intellectual skill, and understanding. While this view might not have the spiritual power of the Augustinian view, it does accord more with our human experience of what happens in the teaching and learning process (Beck, 1964, p. 124–5).

Themes from Thomas Aquinas that have relevance for modern education have been identified (Donohoe, 1958). First, Thomas affirmed the dignity of human intelligence and was optimistic about what it can do. In doing so he presented an intellectual basis both for education and the religious life. Second, his teaching on the role of habit or disposition allows us to recognize that education entails the development of qualities of soul. Third, his teaching that sense experience is integral to the life of the mind suggests that educators be concrete in their expositions. Fourth, Thomas offers the insight that intellectual activity has influence over all aspects of life. Fifth, his attempt to fuse faith and reason, religion and culture gives an overarching aim to Christian education. Finally, there is Thomas's insight that one's approach to education is connected with one's view of humans and of society, which Thomas expresses in this manner:

> In so far as men judge differently about the goal of human life, so will they judge differently about the character of their social life together. Those who make pleasure or power or prestige their goal will think that the best of societies is one in which they can live pleasurably or amass riches or honors or control over others. But those who put a premium on virtue as the purpose of this earthly life will think that the best of societies in which men can best live together in peace and goodness. (In Donohoe, 1958, pp. 107–108)

Comparisons and contrasts have been made between the Augustinian view of teaching and learning and that of Thomas. Since Thomas makes a clearer distinction than Augustine does between learning from a teacher and learning by oneself, he does not hesitate to call the teacher a real cause of learning in students, so long as it is recognized that God is the principal cause of learning and that students are also causes. The difference between the two has been thus expressed:

> St. Augustine's theory emphasizes the ultimate importance of the
> activity of the involved learner and his absolute independence of the
> teacher; on the other hand, St. Thomas's view, marked as it is by his
> Aristotelian realism, makes greater concessions to commonsense by
> showing that the teacher is an indispensable, if temporary participant
> in the ongoing process of every man's earthly education. (Howie,
> 1969, p. 207)

Opposition to Thomas's ideas came from many quarters, especially
from Franciscans such as Roger Bacon, Duns Scotus, and William of
Occam. Some of his writings received condemnation by Church authorities. The arguments among these thinkers are more appropriate for
the history of theology than for the history of education. The main
thrust of their criticisms was that Thomas had reduced Christian faith
to Aristotelianism in not allowing for knowledge of God through direct human experience.

The scholastic emphasis on logic and dialectics or argumenta-
tion in the service of faith produced a remarkable synthesis. In time,
however, the synthesis became arid and full of subtleties. The intellectual reaction to late scholasticism is seen in the new educational
theories of the Renaissance and the criticisms of the Protestant Reformers. As discussed in a later chapter, a revival of interest in the
scholastic philosophy appeared at the end the nineteenth century and
lasted through the first half of the twentieth century. The work of the
scholastics had reached far beyond the thirteenth century for "subsequent centuries would begin to examine their unchallenged assumptions, root metaphors, contradictions of fact, methodologies, and so
forth. That was the beginning of the modern mind. . . . " (Sawicki,
1988, p. 26).

Scholasticism received criticism in the beginning of the fifteenth
century even from a chancellor of the University of Paris, Jean Gerson
(ca. 1363–ca. 1429). Influenced by the Victorine school of theology,
he was critical of the subtleties of scholastic theology and called for a
return to the Scriptures and fathers of the church. Gerson wrote one influential work on Christian education, *On Leading Children to Christ.*
This work focuses mainly on how confessors should deal with children
and their failings. The example and writings of Gerson offered a strong
justification for giving extensive attention to the care of children. Gerson advised that teachers adapt themselves to children, not to step
down to their level but rather to lift them up to theirs. About the teaching of children he remarked:

> Where there is no love, what good is instruction, as one neither likes
> to listen to it nor properly believes in the words heard, nor follow the
> commandments. Therefore it is best to forego all false dignity and to
> become a child among children. Yet, all sins have to be avoided, and
> all signs of impure love have to be held at bay. . . . [The confessor]
> will not be able to convince them unless he smiles kindly at the
> laughing ones, encourages those who play, praises their progress in
> learning, and when remonstrating, avoids all that is bitter or insulting.
> Then the children will feel what he does not hate, but loves them like
> a brother. (In Cully, 1960, pp. 123–124)

A link between the medieval world of the scholastics and the learning of Renaissance humanists, to be treated in the next chapter, is found in the work of Dante. Living in Florence during the Renaissance the great Italian poet Dante Alighieri (1285–1321) can be viewed both as a medieval scholastic and a Renaissance humanist. His *Divine Comedy* has been interpreted as "a progressive education leading to the higher realm of speculation, culminating in philosophy and theology and ending in religious epiphany, yet grounded in the pagan classics and liberal arts" (Kelley, 1991, p. 4). This great work has the characteristics of the medieval mentality, grand in scope, deeply religious, encyclopedic in its learning. Dante differed from the humanists in his commitment to scholastic philosophy, to Aristotle whom he called the master of all those who know, to Thomas Aquinas who ranked high in his estimation, and to theology which was for him the queen of the sciences. He differed from the medieval scholastics in his preference for the vernacular over Latin, his critical attitude toward the church, his love of poetry, and the free rein that he gave to the imagination. However when he expressed opinions which are close to an educational theory, he epitomized the highest ideals of the medieval mind:

> Unerring providence has therefore set man to attain two goals: the
> first is happiness in this life, which consists in the exercise of his own
> powers and is typified by the earthly paradise; the second is the
> happiness of eternal life, which consists in the enjoyment of the
> divine countenance, which man cannot attain to by his own power but
> only by the aid of divine illumination, and is typified by the heavenly
> paradise. These two sorts of happiness are attained by diverse means,
> just as one reaches conclusions by different means. We attain to the
> first by means of philosophical teaching, being faithful to it by
> exercising our moral and intellectual virtues. We arrive at the second
> by means of spiritual teaching, which transcends human reason, in so

far as we exercise the theological virtues of faith, hope, and charity (In Bowen, 1975, p. 185).

Summary

This chapter focused primarily on early developments in both parts of the Roman Empire. Most often educators were bishops who wrote discourses or sermons on Christian formation. The towering figure of Augustine dominated thinking about education as no other. Educational efforts took place in monasteries and in small institutions under the direction of bishops. Religious education received a considerable boost with the rise of universities where theology became a dominating area of study. Among church leaders and scholars debates arose over the nature of education as rational or mystical. By the end of this period the scholastic or rational approach marked education in the universities and in the schools that prepared students for university education. A more spiritual or mystical education prevailed in the monasteries. The arid education that scholasticism often resulted in awaited the scathing criticism of Renaissance humanists and Protestant reformers.

Chapter 3

Christian Renaissance Humanism: 1320 to 1600

> I might also add that a sensible reading of the pagan poets and philosophers is a good preparation for the Christian life. We have the example of St. Basil, who recommends the ancient poets for their natural goodness. Both St. Augustine and St. Jerome followed this method. St. Cyprian has worked wonders in adorning the Scriptures with the literary beauty of the ancients. Of course it is not my intention that you imbibe the bad morals of the pagans along with their literary excellence. I am sure that you will nonetheless find many examples in the classics that are conducive to right living. Many of these writers were, of course, very good teachers of ethics. (Erasmus in Bowen, 1975, p. 333)

The focus in this chapter is on the development of the educational theory of Renaissance humanism, with special notice given to how it laid the theoretical basis for the Christian school that emerged at this time. Developments in Italy, England, and Germany are given the most attention since movements in those countries have had long lasting influence on the direction of education in general and Christian education in particular. The chapter concludes with the treatment of a particular form of Renaissance humanism developed by the Protestant reformers Martin Luther and John Calvin. It was this stamp of humanism that formed the basis of the educational ideals of those who established educational institutions in the United States. Christian education among Protestants and Catholics has been greatly influenced by educational ideals and practices developed in this period of history.

Historians have identified at least two periods within the Renaissance of Western learning. The first phase of the Renaissance, the Ital-

ian Renaissance, took place in Italy from 1320 to the end of the fifteenth century. At this time scholars, especially in Florence, took a renewed interest first in the Latin and later in the Greek classics. They
established schools where secular learning received more study than it
did in the monastic and cathedral schools. This effort was partially motivated by a negative attitude toward the excessive rationalism of medieval theology. These scholars maintained and fostered a religious
faith, but more in the form of a simple or biblical piety than in the mode
of the scholastic theology. The second phase of the Renaissance, called
the Northern Renaissance, took place mainly in Holland, England, and
Germany. Scholars within this revival of learning manifested a decidedly keener religious interest and focused their attention on the reform
of theology and of the church, as well as on the values of the classical
literature.

Though the Renaissance in fourteenth century Europe is rightly
viewed as a broad cultural movement involving changes in politics,
theology, philosophy, and the fine arts, it is also widely recognized that
the essence of Renaissance humanism is found in its educational efforts. While the Renaissance provided the basic texts for study, research, and creative development, its chief educational achievement
was found in the secondary and preparatory schools which were established in European countries, mainly for boys between the ages of
eight and sixteen. The humanist curriculum prevailed in the German
gymnasium, the French lycée, and the English public school. This curriculum traveled with Europeans as they colonized Asia, Africa, and
the Americas. In their curriculum Renaissance humanist schools
melded the classical and medieval, the secular and the religious. The
Renaissance educational theory, which prevailed at least until the early
decades of the twentieth century, marks a high point in the development of both Christian education and Western civilization. Its essential ingredients have been concisely described:

> Combined with continued faith in the Christian tradition as articulated
> by Augustine, as communicated in Jerome's Bible, as rationalized by
> Thomism, as synthesized by Dante, this was to be the essence of
> western civilization down to the early decades of the twentieth
> century. (Cantor, 1993, p.561)

The first Renaissance humanists were teachers of the humanities
or humane studies, which included the studies of grammar, rhetoric,
history, and poetry. They readily distinguished themselves from those

who taught divine subjects or the various branches of theology. Their primary objective in teaching was to deal with the spiritual relationships of men and women with God. Although some humanists posited an opposition between these two types of studies, human and divine, most saw them as complementary. Thus in its beginnings "Renaissance humanism was not so much a philosophical tendency or system, but rather a cultural and educational program which emphasized and developed an important area of studies" (Kristeller, 1961, p. 10). In modern usage, however, the term *humanism* has come to signify a world-view or attitude of mind that places human understanding at the center of study. According to this view:

> By studying the products of the human spirit, especially art and literature, one penetrates to the human mystery in much the same way that the theologian penetrates to the mystery of God through the study of his product, the cosmos. (Coates, White, and Schapiro, 1966, p. 5)

The humanist curriculum consisted of the traditional subjects of grammar and rhetoric (reading, speaking, and writing), poetry, history, and moral philosophy. The broad movement of Renaissance humanism did not, however, have one particular ideology for:

> Renaissance humanism as such was not Christian or pagan, Catholic or Protestant, scientific or antiscientific, optimistic or pessimistic, active or contemplative, although it is easy to find for these attitudes, and for many others, a certain number of humanists who favored them. What they all have in common is something else: a scholarly, literary, and educational ideal based on the study of ancient antiquity. (Kristeller, 1962, p. 12)

Humanist education encompassed the world of letters and action. The Renaissance man (l'uomo universale) was to use his learning for the betterment of society as citizen, lawyer, prince, Christian, bishop, historian, poet, or scientist. As far as we know, only a small number of women received education in the humanities during this period. This humanist education was certainly viewed as the path to knowledge, mastery of one's self, and a vehicle for service to the entire community. At this time women were neither teachers nor public persons (Grafton and Jandine, 1986, p. 57)

Even at the beginning of the twenty-first century there are still powerful voices that attempt to promote the value of this humanistic education against a growing number of critics who propose an education that draws on many cultural traditions. The present-day battle over the canon of books to be taught in colleges and secondary schools reflects a debate over the continuing value for our times of the Renaissance humanist tradition. The argument over the Eurocentric nature of United States education has its roots in the educational theory of Renaissance humanist, which defined what it is to be an educated person.

The Italian Renaissance and Humanist Education

The social context for the Italian Renaissance spread secular and urban culture in the developing Italian cities of Florence, Milan, Pisa, and Rome. In the Italy of this time many currents of thought converged: medieval scholasticism, Byzantine culture, and Muslim learning. Civic and public life grew in intensity, as trading pumped new money and ideas into Italian life. This new urban culture demanded a new alignment of law, communications, politics, and education. Thus while the study of the humanities was an end in itself for some humanists, humanist education also had as its broader purpose the ethical and vocational education of theologians, lawyers, politicians, merchants, and teachers for their professional roles in society. This new humanist education centered on laypersons and their activities in the world rather than on clerics and their responsibilities in the church. Italian humanists in going back to the classic literature of Greece and Rome were generally dissatisfied with the heavy emphasis on dialectics and speculation in education. This dissatisfaction was especially evident in theological matters that characterized the scholastically oriented university education of the times.

As an intellectual movement Italian Renaissance humanism placed greater emphasis on the appealing mystical philosophy of Plato than on the rationalist philosophy of Aristotle. This movement is so called because it accepted the primacy of human values over the institutional values of the church and feudal institutions. In their writings Italian humanists relied more on human reason than on institutional authority. They esteemed the main values of the Greek and Roman classics that they considered rich in both intellectual and moral textures. These Renaissance humanists remained deeply committed to religious values, especially those of the Scriptures. Some humanists even wedded the Gospels with Plato to form a Christian Platonism that stressed a spiritual, mystical, and personal relationship to God. In essence, as classical civilization advanced the letter, so Christianity advanced the spirit of Renaissance culture.

The Renaissance in Italy began with the pioneering work of Francisco Petrarch (d. 1374), a keen student of classical literature, who has been called "the father of humanism." Petrarch authored numerous books praising the great Roman orators and leaders. He also wrote many poems in which he extolled the rare beauty of his beloved Laura as well as the wondrous beauty of creation. Petrarch made a collection of Latin literature under the commission of various popes and cardinals of the church. In the classical past he found the lessons that were needed for his times. Petrarch, as a principal leader in the Latin revival, emphasized classical models with the use of original sources and the exacting application of the principles of literary interpretation. He placed less emphasis on dialectics and fostered the many virtues of the scholarly life. While the revival that he and other Italian humanists inaugurated catered mainly to the education of the ruling classes, their educational program was a radical break with the medieval approach to education. Their program marked the beginning of modern liberal arts education, which eventually reached people of all classes of society.

Petrarch's approach to education promoted the moral discipline needed by individuals for a complete life in the world. He pointed to the great men of the past as striking examples of persons who had achieved moral discipline in acting rightly toward God and their fellow humans. For Petrarch a person's sense of morality came primarily through the knowledge of history, philosophy, and poetry. Of the Greek writers, Petrarch the poet preferred Plato to Aristotle because of his own aversion to the extremes in dialectics that students of Aristotle employed. However, his scholarly interest was more in the Roman camp than in the Greek. Of the Latins his favorite was Cicero, who personified for him Roman virtue and *civilitas*. Petrarch saw in Cicero and other Romans the virtues of the Christian gentleman.

The religious dimension of education appears prominently in Petrarch's later writings. After some severe setbacks in public life he turned for consolation to the writings of Augustine of Hippo and withdrew into a more solitary life. He leaned heavily on Augustine, particularly his *Confessions,* for his views on piety and spirituality. Petrarch was keenly interested in church doctrine and the defense of religious orthodoxy. The highest religious ideal and Christian duty for him was not self-denial but rather self-fulfillment. Like other humanists Petrarch greatly valued the beautiful things of this world which he considered evidences for the existence of God. His concern for himself and for the world was inspired by his Christian faith. Petrarch like many humanists was critical of the church of his times, finding its worship too insipid and its theology too alienated from human concerns. In turning to the writings of the early church fathers such as Augustine he sought out a spirit which would nourish him and his fellow humanists. His spiritual life was thus nourished both by classical and Christian writings. Petrarch's spiritual autobiography found expression in the form of letters to classical and Christian heroes to whom he poured out his doubts and ambiguities, as Augustine had done in his confessions to God. It has been noted that:

> The charm of his art and the immediacy of his personal quest for order and health struck responsive chords in his generation; he, more than any other, was responsible for a rebirth of that respect for the individual personality in its search for self-understanding and the right of free expression which had been founded and at the same time lost in the Patristic age. (Coates, White, and Shapiro, 1966, p. 12)

Although somewhat engaged in public affairs in his early adulthood, Petrarch recommended the *vita contemplativa* or the *vita solitaria,* a contemplative and solitary life retreat for properly developing the mind and the spirit. Yet Petrarch was no total recluse for he could say "No solitude is so profound, no house so small, no room so narrow but it may open to a friend" (In Charlton, 1965, p. 24).

Petrarch's importance in the history of Western culture and education was recognized shortly after his lifetime. Rudolph Agricola, a fifteenth century scholar, expressed gratitude for Petrarch's achievement:

> We are indebted to Petrarch for the intellectual culture of our century. All ages owe him a debt of gratitude—antiquity for having rescued its treasure from oblivion, and modern times for having with his strength founded and revived culture, which he has left as a precious legacy to future ages. (Spitz in Goodman and MacKay, 1990, p. 219)

Giovanni Boccaccio (1313–1375), a disciple of Petrarch, extended the Renaissance revival of classical learning to the study of the Greek language and literature. Like Petrarch he was keenly interested in manuscripts. His renown came, however, through his poetry, especially the *Decameron,* a series of stories told by men and women while they were escaping from a plague that beset Florence. The poems are noted more for entertainment than for education.

Not all humanists followed Petrarch in praising the contemplative life. Leonardo Bruni (c. 1370–1440) sang the praises of the *vita activa et civilis,* and stated that "the contemplative life is, to be sure the more divine and rare, but the active life is more excellent with respect to the common good" (Bruni, 1987, p. 87). In what has been called civic humanism Bruni added the study of history to the humanist concern with preparation for public and political spheres. Of history he noted:

> Knowledge of the past gives guidance to our counsels and our
> practical judgment, and the consequences of similar undertakings will
> encourage or deter us according to our circumstances in the present.
> (Bruni, 1987, p. 245)

Bruni's civic humanism stressed a public life in which liberty, virtue, and republican government play a prominent role. The tradition of civic humanism was continued by Machiavelli and others.

Bruni was a humanist who attempted to revive classical models while still doing justice to Christian studies. Education for him centered on a study of poets, historians, and orators of the past, especially those who emphasized the religious duties of individuals. He made room in his curriculum not only for Plato and Cicero but also for Jerome, Augustine, and Boethius. Although he assigned value to Christian studies for education in morality, there is no doubt of his greater love for the works of the Greeks and Romans.

Another prominent humanist, Petrus Paulus Vergerius (d. 1420), professor of logic and law, considerably widened humanist concerns in education. Vergerius mapped out the first systematic program for humanist education in his *The Education of the Gentleman.* He placed an emphasis on a mild asceticism for the early years of education and echoed Petrarch's concept of education for moral discipline. Vergerius stressed the father's role in the education of sons. A primary purpose of early education in his view was the inculcation of reverence for the church, society, and elders.

Vergerius' chief concern was with higher education. For him the essence of liberal education consisted of studies in history, moral philosophy, and eloquence. He described liberal education in these terms:

> We call those studies liberal which are worthy of a free man; those
> studies by which we attain and practice virtue and wisdom; that
> education which calls forth, trains and develops those highest gifts of

body and mind which ennoble men, and which are rightly judged to
rank next in dignity to virtue alone. (In Bowen, 1975, p. 214)

Within the study of liberal arts Vergerius focused on what he considered the study of philosophy, history, and eloquence, which he defined in these terms:

> By philosophy we learn the essential truth of things which by
> eloquence we so exhibit in orderly adornment as to bring conviction
> to differing minds. And history provides the light of experience, a
> cumulative wisdom fit to supplement the force of reason and
> persuasion of eloquence. For we allow that soundness of judgment,
> wisdom of speech, integrity of conduct are the marks of a truly liberal
> spirit. (In Charlton, 1965, p. 35)

Like Petrarch, Vergerius favored the classical Romans over the Greeks. He rejected the Platonic concept that knowledge was preexistent, arguing that the teacher's role was to mediate between students and knowledge. For him the teacher was important because in his view learning did not occur immediately through some kind of divine illumination, as Augustine and other Platonists thought. Interestingly, Vergerius suggested guidelines for teachers in their task of mediating learning: put material to be learned in order; present small amounts of information at a time; proceed to the next point only after previous ideas are grasped; carefully organize bodies of content of knowledge; and space learning and instruction throughout the school day. Vergerius also recognized that individuals had different qualities of mind according to which their education might be conducted:

> Respecting the general place of liberal studies, we remember that
> Aristotle would not have them absorb the entire interests of life: for
> he kept steadily in view the nature of man as a citizen, an active
> member of the state. For the man who has surrendered himself
> absolutely to the attractions of Letters or of speculative thought
> follows perhaps a self-regarding end and is useless as a citizen or as a
> prince. (In Bowen, 1975, p. 217)

The educational ideals of Italian humanism prevailed despite opposition from many quarters. Some religious leaders contended that humanism gave too much praise and attention to classical figures and pagan modes of life to the neglect of the teachings and examples provided within the church. Defenders of humanism, however, often appealed to the ideas of Basil and others in praise of the classics, which were discussed in the previous chapter. As we have seen, this tension between defenders of classical learning and supporters of Christian sources has marked Christian education from its earliest days. This tension continues in various forms among Christian educators down to our own time.

The ideals fostered by Petrarch and Vergerius found concrete expression in the secondary schools or gymnasiums which humanists established in Italy. From these institutions students went to the university or studium, which, however, only gradually began to advance humanist studies. Some Italian humanists in their desire to advance Platonic ideas even revived the classical academy, a free association where scholars discussed intellectual matters. Within secondary schools and academies the schoolmaster became an important figure.

A notable secondary school was established in Mantua by Victorino da Feltre (1378–1445). Previously he had established the Casa Giocosa in Padua in which he attempted to offer an education leading to moral, ethical, and religious cultivation through a study of classical authors and Christian sources. In his school at Padua Victorino integrated classical ideals with Christian learning and piety, following the lead of Vergerius and Bruni. All the studies of the liberal arts were included in the curriculum. Victorino also highlighted the training of the body, the development of manners, and the formation of a moral character. The study of Roman authors, especially Cicero, stressed at this school, seeped into the educated ranks of the Italian nobility. The curriculum and ethos of the school have been characterized, in sharp contrast to the cathedral and monastic schools, as "active, healthy and happy . . . with a clearly defined ethical character" (Laurie, 1969, p. 6). At the time of his death Victorino, more than any other Renaissance figure, had become the embodiment of the new conception of the schoolmaster.

A narrower approach to humanist education found its niche in Guarino da Verona's (d. 1460) school that tended to view this education as an adornment, valuable only for its recreational value. It should be noted that humanist education never became widespread because of the dual demands for materials and highly educated teachers.

The growth of universities in Italy, beyond Bologna and Padua, was slow. In these universities the influence of Aristotle and scholasticism prevailed. Humanists who were more inclined toward Plato and the Neoplatonists sunk their roots in the classically inspired academies.

The most notable academy was the Platonic Academy of Florence under the guidance of Marsilio Ficino (1433–1499). Ficino translated many classical works and wrote commentaries on Neoplatonic philosophers. Ficino's principal works were *Theologica Platonica de Immortalitate Animae* and *De Christiana Religione.* Ficino attempted to accomplish in his writings reconciliation between Christianity and Plato. Plato's philosophy was accepted by Ficino as a norm and Christianity was explained in terms of it. While Augustine accepted only those parts of Plato that could be reconciled with Christianity, Ficino on the other hand seemed to accommodate Christianity to Platonism. Using Plato as a springboard, Ficino presented his beliefs in human dignity, which he asserted came from the indwelling of the divine logos within each person. The purpose of life for him was to seek union with the Creator and through this union to achieve the greatest happiness. This Platonic and Augustinian form of theology offered much greater warmth and satisfaction than the rationalist Thomistic synthesis which was based largely on Aristotle. The artists of the period also imported the ideals and forms of Plato into their artistic conceptions. Aristotelian ideas, however, were influential in the writings of the Italian humanist Pietro Pomponazzi (d. 1251).

The Platonic ideals as described by Ficino found favor among Renaissance artists. Sculptors and painters attempted to embody the universal truths of beauty and love in symbolic forms. The interest of Botticelli and Michelangelo in the human body represented an effort to hold on high the ideal or higher nature of the human. The main objective of the Platonic artists and philosophers was to present as vivid as possible the beauty and dignity of the human. The idealist humanist vision of the human offered by artists and philosophers alike was no better expressed than by Pico della Mirandola when he placed these words in the mouth of God at the dawn of creation:

> We have set thee at the world's center that thou mayest from thence more easily observe whatever is in the world. We have made thee neither of heaven nor of earth, neither mortal nor immortal. . . . (In Laurie 1969, p. 74)

Another Italian humanist who gave extensive attention to education was Baldesar Castiglione (d. 1529), bishop of Avila. Castiglione wrote *The Book of the Courtier,* a treatise for men and women who were preparing for the service of princes. The education he proposed was both literary and physical or recreational. Greek and Roman classics were studied as well as the fine arts. Castiglione touched upon the moral life and overall bearing of the courtier. For the education of women he advised an education for modesty and humility. Castiglione was also concerned with the education of princes. He devoted much attention to an education in the arts, especially music and painting. His courtly and artistic emphases represented a departure from the ideal of civic humanism in that he restricted himself to a concern with the education of persons around the court.

The darker side of Italian humanism is etched in the writings of Niccolò Machiavelli (1469–1527). In a number of books, but especially in *The Prince* (1513), he reflected somewhat cynically on many aspects of Italian political life. This complex figure has been viewed by historians either as a disillusioned public servant who passionately reaffirmed humanistic values or as a slave to political power and an advocate of force and deviousness in the political sphere. While Machiavelli's commitment to humanist learning was firm, he did harbor a rather pessimistic view of human nature. While believing that human nature is always and everywhere self-serving and cowardly, he still saw humans as the most creative power in the world. Making a distinction between what humans are and what they could be, he attempted to describe a state or republic in which tyranny can be avoided. Machiavelli's advice to rulers of states is still shocking to modern readers:

> It is not necessary for the prince to have . . . [good] qualities, but it is
> necessary that he seem to have them. . . . He should seem to be all
> mercy, faith, integrity, humanity, and religion. (Machiavelli, 1950,
> p. 63)

The prince according to Machiavelli should appear to have these qualities in order that the masses of the people would imitate him. Of the people he remarked that they only "see what you appear to be; few feel what you are, and those few will not dare oppose themselves to the many" (Machiavelli, 1950, p. 66).

While Machiavelli did not directly involve himself with Christian education as such, his work has had some influence on certain forms of moral education for Christians in the world. His rather dark and Augustinian view of the sinfulness of human nature and his questionable justification of achieving good ends through what are considered evil means have raised important issues for the Christian moralist and educator. In developing an ethic for a time of crisis Machiavelli prefigured the ethical stance of Christian realism developed by the twentieth century Protestant theologian and educator Reinhold Niebuhr. Niebuhr attempted to deal realistically with issues of state power, violence, human evil, and Christian faith.

A more optimistic view of human nature and its potential bore fruit in the Renaissance artists of fifteenth century Italy. These artists knew both the real world and the world that could possibly come into being through intelligent human activity. The Renaissance artists attempted to reveal the form, order, and harmony that were realizable in human life. Renaissance artists like Michelangelo and da Vinci were premier examples of Renaissance educators and students. On the one hand, they were scientists in their careful knowledge of perspectives, optics, mathematics, and physics and, on the other hand, they were philosophers who propounded visions of what the world might be. Above all, they were teachers who challenged students with engaging visions of the ideal world "so natural that the beholder would be seduced into believing in it and working for its realization as a program consciously followed" (Coates, White, and Shapiro, 1966, p. 33). Some of these artistic geniuses were in their own right theologians. They used many religious themes to incite beholders to transcend natural life and to reach for the divine. Da Vinci wrote in his notebooks:

> Behold, the hope and desire for repatriation and for the return of the first state is similar to the urge which drives the moth into the flame. Man who with continual longing and full of joy looks always forward to the new spring, always to the new summer, always to new months and new years—he does not realize that he wished for his own destruction. But this wish is the quintessence, the very spirit of the elements, which finds itself imprisoned in his soul, and always longs to return from the human body to Him who has sent it forth. (da Vinci in Panofsky, 1962, p. 182)

The Italian Renaissance became internationalized in the fifteenth century. Italian scholars carried the ideals of the Italian Renaissance to other countries of Europe as they went abroad in the fifteenth century to teach in schools and institutes and to search for manuscripts. Also, scholars from European countries came to Italy to study with great Italian humanists. In addition, there was scholarly correspondence between Italian humanists and scholars in other countries.

Humanism eventually became widespread in other European countries besides Italy. While it flourished in the northern European countries of England and Germany, humanism had only little impact on education in France and Spain. The humanism that developed in England and Germany had a more pronounced religious dimension than Italian humanism. The northern humanism was even more determined to move away from the abstractness of medieval scholasticism. Three most distinguished humanists—Colet, More, and Erasmus—led the movement to strengthen both education and religion. The educational efforts of the Protestant Reformers Martin Luther, Philip Melanchthon, Ulrich Zwingli, and John Calvin depended in great measure on the humanist tradition.

The Northern Renaissance: Christian Humanism in England

English humanism began when scholars at Oxford introduced the study of the Greek language and Greek writings into the curriculum. Humanism was also welcomed into English education, especially into the grammar schools, as a way of strengthening the knowledge and practice of religion. These grammar schools emerged in the fifteenth century to meet the educational and vocational needs of the new commercial classes. The high point of English humanism came when Erasmus, Colet, and More fostered humanist education to support their view of Christianity.

Although not an Englishman, the most significant and influential figure in both Northern and English humanism was Desiderius Erasmus (c. 1466–1536). Born in Holland, he considered himself a citizen of the world and traveled extensively through many countries. His entire scholarly life was driven by the desire to reform religion and education. As Erasmus expressed it:

> My whole purpose in life has been two-fold: to stimulate others to cultivate *bonae litterae* into harmony with theology . . . and to initiate a process which would impart to *bonae litterae* a truly Christian note. . . . Secondly, that the study of theology on its present conventional lines [scholasticism] might itself be improved and enlightened by theologians acquiring a better knowledge of classical Latin and Greek and an improved critical taste in literature as a whole. (In Charlton, 1965, p. 65).

Erasmus's chief religious concern was to free Christian life from the abstractions of scholasticism and to foster the *philosophia Christi,* a simpler and rather undogmatic Christian faith. At the center of Christian life he placed the Scriptures and fathers of the church. Erasmus's great contribution to Scripture studies was his translation of the New Testament from the Greek. His first contribution to pedagogy was *Adages* (1500), a collection of proverbs drawn from the classical authors and the early Christian fathers of the church.

Erasmus's approach to Christianity was shaped by the spirit of *devotio moderna,* to which he was exposed when he spent time in his native Holland with the Brethern of the Common Life. The brethern established schools in which they cultivated a piety that was based on the imitation of Christ rather than on a creed or sacraments. Thomas à Kempis's widely read *The Imitation of Christ* embodied this devotional approach to the Christian life. Its piety is reflected in the often-quoted sentence: "I would rather feel compunction than be able to define it." Erasmus also lived for a while with Augustinian canons. Afterwards, he studied theology at Paris where he developed a negative attitude toward the scholastic theology taught there.

Erasmus's approach to Christianity is apparent in his *Handbook of the Militant Christian* in which he expressed the view that prayer and knowledge should be the armor for Christians in their daily combat with the forces of evil. This treatise was written at the request of a woman who hoped that the work would improve her husband's morals. In it Erasmus offered rules for living the Christian life and stated that prayer and knowledge were complementary; neither was sufficient without the other for living the full Christian life. His handbook was basically a treatment of how Christians should live in the world in the face of the moral problems that they encountered in their daily lives. He also felt that knowledge of classical authors was a valuable part of this learning, with the caveat that the authors were read in a proper manner and were subordinated to the Sacred Scriptures. He offered these admonitions:

> If you but dedicate yourself entirely to the study of the Scriptures, if you meditate on the divine law, nothing will ever terrorize you and you will be prepared against any attack of the enemy.

> I might also add that a sensible reading of the pagan poets and philosophers is a good preparation for the Christian life. We have the example of St. Basil, who recommends the ancient poets for their natural goodness. Both St. Augustine and St. Jerome followed this method. St. Cyprian has worked wonders in adorning the Scriptures

> with the literary beauty of the ancients. Of course it is not my intention
> that you imbibe the bad morals of the pagans along with their literary
> excellence. I am sure that you will nonetheless find many examples in
> the classics that are conducive to right living. Many of these writers
> were, of course, very good teachers of ethics. (In Bowen, 1975, p. 333)

In this devotional vademecum Erasmus, following Plato and Augustine, declared the necessity for a healthy asceticism of the body and a
continual spiritual search.

Erasmus wrote extensively on many educational matters. He
strongly advocated universal education, especially if it included the
study of the Scriptures. In his *Paraclesis,* another work written in the
form of a handbook, he penned these eloquent and often quoted words
on the Scriptures:

> And I would that they were translated into all languages so that they
> could be read and understood not only by Scots and Irish but also by
> Turks and Saracens. Surely the first step is to understand in one way
> or another. It may be that many will ridicule, but some may be taken
> captive. Would that, as a result, the farmer sing some portion of them
> at the plow, the weaver hum some parts of them to the movement of
> his shuttle, the traveler lighten the weariness of the journey with
> stories from this source. For in general our daily conversation reveals
> what we are. (In Cremin, 1970, p. 35)

In his *Praise of Folly* Erasmus satirized many aspects of his society, including teachers and their schools. Offering many criticisms
of the schoolteachers of the time, he was especially hard on those who
made false interpretations of Christianity. Furthermore, he even chided
some early church fathers for their hostility toward classical learning.
This work contains a division of mankind into the vulgar who live to
satisfy their own appetites and the pious who live a life of the spirit and
seek to share in the Highest Good which draws all to itself.

In his *De Ratione Studii* [On the Right Method of Teaching]
Erasmus systematically presented his views on education. This work
has been compared to the educational writings of the renowned Roman
educator, Quintilian. A basic thesis of this work states that:

> All knowledge falls into one of two divisions: the knowledge of
> "truths" and the knowledge of words; and if the former is first in
> importance, the latter is acquired first in order of time. (In Bowen,
> 1975, p. 338)

In this work Erasmus gave to the study of Greek and Latin, as well as the classical writings, a central place in education.

Although Erasmus was critical of schoolmasters of his time, he exhibited a great respect for the position of schoolmaster. In a letter to Colet he commented:

> I thought it a highly honorable office to bring up youth in virtue and learning; that Christ had not despised that age, upon which kindness was bestowed, and for which the richest harvest might be expected, . . . there was no duty by which [one] could serve God better than by drawing children to Christ. (In Bowen, 1975, p. 347)

In his *On the Education of Boys* Erasmus emphasized the development of the power of reason as an important goal in education. He recommended that education should begin at three years of age and not at eight, which was the common practice at the time. Erasmus even indited with sin those parents who refused to educate their children in religion. He contended that in the early years of a child's education special attention should be given to the cultivation of virtue. In Erasmus's view it would not be harmful to the child to begin at such an early age. While he urged starting the process of education early, he also counseled that teachers should show respect for the immaturity of the young child by making use of games, prizes, competitions, and rewards. Though Erasmus encouraged a verbal strain in education, he did give a place to music, arithmetic, and geography for leavening the curriculum. Erasmus also took a strong stance against corporal punishment. For him education should be a positive and helpful process that cultivates reason, extols humanity, leads students to God, all the while using pedagogical methods consonant with these goals.

Erasmus was deeply involved in the acrimonious theological debates that took place between the Catholic Church and Martin Luther. While sympathetic to the criticisms that Protestant reformers made of Church theology and practice, he eventually sided against Luther in his treatise *On the Freedom of the Will.* Notwithstanding this effort, his theological treatises were tagged as theologically dangerous by the Church of Rome, and placed on the prohibited list of books.

Erasmus was also severely criticized by Protestants for not wholeheartedly joining their cause. One reformer unleashed this attack on him:

> I am stupefied and shaken to know what has happened that you who once joined with us to demote the pope, you who detested bulls of

indulgences, who damned ceremonies, expelled papal courtiers,
execrated the canon law and the decretals, in a word you who
denounced universal hypocrisy, that you now turn completely around
and join that enemy, that you now flatter. . . . You have been suborned
by the lure of emoluments. (In Rummel, 1990, pp. 9–10)

While Erasmus did not actually translate into practice any of his
educational reforms, he did influence many others, especially John Colet (1466–1519), who established St. Paul's Grammar School in London. Like Erasmus, Colet strongly advocated reforms in religion and
education. He was also a Scripture scholar who gave influential lectures
on the Epistles of St. Paul. Becoming dean of St. Paul's Cathedral in
London, he was dissatisfied with its cathedral school, and gaining the
support of the merchants in London he established a school free from
church control. His reason for founding the school was "specially to in-
crease knowledge and worshipping of God and our Lord Jesus Christ
and good Christian life and manners of children" (In Cremin, 1970, p.
86). The curriculum of the school followed the Christian humanist approach with a study of selected Latin authors, restricted to Christian
writers. Colet prepared the textbooks for the school which included a
catechism for fostering Christian piety. While the authors studied did
not represent the full breath of humanism advocated by Erasmus, the
founding of this school was an important event in the establishment of
schools outside the control of the Church. Erasmus's treatise *De ratione
Studii* was written to guide the conduct of this school.

Thomas More (1478–1535), a friend of Erasmus, who visited him
often in England, was another leading figure in the English humanist
movement. In one of his letters he offered a vigorous defense of humanist education, which he considered a sound basis for theology;

To whom is it not obvious that to the Greeks we owe all our precision
in the liberal arts and in theology particularly? . . . Few will question
that humanist education is the chief, almost the sole reason why men
come to Oxford . . . some should also pursue law in which case the
wisdom that comes from the study of humane things is requisite; and
in any case it is something not useless to theologians; without such
study they might possibly preach a sermon acceptable to an academic
group but they would certainly fail to reach the common man. From
whom do they acquire skill better than from the classical poets,
orators and historians? . . . They build a path to Theology through
philosophy and the liberal arts. (In Charlton, 1965, p. 64)

More dealt with educational ideas in his *Utopia* (1965), published in 1516, in which he presented, after the fashion of Plato's *Republic,* the image of the ideal society as a way of critiquing contemporary society. In this work he painted an ideal Christian humanist society. More presented the goal of life in terms of making people happy not by satisfying their wants but by helping them to curb their greed and pride. Utopians are seemingly happy because they live a life that is natural, disciplined, rational, and virtuous. In Utopia there is neither war, nor poverty, nor religious differences, nor private property. In this work More expressed his strong conviction that the world could be reformed through education. While he recognized that for some people in society intellectual pursuits were an all-important activity, he realistically knew that many preferred to occupy themselves with their trades or practices, which he also considered useful for the common wealth. While the full meaning of More's Utopia has been disputed for centuries, More clearly added to the concept of Christian humanism the dimension of social conscience and social criticism.

For More the utopian society is formed through the enactment of just laws, the maintenance of sound institutions, and the creation of educational opportunities for all. Learning happens in the home, the church, the school, and in community activities. The children receive education from their earliest years, including an introduction to good literature. Since the inhabitants of Utopia work only a six-hour day, they have sufficient time available for intellectual pursuits, including daily academic lectures. In Utopia education is for both men and women. Education for More entailed not only systematic learning but also the training and experiences which individuals acquired in homes, churches, and the world of trades. *Utopia* has also been called the greatest educational work of the English Renaissance in that it describes an:

> Education that would on the one hand enable every individual to live the virtuous life according to nature since to this end we were created by God and on the other hand encourage the practical application of learning to the benefit of the community. (Cremin, 1970, p. 86)

More struggled greatly with the ongoing humanist debate over the relative advantages of the active life and the contemplative life. In Utopia one of the men was anguished over whether or not he should enter the service of the monarch since such an activity would probably entail making compromises and employing subterfuges in order to survive. More seemed to side with the counsel that the man should enter politics in order to aid society. Rejecting the monastic life for himself, More decided to remain a layman and to become active in politics. He was encouraged by friends to become Chancellor of England under Henry the Eighth, especially since Henry had leanings toward humanist learning. However, when More refused to support the king's request for a divorce, he was jailed and eventually executed by the king.

More was a strong advocate of the education of women both in his writings and in his practice. He gave to his daughters the same classical education that he provided for his sons: Latin and Greek classics, the early fathers of the church, logic, philosophy, music, and even science. His home became virtually a school, as children who lived nearby were included in the education given there. Of More's intensively classical and Christian home school Erasmus wrote:

> You would say that in that place was Plato's Academy. I should rather call it a school or university of Christian religion. For there is none therein who does not study the branches of liberal education. Their special care is piety and virtue. (In Alexander, 1980, p. 82)

Another prominent humanist who made England his home for a time was the Spaniard Juan Luis Vives (1492–1540). While in England Vives taught at Oxford, had contact with both More and Erasmus, and drew on their writings in his work. Later he made Paris his home where he continued to write on educational topics. Vives was similar to other humanists in his opposition to the perceived aridity of scholasticism. He was keenly interested in classical writers and in early Christian writers such as Jerome and Augustine, whose works he edited. His personal goal as an educator and the objective that he placed before other teachers and students were the attainment of learning and virtue through education and self-knowledge. Vives made pioneering studies not only in education but also in psychology.

Vives's main educational work was *De Tradendis Disciplinis* [On the Transmission of Knowledge] (1908), published in 1531. Of this work it has been written:

> With its insistence on the need to observe the child and to adapt both aim and method to his needs, its call for a humane relationship between master and pupil, its advocacy of the vernacular in the earliest stages of education and its thoroughly humanistic approach to the study of the

classics, [it] provided much of the theoretical basis of sixteenth century innovations in English education. (Charlton, 1965, p. 124)

In this humanist work Vives envisioned the central task of education as the achievement of intellectual clarity which comes from knowledge of the structure of the world and a vision of God's design for the world. Vives also discoursed on all areas of knowledge and expanded considerably the curriculum of the liberal arts and the Greek and Latin classics. He included not only the traditional liberal arts but also natural science, medicine, ethics, economics, politics, poetry, and theology. Vives was a determined advocate of schools for young children to be supported at public expense. He devoted, in the tradition of Quintilian on whom he drew extensively, much effort to describing methods of pedagogy.

Vives firmly believed that knowledge of the world with its impressive design would lead students to God. Further, he believed that students should be encouraged to work to their utmost in order that the common good might be achieved. For him once persons become scholars they should be motivated by the example of Christ in their desire to hand on knowledge to others. While he presented ideals and methods for education in all disciplines, he singled out religious and moral education as well as the "humanization" of students. Vives also wrote books on the Christian family and on the education of Christian women.

Among the other scholars who advanced the humanist cause in education in England at this period of time was Roger Ascham. He gave advice for the tutor in his *The Scholemaster* (1790). Another, Thomas Elyot wrote on the education of nobles in *The Governour* (1531). While both gave attention to moral education, religious education as such did not receive extensive treatment in their works. *The Scholemaster* has been called the quintessential English Renaissance work on education (Cremin, 1970, p. 77). This work devotes one section to ethical education and another to methods of pedagogy. The schoolmaster for Ascham was the tutor who prepared boys for the university. He advised tutors to use love rather than fear, gentleness rather than flogging, encouragement rather than punishment, and admonition rather than rebuke (Cremin, 1970, p. 77).

The Reformation and Protestant Humanism

Contemporary scholarship has reached a consensus that the Protestant Reformation in Germany and elsewhere was part of the Renaissance humanist movement and that the Italian Renaissance was instrumental in the development of important aspects of the German humanist movement (Spitz, 1990). Renaissance humanism in Germany incorporated both a cultural nationalism that provided a greater sense of identity to the nation and a religious enlightenment that resulted in the Lutheran Reformation.

Renaissance humanism influenced the Reformation in a number of ways. The humanist's contention that education demanded a return to the original sources inspired and sustained the reformers' commitment to return for their theology and education to the original Scriptures and to the fathers of the early church. Secondly, the Reformation placed equal emphasis on education that Renaissance scholars advocated. Thirdly, the reformers followed the Renaissance's downplay of dialectics in education and its stress on grammar, rhetoric, history, and poetry. Preaching the gospel, the heart of Reformation religious faith and education, depended on the study of grammar and rhetoric. The reformers used the study of history to recover what they considered were the original teachings of Christianity. The Reformation's wide use of music for inspiring religious sentiment sprang from the study of poetry, a favorite Renaissance endeavor.

While the Reformation was within the humanist movement with regard to the subjects taught, there were serious differences between Reformation humanism and the humanism of Italy and England. A real chasm between Reformers and humanists opened up theological issues such as freedom of the will, law and gospel, and sin and grace. Reformation humanism did not have the Italian and English humanist's optimism about human nature since the reformers focused so strongly on human sinfulness and the need for redemption by Jesus Christ. Reformation humanists had less of the humanist confidence in the ability of men and women to shape themselves, emphasizing as they did the necessity of divine initiative and grace for all worthwhile human activity.

Martin Luther (1483–1546) was as deeply concerned as humanists were with the reform of religion and education. Yet he did differ from men like Erasmus, More, and Colet. While humanists made the cultured and pious person the chief goal of education, Luther was more interested in educating a person who would respond to the calling to serve one's fellow humans in churches as well as in the civic and economic order.

Luther wrote three major essays on education: *To the Councilmen of All Cities in Germany that They Establish and Maintain Chris-*

tian Schools, On Keeping Children in School, and *On Christian Freedom.* In these essays he dealt with many aspects of education, especially the politics of establishing an educational system in Germany.

Luther focused on the education of the young because he believed that this emphasis would be the most effective way of promoting the ideals of his reform movement. While humanist education in Italy and England was largely restricted to the upper and middle classes of society, Luther and other reformers called for the education of all boys and girls. In their zeal, they even tried to make such education compulsory by appeals to political leaders. In the humanist tradition Luther extolled the dignity of teachers, considering teaching a divine vocation and placing it next to preaching as the most useful service men and women of God could give to their fellow human beings.

Luther played a major role in developing the first national system of education in Europe since Roman times. His reforms for the church included the advancement of education, for he believed that no true theology could be developed unless based on literary studies. In a letter to a humanist friend he urged: "I beseech you do your utmost in the cause of the training of young people, for I am convinced that the neglect of education will bring the greatest ruin to the gospel. (In Bowen, 1975, p. 361)

In 1524 Luther wrote to the leaders of cities in Germany urging them to establish and maintain schools in order that the Roman Church could not maintain the power it traditionally had over education. He introduced a quietly utilitarian argument that schools would be an asset to cities by providing useful and obedient citizens. In recommending schools throughout Germany Luther launched an argument often used even in modern times in advocating the establishment of schools:

> If it is necessary, dear sirs, to expend annually such great sums for firearms, for roads, bridges, dams, and countless similar things, in order that a city may enjoy temporal peace and prosperity, why should not at least some money be devoted to the poor needy youth. (Luther, 1962, pp. 369–370)

Luther further contended that money could be saved through establishing schools because citizens would no longer have to pay priests for educating their children. In addition, Luther pursued the religious line of argument that young boys and girls would be able to study the Scriptures in the schools. In order that they understand the Scriptures they should learn the classical languages and Hebrew. Schools should also teach German, history, singing, instrumental music, and mathematics. For Luther the school day was to last only two hours so that students would have time to learn a trade and help around the household. In his view:

> The prosperity of a country depends not on the abundance of its revenue, nor on the strength of its fortifications, nor the beauty of its public buildings but it consists in the number of cultivated citizens, in its men of education, enlightenment, and character. (Luther, 1962, pp. 355–356)

Furthermore, Luther criticized the excesses of the scholastic education offered in the universities where arid commentaries and interpretations of Aristotle were central to the curriculum. He opposed the universities' dialectical education and proposed in its place a humanist curriculum in languages, classics, and rhetoric, which he felt would better prepare future ministers for biblical studies and evangelical preaching. Luther called for a theological education that placed emphasis on the exegesis of the Bible, an approach to homiletics or preaching based on humanist principles of rhetoric, and a strong concentration in Church history, poetry, and drama. His scholarly work in the lecture halls and outside the walls made Wittenberg the first Protestant university to deepen its commitment to humanism and the principles of church reform.

Luther was a driving force in the organization of schools throughout Saxony. In 1528 with the help of Philip Melanchthon he developed for this region a plan for schools that would foster his theological ideas. The ideal presented for the schools was an eloquent piety that included the development of persons' intellectual and spiritual power. Schools were organized at three levels: for beginners, for those learning grammar, and for those who were advanced. The humanist curriculum proposed for the school had an emphasis on Latin authors.

Luther has left his mark on Christian education through the various catechisms that he wrote. These signature works were clear and concise summaries of Christian teachings adapted to the mentality of ordinary people and children. He published a *Large Catechism* for pastors and teachers and a *Small Catechism* for children. These catechisms were eventually enlarged by Luther himself and later added to by leaders of the Lutheran Church. His catechetical works were wakeup calls to the churches of the reformation and also the Roman

Catholic Church to the need for systematic education of the young in Christian teachings. The dialogical form of the catechisms echoed the theology of the reformation churches that emphasized the addressing of the Word of God to persons who were thereby called to make an obedient response of faith. While other catechisms predated Luther, he established for centuries to come the catechism as the principal text for Christian education in most churches.

In Luther's judgment, there had not been an adequate response by the German councilors to his first letter on education. Undetermined, Luther wrote another treatise or sermon on education, *On Keeping Children in School.* In this treatise he reiterated forcefully what he had written in an earlier work. He reasserted his contention that only education could guarantee a well-ordered society as well as respect for the rule of law. Luther addressed especially merchants and business people who tended to look down on a humanist education. He served notice to civic leaders that they had the duty of compelling children to attend schools. His rhetoric in this document was scorching. He did not spare parents his wrath in word. If they did not send their child to school, they would be doing the work of the devil and would prepare their child to be "a gross, ungrateful clod" (In Bowen, 1975, p. 369).

In this sermon Luther declared that "it is the duty of the temporal authority to compel its subjects to keep their children in school, especially the promising ones" (In Bowen, 1975, p. 368). Luther asserted that children were given to parents not as their own property but for the service of God. Going to school would, in his opinion, enable children to get good jobs and to render their service to God. Luther by this time put greater emphasis in religious education on learning in the vernacular, contending that German people, including women and children:

> Can learn from German books and sermons more about God and Christ—I am telling the truth!—than all the universities, foundations, monasteries, the whole papacy, and all the world used to know. (In Bowen, 1975, p. 369)

This sermon received a greater response than his previous treatise and resulted in the establishment in the succeeding decade of many schools in Germany along the Lutheran model.

Luther exhibited a certain ambiguity and ambivalence about the role of human reason and secular learning in education. While he approved of secular learning, his scripturally based theology strongly rejected a rational understanding and interpretation. He pointed out the

weaknesses and limitations of natural reason unaided by grace. He regarded the work of the scholastics in extolling human reason an example of arrogance. Arguing for the primacy of Scriptures he castigated human reason as the work of the Devil. He did, however, give
some limited role to reason after divine faith had established God's order. He stated that:

> Philosophy understands naught of divine matters. I don't say that man
> may not teach and learn philosophy; I approve thereof, so that it be
> within reason and moderation. Let philosophy remain within her
> bounds as God has appointed. (In Bowen, 1975, p. 371)

Luther, however, did not accept Thomas Aquinas's view that reason could be a guarantor of faith. He countered forcefully that in matters of faith natural understanding meant little. He proposed faith based
on learning and scholarship and devoted to Christian sources, all under the direction of recognized teachers. In this way Luther was closer
to Augustine in his advocacy of the primacy and mystery of religious
faith, which could not benefit to any great degree from rational doctrine. The schools of the Lutheran reformers focused on the study of
the Scriptures in an attempt to cultivate a learned piety. Many schools
and universities throughout Germany abandoned the scholastic and
philosophical attitudes of medieval Christendom in favor of this approach to learned piety.

The Lutheran reformation thus placed a great emphasis on
schooling and learning but with a distinctive approach to education
that Catholic educators had to deal with in years to come. In Luther's
mind there was a close connection between schools and the advancement of religion. He noted that "when schools flourish things go well
and the church is secure. . . . God has preserved the church through the
schools" (In Bowen, 1975, p. 373).

In his educational efforts, especially in higher education, Luther
was aided by Philip Melanchthon (1497–1560), professor of Greek at
the University of Wittenburg. In his inaugural lecture at the university
in 1517, Melanchthon delivered an address *On Improving the Studies
of Youth*. This address was an eloquent appeal for preparing students
to read and study the Bible. He introduced the study of both Greek and
Hebrew as the sure way for students to reach evangelical truth. For
Melanchthon the purpose of education was to promote learned piety
through a solid classical education. Melanchthon campaigned for es-

tablishing schools in Germany designated for children and dedicated to inculcate a learned piety.

Melanchthon had a hand in the reform of schools in Saxony. In 1527 he personally inspected these schools and found them in deplorable condition, especially in their teaching of religion. Together with Luther he drew up for the reform of these schools proposals in *Visitation Articles,* which contained both articles of Lutheran faith and the proper method of establishing and maintaining schools. Their plan specified the subjects to be taught and even the hours of instruction. Instruction and conversation was to be in Latin. Children were to learn the alphabet, the creed, and the Lord's prayer in addition to passages from the Latin classics. Older children were to learn lessons from Aesop's fables and passages from Latin classical and Christian authors.

Melanchthon, like the English humanists, attempted to reconcile the classics with Christianity. In the foreword to his edition of Cicero's *De Officiis* he expressed his sentiments:

> As it is right for Christians to develop and foster a civil society, so this doctrine of civic morals and duties must be studied. For it is not godly to live like the Cyclops, without a legal order or an ethical doctrine, or the other frameworks to our life which classical literature provides. Those who abuse philosophy are at war not only with human nature, but also and more importantly with the glory of the Gospel; for it teaches that men should be constrained by civic discipline. (In Spitz, 1990, p. 55)

The educational ideals set forth by Melanchthon received effective implementation in the gymnasium, or Latin grammar school, established in Strasbourg in 1528 by Jacob Sturm (1507–1589). This school, which Sturm directed for forty years, had as its main objective the cultivation of a learned and eloquent Protestant piety. Such piety emanated from sound knowledge and was expressed in eloquent language. The classical curriculum of Latin and Greek authors was adopted, with all teaching and conversation held in Latin. Sturm faced the same educational problem that all Christian humanists had to deal with: how to prevent the pursuit of eloquence from subverting the attainment of piety. For Sturm the two could not be separated. The gymnasium had a full curriculum of studies that the students pursued in a graded sequence. The theology that was taught to students was based on the Scriptures, especially the Greek New Testament.

Sturm wrote extensively on educational matters. His school became a model for the large number of schools established in Germany
to foster the Lutheran or evangelical faith. His school and his educational ideals and organization spread throughout Europe and elsewhere
when, according to some scholars, the Society of Jesus, the Jesuits,
drew on it in establishing the *ratio studiorum* for their schools.

Lutheran education today attempts to remain faithful to the chief
insights of Luther. It sees religion as essential to education in providing
a purpose in life. This biblically based education is based on the Scriptures and continues to emphasize Luther's themes of Scripture, faith,
salvation through grace alone, and Jesus as the central Word. For many
Lutherans religious education still means studying the Bible, singing
hymns, and memorizing the catechism. In many places Lutherans have
established schools and colleges in order to integrate religion into the
curriculum. The lasting potential of Lutheran religious education is:

> Its emphasis on the need for a clear distinction between law and
> gospel shows that the law serves theologically to convict the sinner
> and serves in a civic way to control and regulate society. It is not
> intended to serve as a way of life. Christians are to live under the
> gospel, exercising love and forgiveness. Lutheran educators
> understand Christians to be both sinners and saints, sinners because
> they are still in the flesh and daily sin much, saints because they daily
> receive the assurance of God's grace and forgiveness and thus stand
> justified. Lutheran education stresses that the gospel is the power that
> can affect growth in faith and make it effective in the lives of children
> and adults. (Schultz, 1990, p. 389)

The other great leaders of the Protestant Reformation also gave a
central role to the education of the young. Ulrich Zwingli (1484–1531)
was a leader of religious reform in Switzerland. Like Luther he placed
great emphasis on the Scriptures in his reform efforts. In his treatise on
the education of youth he preached a combination of ascetical behavior and humanist learning. Zwingli set high standards for the education
of the young, favoring an education that would result in striving for
greatness in Christian living. In writing to young people he stated:

> The true Christian is not the one who merely speaks about the laws of
> God, but the one who with God's help attempts great things. And for
> that reason, noble youth, see to it that you adorn more illustriously
> and with true adornment the fair gifts of race, physique, and
> patrimony with which you have been endowed. . . . Rank, beauty, and

wealth are not genuine riches, for they are subject to chance. The only true adornments are virtue and honor. May God so lead you through the things of this world that you may never be separated from him. (Zwingli in Cully, 1960, pp. 160–161)

John Calvin's (1509–1564) ideas on education were, like Luther's, situated within the humanist tradition. His fundamental ideal was *pietas literata,* a piety enlightened by classical learning. For four years Calvin was a teacher at Sturm's gymnasium in Strasbourg. He helped establish various schools in Geneva, one for ministers and teachers and another for children. A classical education was provided in these schools. While the curriculum came from the humanists, the tone came from Calvin's theology with its strong emphasis on the Scriptures. After his conversion to evangelical Christianity Calvin's interest in the humanist curriculum waned somewhat so that in his writings he celebrated to a greater extent the Bible and early Christian writers (Kelley, 1991, p. 91). In his highly influential *Institutes* he offered this comparison:

> Now this power [to transform all things] which is peculiar to Scripture is clearer from the faith than from human writings, however polished. The latter are not capable of affecting us at all comparably. Read Demosthenes or Cicero; read Plato, Aristotle or any other of that class. You will, I admit, feel wonderfully allured, delighted, moved, enchanted. But turn from them to the reading of the sacred volume and whether you will it or not, it will so powerfully affect you, so pierce your heart, so work its way into your very marrow that compared with the impression so produced, the power of the orators and philosophers will almost disappear, making it clear that the Holy Scriptures breathe something divine, which lifts them far above all the gifts and grace of human industry. (Calvin, 1:8:1)

Although he continued to find value in Renaissance humanism, Calvin also pointed out some of its dangers from the religious point of view. Such study could lead to too much pride in the human, a lessening of interest in things of the spirit, and a devaluing of asceticism.

Notwithstanding these reservations, in 1559 Calvin established an academy or college in Geneva that had a seven-year classical curriculum. Modeled after Sturm's school in Strasbourg, Calvin's school also had an advanced department for the teaching of Hebrew, Greek, philosophy, law, and theology. The last subject was taught by Calvin and Theodore Beza, the rector of the school. The ideal of his schools was rooted a principle once stated in a sermon: "No one is a good minister of the Word who is not first a scholar." Calvin held teachers of theology in high regard, considering them divinely appointed and equal to pastors and bishops.

Calvin's *Institutes of the Christian Religion* was a fundamental text for teaching theologians, pastors, and adults. There were five major editions of this work, with the final version published in French in 1541. This work included references to the Bible and the Church fathers as well as quotations from some classical writers. In his introduction to the *Institutes* Calvin stated his purpose in reintroducing catechetical instruction into the church. He contended that:

> What we now bring forward, therefore, is nothing else than the use of
> a practice formerly observed by Christians and the true worshippers
> of God and never neglected until the church was wholly corrupted. (In
> Cully, 1960, p. 165)

Calvin of course was deeply committed to the teaching of evangelical faith to children, a ministry that he viewed as crucial for the spread of the Reform movement. In 1537 he wrote *Instruction in the Faith,* a catechism for children. In a letter to a friend he wrote, "Believe me, my Lord, the Church of God will never preserve itself without a Catechism" (In Wallace, 1988, p. 8). Since this first catechism was rather long and difficult for children, Calvin wrote another catechism in 1545 for religious education in Geneva. However, the most influential of all the Calvinist catechisms was the *Heidelberg Catechism* of 1563.

Education in the Reformed and Presbyterian Churches today finds its foundational inspiration in the ideals of Calvin. The designers of the new curriculum in 1988 characterized Reformed education as biblical, historical, ecumenical, social, and communal. Reformed education is grounded in the Bible, informed by the history of the church, committed to the unity of the church, engaged with issues in contemporary society, and nurtured within the faith community. Three additional aspects supplement these adjectives. A primary role of the minister is to be a teacher. The catechetical method is the preferred one. The confession of the church is the content of the message (Brown, 1990, p. 542)

Summary

In the Renaissance period Christian humanists made extensive use of the classical tradition in educating Christians. However, they attempted to always subordinate this tradition to their ideal of *pietas literata.* They developed the notion that this form of education, which had been restricted to the elite in previous times, could now be open to all. It was Luther himself and later the Jesuits who were strongest in pursuing this ideal of leading all to a life of learning and piety.

Also, at this time education became closely connected with the political and religious struggles. While it once served as a unifying force in Europe, education itself now became one of the most powerful instruments for fostering divisions. In later chapters it will be necessary to separate Protestant efforts in education from Catholic pursuits. While in the medieval period education was an instrument of Christian civilization, at this revolutionary time with the breakup of the Christian West, education became an instrument of particular religious beliefs and of religious dissent. In the next chapter I will show how the Roman Catholic Church reacted in an educational manner to the use of education by Protestant Reformers.

Chapter 4

The Emergence of Catholic and Protestant Education: Sixteenth to Nineteenth Centuries

[Members have the obligation to set] a good example, [and, since] learning and methods of presenting it are necessary for the attaining of this end, therefore, after it seems that a fitting foundation for self-denial and for the necessary progress in virtue has been laid for those who have been admitted to probation, the education in letters and of the manner of utilizing them, so that they can add to a better knowledge and service of God, our Creator and Lord. (Constitutions of the Society of Jesus, in Bowen, 1975, p. 421)

The distinguishing mark of New England's cultural identity was symbolized by the one book that stood beside the Bible in their regard—the catechism. For the New English child the catechism not only symbolized his Protestant inheritance but tangibly inaugurated his education in the elements of his new faith. (Axtell, 1976, p. 5)

Religious education before the Protestant Reformation was designed primarily to support the ideal of a Christian civilization. After the Reformation religious education increasingly took on the task of furthering the goals and needs of particular religious denominations. This chapter will discuss some of the main efforts and ideas of Catholic and Protestant educators to propagate their faiths in the years after the Protestant Reformation. While significant Catholic initiatives in education took place in France, the educational efforts of the Jesuits and other religious orders of men and women in this period were felt in most European countries. Protestant initiatives in education occurred in Germanic countries as well as in England, France, and the United States.

Education in these centuries in both Protestantism and Catholicism followed in the footsteps of Renaissance humanism and its ideals. The educational forays of both the Jesuits and Lutherans drew largely on the spiritual and literary values of humanist scholarship. As time went on, however, other educational forms developed that focused almost exclusively on Christian sources, mainly the biblical writings. This was truer in Protestantism than in Catholicism.

Developments in Catholic Education

Developments in Roman Catholic education during this period included the educational mandates of the Council of Trent, the highly influential efforts of the Society of Jesus, and the work of teaching orders of men and women in France and other countries.

Catholic education was shaped definitively by the Catholic response to the Reformation. The response focused on four elements, all connected to education: the Council of Trent, the Inquisition, the Index of Forbidden Books, and the Society of Jesus. The Council of Trent, which defined Catholic doctrine in opposition to the Reformers, set in motion through its decrees a thorough reshaping of Catholic education. Not until the reforms stemming from the Second Vatican Council were any significant changes introduced into Catholic education. The thrust of the Tridentine reforms was carried out not only by bishops and pastors but in a special way by the emergence of new Catholic religious orders of men and women and the redirection of efforts by older religious orders. In both Europe and the United States as well as in the entire Catholic world a defensive and apologetic approach to theology and education prevailed.

Educational Reforms of the Council of Trent

The chief doctrinal response of the Roman Catholic Church to the Protestant Reformation took place at the Council of Trent (1545–1563). Through its many decrees the council reaffirmed the rights of the Church in the area of theology and education. The council explained the correct interpretations of church teachings and pointed out the errors in Protestant interpretations. The council especially defended and affirmed those doctrines that were disputed by various reformers of the church. Trent was also noteworthy for the attention that it gave to the education of the clergy.

The council was keenly interested in strengthening Catholic education, especially in areas of church teachings. In 1566 it issued the *Catechismus Romanus,* a catechism intended to aid pastors in their preaching and teaching. The Catechism had four sections that treated the Apostles Creed, the seven sacraments, the Ten Commandments, and prayer including a commentary on the Our Father. Within the scope of the council's directives, suggestions were made about using the catechism for sermons and the need to make adaptations according to the age, capacity, manners, and social condition of those being instructed.

Other influential catechisms date from this period. Peter Canisius (d. 1597), a Dutch Jesuit, published a compendium of Catholic teachings to be used in colleges, an abbreviated version of the compendium to be used for those not well educated, and a small catechism with 122 questions and answers which was used in German-speaking countries. The Jesuit Robert Bellarmine composed the most popular catechism in Italy in 1597. He followed Augustine's division of doctrine according to faith, hope, and charity. Besides spawning these and numerous other catechisms, the Council's teachings were clearly expressed in the Catechism of the Third Plenary Council of Baltimore in 1885 which became for the next century the standard text for religious education in the United States.

Interest in teaching the catechism resulted in the post-Tridentine establishment of the Confraternity of Christian Doctrine. Proposed in 1560 and finally established in 1571, the CCD, as it came to be known, consisted of a group of lay men and women who were specially prepared to teach the catechism to both children and adults. While the Confraternity made great strides under leaders like Charles Borromeo, archbishop of Milan, its full flowering did not occur until the very beginning of the twentieth century.

In another educational effort the council promulgated an Index of Forbidden Books which proscribed authors and writings that were considered dangerous to Catholic faith and morality. In time many celebrated books, including works that bear on education, were placed on this list. The church also reactivated at this time the medieval Inquisition that investigated false teachings or heresy, issued sentences, and enforced punishments on offenders.

Shortly before this council Pope Paul III approved the new Society of Jesus of Ignatius Loyola. The men in this new group were destined to become intellectual leaders in the Catholic Church's effort to combat Protestant teachings and to promote Catholic teachings. The Jesuits became the most formidable foes of Protestantism throughout Europe. In this crusade they made extensive use of a network of schools and colleges established throughout Europe and also in other parts of the world. They also systematized a form of education that had great impact in the succeeding centuries.

Jesuit Education

Sixteenth-century educators were in quest of a ratio, a systematic approach to education that arranged or ordered elements of education. A ratio was sought for the teaching of languages and literature and likewise for the sequence of learning that would take place in a school. The most influential ratio in the late Renaissance period was developed by the Society of Jesus or Jesuits. This Catholic order established schools and colleges throughout Europe, coming to be called the schoolmasters of Europe. They also established educational institutions in other parts of the world.

The founder of the Jesuits, Ignatius Loyola (d. 1556), made the spiritual good of souls the primary objective for Jesuit ministries. However, it was not many years after the founding of the order that the work of combating the religious heresies of Protestantism became a major focus for Jesuit ministries and education. Among the Jesuits learning and religious obedience were the weapons for the crusade against opponents of the Catholic Church. While Jesuits established no schools during the first decade of their existence, at the time of Ignatius's death the order had established over a hundred schools and colleges in Western Europe. The number doubled by the end of the sixteenth century and in the eighteenth century there were 700 schools and seminaries spread over Europe. At first the schools were only for members of the society, but in short time the Jesuits began to accept other boys into their schools (O'Malley, 1993).

The *Constitutions* of the Jesuits, written in 1556, the year of Ignatius's death, clearly indicated that education had become an essential task of the order. While the society still aimed to help its members to save their souls, it recognized that education was essential for achieving this purpose. Members of the society had the obligation to set:

> A good example, [and, since] learning and methods of presenting it
> are necessary for the attaining of this end, therefore, after it seems that

> a fitting foundation for self-denial and for the necessary progress in
> virtue has been laid for those who have been admitted to probation,
> the education in letters and of the manner of utilizing them, so that
> they can add to a better knowledge and service of God, our Creator
> and Lord. (In Bowen, 1975, p. 421)

The constitution described the education for members of the society. Its basic principle is: learning and piety are closely linked. Members were to study the humanities and the philosophy of Aristotle as
interpreted by Thomas Aquinas. The foundation for these studies was
grammar, rhetoric, logic, moral philosophy, and metaphysics. After
these studies Jesuits studied positive theology (a study of the Scriptures, Fathers, and doctrines of the church), and speculative theology.
Added to this program of studies were many works of piety: the Spiritual Exercises, prayer, meditation, examinations of consciences, confession, and works of mercy.

The definitive *Ratio Studiorum* of the Jesuits was published in
1599. This thirty-chapter expansion of what was written in the Constitutions presented the rules for the various persons that were involved
in running the Jesuit schools and universities. This work has been
called "the most comprehensive and certainly the most enduring set of
regulations for the conduct of education ever compiled" (In Castle,
1958, p. 79). The *Ratio* is not a set of principles but rather a book of
rules for establishing a uniform system of education. The philosophy
of education presumed by the *Ratio* is Renaissance humanism, supplemented by some classical and medieval ideas. The content of the
education prescribed was the humanistic studies or *pietas literata* of
the time. The primary institution was the college that was divided into
various grades. The Jesuit institutions took in both interns, those who
planned to enter the society, and externs, those who did not have such
plans. In some places they even took in Protestant students. The *Ratio*
recognizes that the difficult task of teaching required professional
training.

The *Ratio* describes the daily schedule and the procedures to be
used in the classroom, systematizing all aspects of school teaching. It
contains a virtual course in teacher training. It prescribed the *prelectio*
in which the master reads and interprets a text for the students. He then
explains the topic and its connection with what proceeded, explaining
especially any obscure parts that call for interpretation. The vernacular and Latin can be used. Another method was the *concertatio* (debate

or discussion) whereby masters or fellow students posed questions for discussion. Written exercises and repetitions provided reinforcement of what was learned.

Emulation or rivalry was an important motivating factor in Jesuit education. Students competed with one another to become learned. Rivalries developed within classes and between classes. Student rivals were to be alert to mistakes and inadequate preparation. Rivalries were especially strong in debates and disputations.

Jesuit education was deeply concerned with fostering piety and virtue. Teachers were to ensure daily attendance at Mass, repetition of Christian doctrine, daily prayers, examination of conscience, confession, and meditation. Prescribed reading included the lives of the saints. The spiritual life of the students was fostered by private conversations with a view to strengthening religious convictions. An early Jesuit educator observed that a single private talk would "work more powerfully than many lectures and sermons given in common" (In Castle, 1958, p. 81). Expurgated versions of the classics were used to guard students from temptation.

Punishment and admonition were part and parcel of the educational process. It was pointed out that teachers should ignore minor misdeeds. Punishment was to be left to an official Corrector who was not of the Society, thus separating the punishing act from the teaching act. Pupils were to be called by their right names. Teachers were not to play favorites or to speak to students outside class, except in an open area. Students were not to be used as copyists nor were students to spend their own money in schools (Fitzpatrick, 1933, pp. 212–213).

The curriculum of Jesuit schools followed the standard humanistic education of the time. The Jesuits were in the vanguard in building a system of schools where this education could take place effectively. After a study of grammar, students were introduced to the Latin and Greek classics as well as some Christian writers. Philosophy was to be studied for three years and then students were to embark on the study of theology. The quintessential guide to the study of theology was Thomas Aquinas. Professors were warned "never to speak except with respect of St. Thomas, following him readily as often as is proper, or reverently and gravely differing from him if at any time he does not approve of him" (In Bowen, 1975, p. 42).

The Jesuit system of education spread throughout Europe was a centralized system with colleges placed strategically. By the end of the sixteenth century they had produced numerous graduates throughout

Europe who moved into pivotal positions of power. By the seventeenth century these schoolmasters of Europe dominated the education of boys in Catholic parts of Europe.

The Jesuit achievements in education and schooling were truly remarkable, especially in Spain, Portugal, and Italy. Later the order spread its work to France, Germany, and Poland. They marshaled the most formidable opposition to Lutheranism in Germany. In England they directed their attention to the universities in order to keep Catholicism alive. Penal laws in England were aimed against Catholics and Jesuits who continued to teach and practice the Catholic faith.

Early Jesuit education was not, however, without its failures, frustrations, and crises (O'Malley, 1993). The schools had their share of incompetent teachers and unruly students. Early on they laid down a rule that students could not enter school buildings bearing arms. They argued against the use of physical punishment. The Society had schools that failed as well as school closings, but in the end their successes were much greater than their failures. Their example encouraged many of the more established religious orders to enter the field of education and inspired the founding of teaching orders of men and women.

Jesuit education marked the end of an era both for the Church and for education. Their educational influence waned as the hold of the Church over education weakened with the onset of the Enlightenment in the eighteenth century. Their commitment to the Latin language of the Church became antiquarian in a world where vernaculars became increasingly important. Their adherence to the Thomistic synthesis could not withstand the assault of enlightenment thinkers. Dependence on Aristotle even in astronomy prevented them and the Church to take cognizance of the Copernican revolution in science.

The limitations of this educational approach became apparent over the years. The curriculum was heavily oriented toward language, with little attention to mathematics and sciences. Also, the system of education in which the curriculum was placed proved to be too rigid to adapt to changing conditions. The commitment to classical languages hindered their progress in the vernacular languages that were achieving a prominent place in education and scholarship. Jesuit education of the past had been criticized for not allowing freedom of expression for students and for its rigidity in content. Modern Jesuit educators have successfully addressed these limitations. Notwithstanding the limitations of early Jesuit education, even such a severe critic of Jesuit education as Voltaire made this judgment on his Jesuit education:

During the seven years that I lived in the house of the Jesuits, what did I see among them? The most laborious, frugal and regular life, all their hours divided between the care they spent on us and the exercises of their profession. I attest the same as thousands of others brought up by them, like myself; no one will be found to contradict me. (In Castle, 1958, p. 85)

While many have praised Jesuit education, the Society of Jesus has lived with much controversy in its history. The Jesuits met their strongest opposition in the seventeenth century France where conflicts between Catholics and Protestant Huguenots were most severe and both sides struggled for control of the schools. Jesuits eventually controlled the intellectual life at the University of Paris, which remained decidedly in favor of Roman authority and Thomistic theology. They became defenders of Catholic orthodoxy especially when it came under attack. The education at the university and education throughout France came under the bitter criticism of the former monk Rabelais. With his rapier-like pen he attacked religion, education, and the Church in a series of books. The Jesuits were also locked in a battle with Petrus Ramus who strongly opposed the teaching of Aristotle from a humanist perspective. After the smoke cleared the Jesuits saw to it that his books were placed on the Index and in his being forbidden to teach philosophy at the University of Paris. Eventually he was allowed to teach there but was murdered in his study on St. Bartholomew's Day, 1792.

So deeply were the Jesuits involved in religious and political disputes with Huguenots in France that in order to maintain religious and civic peace Henry IV expelled them in 1595, calling them "corrupters of youth, disturbers of public peace and enemies of king and state" (In Bowen, 1981, p. 33). Henry favored the cause of the Huguenot Protestants in the Edict of Nantes of 1598 that granted them civic freedoms. With the Jesuits out of the country from 1596 to 1606 other Catholic religious orders, of a less aggressive nature, took up their work in Catholic grammar schools. After Henry's conversion to Catholicism the Jesuits returned to Paris and led a Catholic restoration at the University of Paris and at the new college at La Fleche, where the philosopher René Descartes studied.

In the course of years the Jesuit educational system won many converts but also made many foes. Increasingly it went on the defensive. Jesuits upgraded their Order of Studies in 1752. They issued new procedures in 1828. Yet the educational innovations of the Enlightenment eclipsed for many years the Jesuit system and ideas. In the twentieth century the order has recouped much of its early influence. While there are fewer members of the Society, Jesuit schools and universities operate in many of the major cities of the world. What is chiefly at issue now is the Jesuit identity and mission of these institutions now that there are fewer Jesuits and the curriculum has become considerably broadened beyond the humanism that has formed the historical basis of Jesuit education.

Catholic Religious Teaching Orders in Seventeenth-Century France

The conduct of Catholic education in the centuries after the Reformation was dominated by the work of new congregations and orders of men and women dedicated to teaching. While teaching had been part of the mission of the older orders—Benedictines, Franciscans, and Dominicans—the new orders were founded precisely for purposes of education. These groups were in some way influenced by the activities of the Jesuits. It was in France during the seventeenth century that these orders came to prominence, especially in the education of working class and poor. While these orders promoted a strict doctrinal orthodoxy there were differences among them in their approaches to education. Of the many orders that engaged in religious education at this time only a few will be highlighted, those that had a distinctive approach or those that have continued their educational work in the United States.

Although the Ursulines were founded in Italy in 1535, they flourished in France when they began educating girls in Jesuit-like institutions. Founded in France in 1609 by Anne de Xaintonge (d. 1621), they committed themselves to the education of the poor. Many of the women who joined the order in France were widowed. The goals of their schools were religious and devotional, although some practical elements such as singing and embroidery of church furnishings found space in the curriculum. The literary component of the curriculum was minor. Ursuline schools were established throughout France and French Canada.

A book of regulations for teachers written in 1621 gives the basic ideals of this education. Teachers are to help pupils in living the Christian life by giving them advice concerning life at home, in the world, and in church. Obedience and modesty are to be stressed. Teachers are to exhibit the tenderness of mothers and avoid anger and scolding. They are urged, however, when facing serious problems "to evoke shame and penitence, for example by making the offender kneel in the classroom and ask pardon for their offences or recite an act of contrition with folded arms" (Barnard in Castle, 1958, p. 119).

Various teaching congregations provided basic education for boys in France. While Jesuits offered free education to even poor boys, their education was rather rigorous. The Oratorians, Piarists, and Brothers of the Christian Schools provided an education accessible to a larger portion of the population.

Like the Ursulines, the Oratorians were originally founded in Italy. Philip Neri (d. 1695) gathered a group of men who lived together and dedicated themselves to the religious life. Pierre de Berulle (d. 1629) established the Oratory in France where it took on the work of education. The first Oratorian college was established in 1614 and by the end of the seventeenth century there were over thirty colleges and two teacher training institutions. Their curriculum included Cartesian philosophy and was considered modern in contrast to the Jesuit classi-cal curriculum, since their schools included the study of history, math-ematics, and the natural sciences (Castle, 1958, p. 113). In their schools, which were free of charge, they used both Latin and the vernacular. Though their educational ideal was the *pietas literata,* they also in-cluded history and geography. The Oratorians stressed mathematics as a serious study, because of the growing influence of science and Descartes' ideas. One historian of the French tradition in education has made this judgment of Oratorian education:

> The Oratorian system shows up with a lustre all its own. Its absence of artificiality, its practical usefulness, its gentleness, its cheerfulness, its progressiveness, its high moral tone—all these characteristics lead us to feel that it was the best education of its kind that was given in France or indeed in any European country, during the seventeenth and eighteenth centuries. (Barnard in Castle, 1958, p. 114)

Another Roman group, the Piarists, founded in 1602, established popular schools in Italy, Spain, and France. In Italy the schools served large numbers of poor and homeless boys. In France, while claiming to educate all boys, their efforts were restricted to a minority of the population, a wealthy part.

Perhaps the most influential congregation that emerged in France at this time was the Brothers of the Christian Schools founded by Jean

Baptiste de La Salle (1651–1719). A priest and theologian Jean early on dedicated himself to the education of poor boys by gathering around him a group of men who came to be called Brothers of the Christian Schools. Unlike the Jesuit educators who became priests, the Brothers decided to remain lay persons.

The Brothers organized elementary schools that stressed reading, writing, singing, and religion. They educated children from the poorest and least cultivated homes in classes of a hundred. De La Salle also established a Christian Academy in which boys were given instruction in geometry, architecture, drawing, and other subjects. They also founded a Sunday program of advanced courses in practical subjects for working teenagers to continue their education. The Brothers were also pioneers in special education and institutions for the care and education of delinquent boys. Because of the success of de La Salle's efforts it is claimed that "in some ways his was the greatest achievement in Catholic education" (Castle, 1958, p. 114). Besides schools for the poor, de La Salle also established a teaching institute at Saint-Sulpice, perhaps the first institution of its kind in the world.

The educational rules of the Brothers are found in their manual, *La Conduite des Ecoles Chretiennes* (1695). Its pages emphasize the authority of the teacher and classroom management since classes of one hundred boys to a single master were common. Lessons were given in the basics and in the vernacular (in contrast to the Jesuits who used Latin). Practicality was paramount. The strict and systematic moral and religious training was coupled with such punishment as caning and strapping. Teachers were bidden to maintain silence, which was considered one of the principal means of establishing and maintaining order in school.

The Christian Brothers' manual gave detailed instructions for the teaching of the catechism. Teachers were to avoid preaching during the teaching of the catechism lesson, restricting themselves to asking questions of all the students. Special attention was to be given to those who had difficulty learning the answers. The catechism lessons were to be made relevant to the students' lives. Student answers should be short, make complete sense, be accurate, and suitable to the students' intelligence. Teachers should make use of rewards and avoid punishing students during such sessions. When a longer catechism lesson is called for on Sundays, the teacher will

> Always choose some story that the pupils will enjoy and tell it to them in a way that will please them and renew their attention. He will tell it

with details that will prevent them from being bored. He will say nothing during the Catechism lessons that he has not read in some well-approved book and of which he is not very certain; he will never decide whether a sin is venial or mortal. (In Cully, 1960, p. 220)

At the outbreak of the French Revolution the Brothers were a major teaching force in France. Banished by the revolutionaries they were allowed to return by Napoleon and were included in the national system of education. Brothers now operate educational institutions worldwide, including the United States.

Although not strictly speaking a religious congregation, French Jansenists introduced a puritan or rigorist mode of education into seventeenth-century France. Indirectly this educational strain influenced schooling conducted by a number of religious congregations. Jansenists, the followers of Cornelius Otto Jansen, bishop of Ypres, were opposed to the wealth and luxury found in the Catholic Church. They proposed Christian life as a rigorous daily devotion to God in all of one's actions. Education was a prime way for persons to achieve moral and spiritual perfection. The Jesuits lined up against these ideas. Although the theology of the Jansenists was eventually condemned as heretical, these ardent reformers had a great influence in French educational practice within the Church. Some of their ideas were incorporated into the religious congregations that came to the United States in the nineteenth century.

For their educational ideals the Jansenists returned to the Christian Neoplatonism of Augustine. The ultimate aim of education is salvation to be achieved through a process of moving up from degradation. Jansenists believed that although the grace of baptism restored persons to innocence, individuals were still prone to sin. Their education proposed to help children avoid sin was a closely guarded education. Consequently children in their spiritual lives were to be guided by "the day-by-day, minute-by-minute search to serve God, to offer atonement, to seek grace for one's soul in the afterlife of eternity" (Bowen, 1981, p. 114). In orderly fashion education proceeded by a training of the intellect through the humanities, the will by the practice of virtue, and the person by good manners. The vernacular was used in education, with Latin learned as a second language. For the education of girls the Jansenists proposed a concentration on prayers, housekeeping, attendance at Mass, as well as the study of the Scriptures and Christian writings. The Jansenists in effect offered children many elements of the monastic education that had long influenced education in certain church circles. Vigilance was the password. Children's contact with the outside world was limited once they entered the school. They were supervised day and night. Travel and the theatre were condemned. Reading was carefully controlled. Notwithstanding this strictness loving relationships between teachers and taught were fostered. Excessive preaching by teachers was to be avoided. A judicious use of punishment was utilized in extreme cases.

The small schools of the Jansenists survived for only ten years, existing under great opposition from the Jesuits. The impact of this education was seen more in the attitudes found in many of the teaching orders of men and women that originated in France, some of which engaged in educational efforts in England, Ireland, and the United States. This guarded type of education was provided in many monastic schools for boys and convent schools for girls.

While the education of girls in French convents tended to be strictly supervised, a saner approach to the education of girls was proposed by Bishop Francois Fenelon (d. 1715). In his *Traite de l'education des filles,* published in 1681, he suggested that girls should receive an education suitable for their place in society. Girls should receive dual or two-pronged education, which he defined as character formation and instruction in various studies. He proposed an education suitable to natural development of girls. The curriculum he drew up was the humanist one, including Greek and Latin authors (properly censored). He included instructions for establishing schools and other charitable institutions.

Fenelon's treatise comprises a general theory of education. He stressed developing the powers of reason, using girls' natural curiosity, incorporating play as a means of learning, and making school work as pleasant as possible. He offered this questionable advice: "let us make study agreeable and disguise it under the appearance of liberty and delight" (In Castle, 1958, p. 120). Fenelon urged teachers to appeal to the girls' imagination by using stories from the ancient world and the Scriptures, preferring these to the tedious memorization of the catechism. In general he substituted the principle of attraction for the method of compulsion. He counseled that even in severe discipline cases punishment is to be avoided as far as possible. For such cases he does advocate use of some threats and appeals to shame. If the teacher has difficulties with a student, she is to ask for the help of a third person to make the reconciliation. Fenelon's treatise was widely read and was influential. The eighteenth century American political leader and educator Benjamin Rush drew heavily on it in his treatise on education, making a strong case for the education of women.

Developments in Protestant Education

Between the sixteenth and eighteenth centuries Protestant efforts in the Germanic lands, England, and France aspired to instill the spirit of the Reformation among their people. Various Protestant groups developed approaches to education that placed greater emphasis than Catholics did on the Scriptures and personal religious experience. In this section more attention is given to developments in England since developments there had a great influence on what happened in colonial America. When the various Protestant churches settled the United States, they banked on education to help spread the theology of the Reformation.

Lutheranism and Pietism in Germany

Luther and Melanchthon's campaign to establish state-controlled schools in which the Protestant faith was taught had some success in Germany in the sixteenth century. In their curriculum these schools tended to follow the example of the humanist curriculum found in Sturm's school in Strasbourg.

Within the Protestant churches in the Germanic lands the most influential approach to education came from John Comenius (1592–1670), a Moravian bishop, who believed that people would find truth not through secular studies but through religious faith. Comenius was a Czech who followed not in the tradition of Luther but in that of the martyred church reformer, John Hus. Comenius's impact, however, was greater in secular education and religious education in general than it was on Protestant education as such. He is considered by some the founder of modern educational theory since he treated the main elements of a modern system of education:

> A definition of goal, a psychology of human nature as a basis for interconnecting the methods of education with the laws of mental growth, and finally, a consideration of the role of education within human society. (Ulich, 1947, p. 339)

Like all religious educators Comenius dealt with the educational reconciliation of religious faith and human reason. At a time of increased extolling of the power of reason, Comenius like Luther asserted the supremacy of religious faith. He perceived in people:

> A twofold clear inward light—the light of reason and the light of
> faith—and both are guided by the Holy Ghost. For he who enters [into
> the Christian faith] must put away and renounce his reason, yet the
> Holy Spirit returns it to him, purified and refined. . . . Then the light of
> faith gleams on him so brightly that he can already see and know, not
> only that which is before him but also everything that is absent and
> invisible. (In Bowen, 1981, p. 84)

From his religious beliefs Comenius drew an educational vision of the
unity of all human experiences, material and spiritual, sensual and intellectual, and secular and religious. Just as the world has a unity, so
knowledge is unified. To achieve all knowledge is to achieve God, the
source and goal of human learning and striving. This universal knowledge Comenius called Pansophism (literally, all wisdom, according to
which all elements of knowledge are connected among themselves).

It is this spiritual vision of Pansophism that inspires and inte-
grates Comenius's most important work *Didactica Magna* (*The Great
Didactic*) first published in 1638. The subtitle of the book indicates the
grand sweep of his treatment: setting forth a universal system for
teaching everybody everything. This work, considered one of the great
educational treaties in the history of education, was highly influential
among educators in the ensuing centuries. In this work Comenius suggested that individuals achieve their natural end by attaining a unified
vision of all reality, corporeal and spiritual. For Comenius the ultimate
purpose of this life is to so live as to be worthy to achieve blessedness
in the life to come. For him this goal is reached through learning,
virtue, and religion. It is nature itself that gives the seeds of knowledge,
morals, and religion. Education brings these seeds to fruition.

Comenius proposed an approach to education that is based on the
development of the child's mind, that is, an education in accordance
with growth in nature. He explained that children should be taught not
according to the logical structuring of disciplines but according to their
nature or psychological development. His method of education is thoroughly deductive since it proceeds from fundamental principles drawn
from the very nature of things. Comenius, unlike Luther, was not a humanist in educational matters. He stated that:

> If we wish schools to be wholly reformed in accordance with the true
> standards of true Christianity, either the books of Pagans must be
> removed from them, or they must be treated more cautiously than
> hitherto. (In Adamson, 1971, p. 67)

Describing various stages in the development of the child he proposed an education suitable for that period. Believing that within the child there was potential for development, he advised educators to teach according to these natural stages rather than through the formal curriculum then in use. Comenius described the education that was appropriate for infancy, childhood, and adulthood. He also presented his ideas on how classrooms and schools should be organized in order to accomplish what we might call a child-centered education. He showed, however, little interest in university education, though he did offer proposals in another work for a College of Light or Pansophic College.

While Comenius's educational thought stresses the mystical and religious, he also enunciated practical principles of teaching: begin early before the mind is corrupted; prepare the students' minds to receive knowledge; proceed from the general to the particular, and from what is easy to what is more difficult; do not overburden the student with too many subjects; make progress slowly; do not force the mind to understand anything that is not in its natural bent; teach everything through the medium of the senses; show the utility of what is taught; teach everything by the same method (Ulich, 1968, p. 194). Comenius found concrete outlets for his vision of education in the illustrated textbooks he wrote.

While there is so much to praise in Comenius's work, over time some weaknesses in it have become apparent. His approach to teaching at times creaks of the mechanical. He overburdens the curriculum of the grammar school. His overly cautious approach to the humanist curriculum has been noted. The psychology of the person he presents now seems to be rather artificial. Nevertheless, *The Great Didactic* remains an educational classic because the author "united the purely theoretic study of education with an extensive knowledge of pedagogic questions as they present themselves in the schoolroom" (Adamson, 1971, p. 75).

Seventeenth-century Germany also witnessed the establishment of schools by A. H. Franke (1664–1727) in the Pietist tradition. The Pietists were a Lutheran sect originated by Jacob Spener in 1687–88, who reacted against what they considered the moral decadence of the times. The movement was a mystical one centering on the individual's personal experience or union with God. The otherworldly Pietists emphasized the personal side of religion, stressed private devotions, abstained from secular pleasures, studied the Bible as God's revelation to the individual soul, and were concerned with the continuing reformation of the church. Like Thomas à Kempis the Pietist favored living faith rather than chasing after an intellectual grasp of faith. Pietism is similar to the Methodism of John Wesley that emerged in England around the same time (Brown, 1978, pp. 27–28).

After a controversial career as a university professor, Francke became a pastor and devoted himself to establishing in Halle elementary and secondary schools as well as a course for training teachers. Considered the father of the elementary school in Germany, he began schools for both boys and girls as well as for the wealthy and the poor. In education he stressed the training of the will. His influence was basically restricted to the town of Halle.

Francke's writings on education were neither as extensive nor as influential as those of Comenius. In 1702 he published *Short and Simple Instructions,* a handbook on religious training for guiding children to piety and wisdom. Education for Francke had as its highest goal the glory of God realized in the heart of the believer. Francke wrote that "the chief object in view is that the children may be instructed above all in the vital knowledge of God and Christ, and be initiated into the principles of true religion" (In Adamson, 1971, p. 248). Since educators were to cooperate with God in helping to bring this about, they themselves should be awakened to the faith. Francke insisted that children understand all the prayers and the passages from Scriptures that they recited. Perhaps overkill, religion was taught for four hours a day in the Halle schools, with the Bible and Luther's catechism being the principal texts.

For the secondary school or *Pedagogium* Francke added the study of Greek and Hebrew for the purposes of understanding the Bible. Francke also included in the secondary school curriculum workshop activities and the scientific exploration of nature. Francke's utilization of real or practical activities in the schools is viewed as one of the beginnings of modern German technical schools that provide instruction for apprenticeships. Following the example of Comenius, he gave little place to classical literature in the curriculum.

Under the influence of Enlightenment ideas the religious emphasis in the Halle schools lost considerable ground as other subjects crowded the curriculum. Even though the Halle schools became part of the general educational establishment, "German education, however, never shook itself entirely free of the religious element that the Pietistic schools propagated so assiduously" (Bowen, 1981, p. 166).

Developments in France

France between the sixteenth and eighteenth centuries was divided almost equally between Catholics and Protestants. Catholic developments consisted chiefly of the efforts of the religious congregations to propagate the spirit of the Counter-Reformation. The conservative hallmark of these schools was participation in Catholic devotional activities and the teaching of Catholic doctrine. Not to be outflanked Protestant efforts centered on efforts by Huguenots, followers of John Calvin, to expand the influence of the Protestant Reformation.

In the sixteenth century French education, as well as the Catholic Church and French society, came under a severe attack by Francois Rabelais (1495–1553). In a number of writings he abandoned Latin, the language of academics, and used French to criticize the universities for their Aristotelian scholasticism. Rabelais proposed a humanist curriculum, based on Neoplatonic philosophy, which included not only the classics but also a study of the Bible and a study of nature. Rabelais proposals while strongly negative included:

> An affirmation of life and promoted zest and honesty where he perceived *ennui* and deceit; he attacked the greed and concupiscence of the church, the pretensions of scholars and the shallowness of so much learning. Rabelais's work helped to create a climate of criticism in mid-sixteenth century France. (In Bowen, 1981, p. 30)

The Huguenot humanist Peter Ramus (1515–1572), a leader of the Protestant faction at the University of Paris, continued Rabelais's attacks on traditional schooling. Locked in battle over his Calvinism with the Jesuits at the university, he went into exile and upon his return was murdered in his study. Within his humanism the study of mathematics and science had reigned supreme.

In 1598 when Protestantism was finally tolerated in France, the Huguenots lost no time in establishing schools for children and academies for training teachers in the Calvinist Reformed tradition. Ironically, the Huguenot educational system was similar to the Jesuit system in education. After 1610 with the assassination of the monarch who protected the Huguenots, their schools were considerably weakened. After a bitter struggle the schools were finally suppressed at the end of the seventeenth century.

Developments in Great Britain: Anglicans and Nonconformists

In sixteenth-century England educational changes swept in also when
the Anglican Church was established. With the closing of monasteries
and chantries and the imposition of required texts in schools, Roman
Catholic influence over education disappeared. Under the reign of
Queen Elizabeth I (d. 1603) education became the instrument for making the nation Protestant. All schoolmasters and university graduates
were compelled to take an oath of allegiance to the Queen. All books
had to be approved and children were required to take instruction in
the English catechism. The battle to control the universities of Oxford
and Cambridge continued well into the seventeenth century.

Puritans and Catholics found themselves at odds over the religious and educational policies of the nation. Catholic education went
underground; priests were sent to France and the Netherlands to be educated. The Jesuits, notably Robert Parsons and Edmund Campion,
made efforts to infiltrate the universities. By the end of the Queen's
reign the Church of England had won out and the campaign against Puritans and Catholics continued throughout the seventeenth century.

The struggle between the Anglicans and the Puritans continued
through the seventeenth century. The Puritan faith was a form of evangelical fundamentalism and piety that spread among the middle-class
mercantile class, which looked to the universities, especially Cambridge,
for a humanist education and a learned piety. Between 1560 and 1640
Puritans resisted the established Anglican church in the sphere of education by proposing a number of educational reforms and by establishing some schools (Morgan, 1986). They ventured even more revolutionary reforms after they achieved power in 1649 when after a bitter
civil war England became a republic for eleven years under the Puritan
Oliver Cromwell (1599–1658). The Puritans sincerely believed that they
were ushering in the Christian millennium. During their short-lived time
in power some Puritan educators attempted to bring about reforms in education through utopian treatises and grand schemes. Needless to say,
these visionary plans were to some degree inspired by the religious philosophy of John Comenius as well as the empiricism of the Englishman
Francis Bacon (d. 1626), whose ideas are discussed later in this chapter.

While Bacon did not advocate religious knowledge in the curriculum, Puritan writers influenced by him did tie the empirical to the religious. These writers included the noted poet John Milton (1608–1674)
who wrote a *Tractate of Education* in 1641 in which he criticized the

then accepted educational efforts and called for an education which stressed *pietas literata,* with less study of classical languages and more literary studies. In his educational theory Milton combined the ideals of classical humanism, Puritanism, and utility. William Perry (1623–1687) went further when he advocated middle-class Puritan ideals in proposing that practical, scientific, and technical education be added to language and literary studies.

However, the most important Puritan treatise on education from this period was John Drury's (1598–1680) *The Reformed School.* In this work Drury iterated the religious ideals of Comenius and Milton, advocated the use of the vernacular, stressed real-life experiences for the teaching of practical subjects, and argued for the introduction of technical subjects. Drury also paid attention to methods of instruction, the organic nature of knowledge, the faculties of the mind, and the careful sequencing and timing of lessons according to the developing mind of the child. With the fall of the Commonwealth government in 1649, the Puritan thrust in education considerably waned (Greaves, 1972).

Puritan writers debated vigorously the roles of reason and faith or Spirit in religion and education. They were aware of the dangers of giving reason too much of a role in religion and education. Some writers stressed that the Spirit gave knowledge to individuals that could not be gained by reason. One Puritan writer explained the relationship between faith and reason in this manner:

> I do not contemn nor despise the use of reason. Only I would not have you to establish it for the chief good; but I would have you to keep it under. . . . I would have you more strong in desire than curious in speculation; and to long more to feel communion with God than to be able to dispute of the genus or species of any question, either human or divine, and to press hard to know God by powerful experience. (In Greaves, 1972, p. 116)

At the beginning of the seventeenth century many grammar schools were established in England through private philanthropy to serve the middle and upper classes. The universities were favored in the same manner. The education of the poor, however, was totally neglected. With the restoration of power to the monarch, the Anglican Church exercised great power over education.

Theorizing about education was not extensive in England, especially as educational efforts became a politically charged struggle among various religious groups. Puritans offered a great deal of resistance to the uniformity imposed by the Anglican Church. Their main educational effort was the establishment of dissenting academies that offered theological and general education. In the period 1662–1843 seventy-three such academies were in existence. The chief function of the academies was to turn out prepared parish clergy for non-Anglican churches. As time went on the curriculum of these academies was considerably broadened to include practical and technical subjects. Science received its due respect in these academies rather than in the universities where the scholastic and humanist curriculums still prevailed. With the Act of Toleration of 1689 the academies grew considerably and even took in some Anglican students.

The population explosion of the poor in the cities of England stiffened the traditional reluctance to provide education for the masses. In a counterattack to such a policy religious leaders led one of the great social movements in modern times, the charity school movement. The Society for Promoting Christian Knowledge (SPCK) founded in 1689 by the Anglican priest Thomas Bray and lay associates opened numerous schools for the poor. Against the prevailing view that the masses should be left in ignorance respecting divine providence, the society decided that the poor should receive sufficient education to allow them to read the scriptures for their salvation. The society raised money from the wealthy for the education of the poor. In one-room schoolhouses children learned the Anglican catechism and sections of the Book of Common Prayer, the Psalms, and sections of the New Testament. Nonconformists, Methodists, Quakers, Jews, and Huguenots also created charity schools. The society extended its work also into Scotland, Wales, and Ireland. The schools ran into strong opposition in Ireland where Catholics preferred to have their children attend hedge schools, conducted around hedges, barns, farm buildings, and stables rather than attend schools which imposed the Anglican religion on them. In 1701 the society received a royal charter in the American colonies as the Society for the Propagation of the Gospel in Foreign Parts (SPG).

A sectarian group in England that emerged in the seventeenth century and developed a distinctive piety and approach to education was the Society of Friends or Quakers. Founded by George Fox (1624–1691) the society established schools for children and adults in which the Quaker way of life was passed on. The Friends who came to colonial America also set up many Quaker schools in the middle colonies and a few in the South.

Quaker piety stressed the presence of God as an inner light within individuals gathered in a group. The Friends came together without benefit of clergy and ritual in worshipful silence and in expectation that the Inner Light would move individuals to share their reflections. The primary doctrine of the Society is that:

> The Presence of God is felt at the apex of the human soul and that man can therefore know and heed God directly, without any intermediary in the form of church, priest, sacrament, or sacred book. God is for man both immanent and transcendent. . . . God dwells in man to guide him and transform him into the likeness of His Son. (Brinton, 1958, p. 11)

Quakers reacted against whatever they believed to be unessential for living the Christian life. Their fundamental beliefs revolved around a search for community living in which decisions are made by consensus; a seeking for respect, harmony, and pacifism in which conflicts and disturbances are avoided; equality among sexes, races, and classes; and simplicity in living style.

George Fox established the first Friends schools in 1668, one for boys and one for girls. In a few years there were fifteen schools in England, including some boarding schools. The curriculum of these schools included "whatever things were civil and useful in creation" in the words of an early Quaker educator. The schools stressed practical subjects such as the sciences, mathematics, and practical skills and omitted the humanities, arts, music, and literature, considering them unnecessary ornaments. In the nineteenth century, however, the humanities were introduced into Quaker schools (Smith, 1990, p. 529).

Quaker schools provided a religiously guarded education, one in which children were shielded from influences that would go against Quaker religious principles. In the early years the Friends composed textbooks for their schools. Quaker schools attempted to inculcate a sense of belonging to a religious fellowship through the daily worship experience. Teachers in the schools were to have sensitivity to the presence of God within them and their students as well as to the students' inner sense of rightness. For religious education:

> The most important instruments they used were corporate community worship, largely silent periods when the individual student could be quiet and undistracted, and many periods of silence throughout the

day. There was study of the Scriptures and Quaker principles. (Hole,
1978, pp. 28–29)

Quaker educators argued against an excessively rational education.
They contended that mere knowledge in the head had to give way to a
saving acquaintance with divine things obtained through experiential
knowledge of the Spirit of Truth (Hole, 1978, p. 32).

While in the early years their schools at times resorted to violent
forms of punishment, the Friends became more consistent with their
ideals and later adopted nonviolent forms of discipline. The education
of girls did not differ in essentials from the education of boys.

Anglican efforts in education encountered opposition by nonconformists not only in England but also in Scotland, Wales, and Ireland. In Scotland John Knox (1513–1572), a follower of John Calvin,
introduced a Presbyterian form of church government in which elders
not bishops managed church affairs. Knox persuaded officials to allow
the theological principles of Calvinism to permeate government-
maintained schools. In Wales dissenting academies took the offensive
against Anglican attempts in education. In Ireland resistance came not
only from Catholics but also from a large number of Calvinists. The
SPCK was active in establishing charity schools in all of these areas.

Besides the educational efforts of Anglicans and Puritans there
were also educational efforts initiated by nonconformist churches. One
English church that was highly influential in the dissenting academies
and in other forms of Christian education was the Methodist Church.
Founded by the Anglican clergyman John Wesley (d. 1791), this
movement charged that the Anglican Church was not meeting the
needs of the masses of the people. In his approach to religion Wesley
attempted to incorporate personal religious experience, clarity of
thought, and a desire to accomplish things methodically (hence the
name Methodist). Wesley's ideas found haven and harvest in the
colonies and the republic because of the efforts of the great preacher
George Whitfield.

In theology Wesley attempted the difficult task of uniting elements of Catholicism and Protestantism. Of this attempt a prominent
Methodist theologian has written that:

> He believed in faith and good works, Scripture and tradition,
> revelation and reason, sovereign grace and human freedom,
> particularism and universal redemption, the witness of the spirit and

an ordered polity, repentance and the expectation of perfection, the priesthood of all believers and an authorized representative ministry. (Outler in Vernon, 1993, p. 422)

Further, Wesley is considered an important educational leader in eighteenth-century England. He tried to stir up Anglicans in Britain through charismatic preaching and the hymns of his brother Charles. The movement that he led was part of the First Great Religious Awakening (1730–1760), a popular evangelical effort in Britain and the United States, which attempted to move people to a conversion experience. The prominent American preachers on the stump during this awakening were the great preachers Jonathan Edwards and William Tennent.

It was Wesley's belief that education and religion needed each other. He is responsible for four educational developments. First he founded elementary and secondary schools that were marked by a close community among students and teachers, a set of rules for living a religious life, and a curriculum of educational basics, with less attention given to classical studies. Secondly, he was a leader in the Sunday school movement that became a forerunner of the English day school. Thirdly, he organized groups and classes of adults for weekly meetings and Bible study. Fourthly, he was influential in publishing and distributing popular religious literature (Moore, 1990, p. 409).

For his educational ideas Wesley possibly drew upon Bishop John Comenius and the English philosopher John Locke. Believing as many did in his time in the depravity of human nature, Wesley proposed a guarded education in which children would "turn from self will, pride, anger, revenge and the love of the world, to resignation, lowliness, meekness and love of God" (Wesley in Towns, 1970, p. 322). For Wesley the purpose of religious education of children was to produce conversion:

The goal of all work with children at home, in the schools, in the Methodist society is to make them pious, to lead to personal religion, and to insure salvation. It is not merely to bring them up so that they do no harm and abstain from outward sin, nor to be accustomed to the use of grace, saying their prayers, reading their books, and the like, nor is it to train them in right opinions. The purpose of religious education is to instill in children true religion, holiness and the love of God and mankind and to train them in the image of God. (Prince, 1926, pp. 87–88)

Wesley's principles of religious education have been summarized (Towns, 1970). The child is to be considered a unit of salvation. A deeply religious life is possible in childhood. Religious instruction should begin when the child arrives at the ability to reason. Children should be so educated that they are cured of the ills and diseases of human nature. Wesley conceded that education might at times have to include breaking of the will of the child toward sin, even if this meant the infliction of physical punishment.

The Beginnings of Education in Colonial America

In the sixteenth and seventeenth centuries colonies were established in America by the Spanish in Florida, the Dutch in New Amsterdam (later New York), and the English in New England, Pennsylvania, Virginia, and later in New York. The various colonists established educational institutions similar to those with which they were familiar in Europe. The most successful educational institutions, however, were established by the English. For the most part colonial schools were instruments of the Protestant Reformation (Welter, 1962, p. 17).

Religious groups were leaders in educational efforts throughout the colonies. The Anglican Church through the Society for the Propagation of the Gospel in Foreign Parts established a number of schools in New York and New Jersey. Quakers and German Lutherans and Pietists started schools in Pennsylvania in the seventeenth century. Presbyterians set up schools in New Jersey in the eighteenth century. Little effort was expended in starting schools in Virginia and the southern colonies. However, the most extensive and influential educational efforts in colonial America were those of the Puritans in the Congregational church in Massachusetts.

The political leader of the Puritans in Massachusetts was John Winthrop. In establishing the Puritan colony as a Christian commonwealth he declared: "We must consider that we shall be as a city upon a hill, the eyes of all people are upon us" (In Cremin, 1970, p. 15). To achieve this goal Puritans pushed through legislation in 1642 and 1647 that set up elementary and grammar schools for the express purpose of fostering literacy and the Puritan version of the Protestant faith. For Puritans salvation could not come without some basic education in the Scriptures. Education in both primary and grammar schools was intended chiefly to provide moral instruction and sufficient literacy to enable children to read the Bible. Harvard College was established in

1636 to train ministers for the Puritan or Congregational ministry. The other colonies in New England followed the Massachusetts example.

The religious nature of early colonial education in New England took up ample space in books used for instruction. The *New England Primer,* a popular text for primary education, contained not only the alphabet but also the Lord's Prayer, the Creed, and the Ten Commandments. The primer included a catechism for instructing children in the Protestant faith (Spring, 1986, pp. 5–6). Of the importance of the schoolroom catechism it has been noted that:

> The distinguishing mark of New England's cultural identity was symbolized by the one book that stood beside the Bible in their regard—the catechism. For the New England child the catechism not only symbolized his Protestant inheritance but tangibly inaugurated his education in the elements of his new faith. (Axtell, 1976, p. 5)

The most outstanding religious leader and educator in Puritan New England was Cotton Mather (1663–1728). In numerous writings he addressed educational issues concerning parents, teachers, ministers, and learned associations. He showed a bit more toleration for various Protestant groups than did the earlier Puritans. His works had currency throughout America and even in England.

For Mather the main objective of education in the Congregational Church was a piety in which one achieves a saving knowledge of Jesus. Purposively, education prepared children for conversion that comes through knowledge of the Scriptures and the catechism. In his view children needed conversion because they were born not only in ignorance but also in sin. Piety for Mather went beyond merely accepting correct doctrines to doing good works. Mather described the relationship between education and religious conversions in this manner:

> God initiated conversion; he drew men to himself by infusing their souls with grace; without him, men were helpless. In education too the process was initiated from outside the mind of the child. Something had to be put in before he could act, even if his reason were conceived of as a storehouse of unborn ideas. The release of ideas could be triggered only from without; but once release was given, once the trigger was pressed, the child could do much, indeed, he had to do much for himself, just as the soul that craved salvation had to do much once it received so little as a deed of grace. (In Cremin, 1970, p. 291)

For the education of children at home and at school Mather composed a reader entitled *Good Lessons for Children* which he designed so as "to have the Child improve in Goodness at the same time, that he improved in Reading" (In Morgan, 1966, p. 101). He warned against children learning the catechism by rote and without understanding. For Mather not only parents but also teachers in schools should catechize children. Mather like other Puritans advocated the use of corporal punishment for correcting children. He also highlighted the importance of education within the family and advocated societies of associated families that would assist one another in mutual education and the education of children, under the direction of the clergy. Of family meetings he wrote:

> It hath been a laudable custom, in many places, for a dozen families in a vicinity to combine into a design of meeting at each other's houses, at fit seasons, to spend an hour together, in prayers and psalms, and repetition of sermons and religious conferences about the things of God. It would be a real service to religion, yea, and unto themselves also, if the pastors of our churches would animate and encourage such family meetings among their well-disposed people. (In Cully, 1960, p. 236)

Mather's interest in education also extended to the education of adults. His *Essays to Do Good* in 1710 is considered the first work treating adult education published in America. In this work Mather described the formation of adult discussion groups designed for personal and social improvement. Mather advised that:

> A proper number of persons in a neighborhood, whose hearts God hath inclined to do good, should form themselves into a society, to meet when and where they shall agree, and to consider: What are the disorders that we may observe rising among us; and what may be done either by ourselves immediately, or by others through our advice, to suppress these disorders. (In Grattan, 1959, pp. 15–16)

Mather then gives specific directions on how the discussion should proceed and the measures which should be taken to deal with the problems.

In contrast to the Puritans in New England the Society of Friends established schools in seventeenth-century Pennsylvania with a somewhat different approach. Quaker educational theory differed from Puritan beliefs about education since its starting point was not the depravity but rather the basic innocence of the child. Holding as they did that the Inner Light was inside the child, Quakers believed that children were inherently neither good nor evil but innocent, with both good and bad propensities, either of which they could follow. The early Quakers were convinced that the Inner Light shone into the conscience of children as well as adults:

> Enabling them to distinguish between right and wrong. This does not mean that conscience is always right, but rather that, as the individual becomes more sensitive and obedient to the Divine Light, the conscience develops reliability and insight. The schoolmaster endeavors to educate the conscience by appealing to it. (Brinton, 1958, p. 61)

Notwithstanding these beliefs students in early Quaker schools were burdened with many rules.

The highest ideal in Quaker moral and religious education is to allow the opportunity for the Divine Light to be sensed in the soul in such a way that evil propensities do not come to the fore. This philosophy of a religiously guarded education in which the dictates of individual conscience are tested against the consensus of the group has guided Quaker education in theory and practice. Ideally, Quaker education attempts to go beyond the law to establish a Christian spirit of freedom.

The Quakers were deeply involved in the charity school movement that flourished in the United States after the revolution in the late eighteenth and early nineteenth century. The movement became the forerunner of the common school. Religious leaders and philanthropists established Sunday schools, charity schools, and infant schools modeled after English institutions. While in England there was debate on the merits of schooling for the masses, no such debates took place in the United States. Quakers led the way in establishing charity schools in New York, Philadelphia, Baltimore, and other Atlantic coast cities. They even established schools for Negro and Native American children in accordance with George Fox's admonition "Let your Light shine among the Indians, the Blacks and the Whites that ye may answer the truth in them" (In Brinton 1958, p. 68). In the charity schools the monitorial method devised by Joseph Lancaster, an English Quaker, was used according to which older children, once taught by instructors, instructed small groups of younger children. The focus of charity school education was on nonsectarian moral education that had as its purpose the inculcation of obedience, promptness, and industry. The catechism was also part of the instruction (Kaestle, 1983, pp. 38–44).

Another educational institution from the eighteenth century was the Sunday school, first established in England by Robert Raikes. Sunday schools reached out to educate poor children in large American cities; they welcomed children of all Protestant denominations. Besides teaching nondenominational religion, including prayer, hymn singing, and memorizing the Bible, the schools taught the rudiments of literacy. Some Episcopalians and Methodists opposed the nondenominational nature of these schools and formed their own associations. The stated purposes of these educational efforts were to keep children from a life of vice and sin and to foster the proper observance of the Sabbath.

Similar in religious intent to the charity schools and the Sunday schools were the infant schools. First established by Robert Owen in Scotland, they appeared in this country in the early nineteenth century. While these schools taught the rudiments of education, advocates also had a strong religious agenda: "saving children's souls through religious education, saving one's own soul through good works, or preparing for the millennium, which some people expected imminently" (Kaestle, 1983, p. 49). Expectation of the millennium was part of evangelical Protestant belief that Jesus' return was imminent.

First Challenges to Christian Humanism

The development of new knowledge, especially scientific knowledge in the seventeenth century, further increased the conservative orthodoxy of Roman Catholic and Protestant forms of education. The full flowering of these challenges to religious education was reached in the eighteenth century Enlightenment, which proposed a secularized theory of education, with decreasing ties to religious bodies.

The Christian Churches in general reacted negatively against the new cosmology proposed by Copernicus, Tycho Brahe, Kepler, and Galileo. The new cosmology contradicted the biblical accounts that placed the earth at the center of the universe. These new scientific narratives challenged the religious views of the world and of human knowledge, teachings that were the underpinnings of Christian doctrines. The new science also eclipsed the cosmology of Aristotle to which churchmen remained committed. In 1600 the Dominican scholar-priest Giordano Bruno was burned at the stake because his ideas on the nature of the universe were declared dangerous to social, political, and religious stability. (One can note that the Jesuits were deeply involved in all of the disputes, notably Robert Bellarmine, whose efforts were decisive in the condemnation of Galileo.)

One of the thrusts of the new cosmology was to separate the natural sciences from philosophy and theology and thus from the intellectual control of the Catholic Church. Cosmology was a branch of philosophy and theology under the Aristotelian and medieval schema. To the new enlightened ones, science needed no such authority, especially since it was based on observation and not on received opinions. The Catholic Church continued to retain science as a part of natural philosophy and theology because it sustained the traditional religious interpretation of the world and human knowing.

The classical humanist tradition was seriously challenged by the empirical approach to knowledge taken by Francis Bacon (d. 1626). In arguing that knowledge is derived solely from sense experience he questioned and doubted the reliance on authority, tradition, and reason which prevailed in humanist education. John Locke, as will be seen in the next chapter, applied his concepts to education. Bacon's main ideas are found in his *Novum Organum,* a work in which he extolled empirical and inductive knowledge in opposition to the *Organon* of Aristotle, based totally on the deductive method of reasoning. He condemned the preoccupation with Aristotelian logic and argued for adherence to sense knowledge. His ideas provided the basis for the development of the empirical sciences. The churches and the universities were not able to stifle the efforts of scientists and philosophers of science who situated themselves mainly in academies since access to universities was prohibited.

A strong challenge to the classical humanist tradition and to Jesuit education came from René Descartes (d. 1650), a graduate of the Jesuit college at La Flèche. Disillusioned by his Jesuit education he decided "to entirely abandon the study of letters . . . and to seek no other science than the knowledge of myself, or the great book of the world" (In Bowen, 1981, p. 58). Descartes focused on logic and science, all the while holding to God's existence to justify the existence of material things. Although identified with the empirical tradition, he has come to be known as a rationalist since he attributed great power to human reason to formulate clear and distinct ideas about the self and the world. He also maintained that there were some ideas that were divinely implanted in persons. While empiricists contended that all ideas come from sense experience, Descartes developed a system of dualism describing the operations of the mind and matter, seeing these in opposition.

The classical humanist tradition was also under the attack of scholars who preferred the vernacular in education instead of the classical languages. Italian scholars such as Giambattista Gelli scoffed at Latin studies as a vested interest of academic establishment and the church. He proposed a simpler faith than classical humanists, one dependent more on the Bible. Such scholars denied that humanist studies prepared people for life in society. The French scholar Montaigne (d. 1592) took a skeptical and cynical view of humanist education, emphasizing studies in the humanities. He challenged the claims of reason and argued that it was faith that was necessary for the journey to God.

Summary

Europe and to a lesser degree the United States was the ground on which distinctive approaches to Catholic and Protestant education emerged after the Reformation. Catholicism developed a doctrinal approach, following the decrees of the Council of Trent. A cadre of men and women in newly established religious orders preached and taught the doctrines of the church. Protestant education took various forms, in all of which the Bible and personal experience played a major educational role.

By the end of this period new voices were raised extolling human ways of knowing and learning that challenged the religious modes of revelation, faith, tradition, and authority. Empirical and rationalist approaches rapidly gained influence in intellectual circles and eventually in the universities of this period, first in France, then in England, and then in other countries of Europe. These were the ideas that paved the way for the Enlightenment that presented an all-out challenge to the theology and education of the Christian Churches.

Chapter 5

The Enlightenment and Christian Education

> Moralists have unanimously agreed, that unless virtue be nursed by liberty, it will never attain due strength—and what they say of man I extend to mankind, insisting that in all cases morals must be fixed on immutable principles; and, that the being cannot be termed rational or virtuous, who obeys any authority, but that of reason. (Mary Wollstonecraft, 1992, 1792, p. 316)

> In all good education, in all real instruction, in all true teaching, necessity should evoke freedom, law should induce self-determination, external compulsion should develop internal free-will, outer hatred should beget inner love. But all education, instruction, and teaching fail when hatred gives birth to hatred, law to deceit and crime, compulsion to slavery. (Friedrich Froebel, in Castle, 1958, p. 215)

The age of Enlightenment, the period between the English Revolution in 1680 and the French Revolution in 1790, offered many serious challenges to the Christian theology and the practice of Christian education. Many of the Enlightenment thinkers were highly critical of the philosophical assumptions of Christian theology and education. In proposing that knowledge comes from senses, experience, reason, and feelings rather than from authority, history, and tradition, Enlightenment thinkers or philosophes tended to undermine the traditional basis of Christian theology and education. To combat and respond to these ideas Christian leaders and educators became overly defensive of church teachings. The struggle with the philosophes was especially acute with the Roman Catholic Church, which issued many condemnations of Enlightenment writings. In time, however, many of the ideas of the Enlightenment as well as their educational theories and practices gained reluctant acceptance by Christian scholars and educators.

First of all, Enlightenment thinking was a continuation of the thrust of Renaissance humanism. Its manifesto made individuals the centers and creators of meaning, truth, and value. It also greatly extended the focus on the individual, which marked the work of René Descartes in the sixteenth century. The best-known pre-Enlightenment and Enlightenment thinkers are the French philosophes Montesquieu, Voltaire, Diderot, and Rousseau; the English scholars Newton, Locke, and Hobbes; the German philosophers Kant and Lessing; the Scottish philosophers David Hume and Adam Smith; and Thomas Jefferson, Benjamin Rush, and Benjamin Franklin in the United States.

Enlightenment advocates believed in human reason and not faith or tradition as the principal guide for all human conduct. The philosophes spared no authority, political or religious, from the criticism of reason. They developed an ambitious agenda that included:

> A program of secularism, humanity, cosmopolitanism, and freedom, above all, freedom in its many forms—freedom from arbitrary power, freedom of speech, freedom of trade, freedom to realize one's talents, freedom of aesthetic response, in a word, of moral man to make his own way in the world. (Gay, 1966, p. 1)

This commitment to freedom and reason led those wedded to Enlightenment ideals to be highly critical of traditional supernatural religion. They replaced this otherworldly view with a natural religion or deism that limited God's activity to creation and providence. These thinkers, especially John Locke and Voltaire, were insistent in their demands for religious toleration of all faiths. A bitter struggle, especially with regard to education and the schools, erupted between these thinkers, notably Voltaire, and religious leaders.

Some have compared the philosophy of the Enlightenment to a natural religion that embraces shared beliefs about human life. Becker (1959) defined the essential articles of the Religion of the Enlightenment:

> (1) man is not naively depraved; (2) the end of life is life itself, the good life on earth instead of the beatific life after death; (3) man is capable solely by the light of reason and experience of perfecting the good life here on earth; and (4) the essential condition of the good life here on earth is the freeing of men's minds from the bonds of

ignorance and superstition, and of their bodies from the arbitrary
oppression of the constituted social order. (pp. 102–103)

While not all philosophes were as negative on religious beliefs as these
principles indicate, these principles are quite representative of the
philosophes of the eighteenth century. The Enlightenment has also
been interpreted as a synthesis resulting from a conflict between the
classical and Christian traditions in which "the classical tradition with
its rationalism, naturalism and humanism provided much of the ground
work on which the philosophes built" (Gay, 1959).

Enlightenment thinkers set their eyes on the new science that
originated with the work of Francis Bacon (1561–1626). In particular,
Isaac Newton (1642–1727), arguing against Descartes, held that all
ideas come from sense knowledge. He contended that real knowledge
was scientific knowledge, gained painstakingly through designed experiments and careful observation of natural phenomena. Newton's
thought gave rise to scientific empiricism that formed the basis for a
new understanding of the world. His mechanical view of nature did offer some place for God as the clockmaker of the well-ordered universe.
In his view and that of other Enlightenment figures, it was science that
would ameliorate human life and become the chief instrument for social reform. Belief in science led these thinkers to a belief in progress
and in the perfectibility of the human condition. Ultimately science
would be the key to greater human happiness.

Enlightenment thinking spawned the political and economic liberalism that came to characterize European nations and the United
States in the eighteenth and nineteenth centuries. Locke's ideas on
government paved the way for the rejection of the divine right of kings,
lessening of the authority of the church, and the advance of religious
toleration, which called for the end of religious wars. His concepts of
the natural rights of individuals were influential in inspiring revolu-
tions in America and in France. Rousseau's social contract theory underscored a secular understanding for the origin of societies and nations. Liberalism in economics, as advocated by Adam Smith, set the
stage for human reliance on a free market that would ensure the happiness of all. Enlightenment thinkers believed that this freedom would
eventually lead to equal opportunity for all.

For European Enlightenment thinkers the United States became
the principal experiment for their ideals. De Tocqueville in the nineteenth century judged that the good that he saw in America could be

traced to the acceptance of the Enlightenment. In the United States religion had no public role and was relegated to the private sphere. Science and technology, represented powerfully by Benjamin Franklin,
held much more sway in the New World than in the Old. Liberal ideals
in politics permeated the thinking of those that struggled for independence and established the republic. Human rights, so dear to Enlightenment thinkers, were enshrined in the Constitution of the United
States. With no aristocracy in the United States economic opportunity
and equality were seen as real possibilities.

The Enlightenment not only introduced new ideas about human
nature and human society into the intellectual sphere but also was instrumental in increasing the power of the state over education. In doing this, the control of the churches waned and weakened. Eventually
what resulted were state-controlled systems of education over which
churches had little or no control. While in many countries religion has
remained a part of the curriculum of schools, in other countries such
as the United States the public schools have become completely secularized both in control and in curriculum. Different Christian churches
in the United States have reacted in different ways to this secularization. Some have long maintained their own systems of schools, for example, Catholics and Lutherans. In recent years religious schools
among evangelical Christians, Orthodox Jews, and Muslims have pro-
liferated. All churches have offered out of regular school religious education for their young members.

This chapter presents the educational ideas of key Enlightenment
figures, especially those concepts that relate to Christian education. In
the second section it describes how Enlightenment and liberal ideals
influenced the development of national and state-controlled systems of
education in many nations. This takeover resulted in less church control over education as well as the lessening or in some places the actual elimination of the teaching and practice of religion in state-
controlled schools. Although in recent years the limitations and the
excesses of the Enlightenment have been the subject of much criticism
and controversy, it is hard to deny the many positive achievements of
this eighteen-century movement.

The Enlightenment and Religion

The ultimate objective of the philosophes with regard to religion was
to promote intellectual and religious freedom for all citizens. In their

zeal to achieve this goal they took various stances toward religion ranging from acceptance of supernatural religion to commitment to the natural religion of Deism and for some the adoption of an agnosticism or even a materialistic and antireligious atheism. The philosophes bristled under the censorious control that churches exercised in Europe in the political and social spheres, especially the efforts of churches to ban certain books and opinions. Only a representative sampling of Enlightenment ideas on religion is presented here; later in the chapter Enlightenment views on religion will then be treated insofar as they relate to education in religion.

Though remaining a religious believer, Voltaire (1694–1778) was the severest critic of all revealed religions, especially of Roman Catholicism. In short, he considered Catholicism depraved and absurd. While Locke and Newton had viewed Christianity as compatible with natural religion, satirically and bitterly Voltaire attacked not only the Bible but also church theologies, and even debunked the lives of some Christian saints such as Joan of Arc and Francis of Assisi. Voltaire, however, did accept the natural and rational creed of Deism that included belief in the existence of God as creator, his providence over individuals, and immutable natural laws. In his writings he offered rational proofs for the existence of God. His credo asserted the natural goodness and reasonableness of human beings. Voltaire grappled in his play *Candide* with the problem of evil, dramatized for him by the earthquake in Lisbon in 1755. He subscribed to the belief that all religious faiths should be tolerated in society and that established religions should be abolished. For him civic peace would prevail only if all religious faiths were permitted to function openly in society. In an often-quoted statement Voltaire declared that:

> If there had been in England only one religion its despotism would have been fearful. If there had been two religions they would have cut each other's throat. But as there are thirty they live peacefully and happily. (In Coates, White and Shapiro, 1966, p. 254)

Voltaire actually did recognize the social value of a supernatural religion that inculcated fear of divine punishment which would keep the masses under strict control. In his condescending view the educated classes had no need for supernatural religion; for them a rational Deism was the more rational alternative. On balance Voltaire's influence with regard to religion in society may be cast as positive since he issued many warnings against religious intolerance and fanaticism. Though he was not successful in eliminating the French laws that established the Catholic Church and called for the repression of Protestantism, these laws, thanks in no small part to Voltaire, were eventually disregarded and then revoked.

More temperate than Voltaire in his critique of religion, David Hume (1711–1776), a prominent figure in the Scottish Enlightenment, shaped a more skeptical attitude toward religion. Throughout his lifetime he did, however, maintain an interest in religion and wrote about God, natural religion, miracles, and superstition, always claiming that he was more agnostic than atheistic. What Hume most decidedly rejected were the abstract metaphysics behind the theologies of the churches. For Hume the existence of God was merely a religious hypothesis that could neither be proven or completely rejected. Hume was also wary of the danger of superstitions in religion. Different from Voltaire Hume thought that religious belief could be on the side of civil liberty.

The more radical French philosophes Diderot and Helvetius came close to proclaiming atheism, something that the German philosopher Holbach definitely did. These men incurred the wrath not only of traditional believers but also of both Voltaire and Rousseau, both of whom still held out for a niche called natural religion.

Of all the Enlightenment figures Jean Jacques Rousseau remained a deeply religious person throughout his life. His quarrel was chiefly with Roman Catholicism. Rousseau criticized not only dogmatic religion but also the overly rational explanations of religion. In his religious faith he avoided dogmas and centered on a simple love of God and a reverence for the Bible and the personality of Jesus. Like a closet Quaker or Pietist, religion for him was a natural sentiment that God implanted in the human soul.

In his *Social Contract* Rousseau proposed a civil religion for society, one that is distinct from particular religious faiths. Society needs religion in order to dispose citizens to obey the laws and to respect one another. For Rousseau:

> The dogmas of civil religion ought to be simple, few in number, precisely fixed, and without explanation or comment. The existence of a powerful, wise, and benevolent Divinity, who foresees and provides the life to come, the happiness of the just, the punishment of the wicked, the sanctity of the social contract and the laws: these are its positive dogmas. Its negative dogmas I would confine to one – intolerance. (In Bellah and Hammond, 1982, p. 43)

For Rousseau civil religion's sole purpose was to legitimate and strengthen the state. Drawing on this thesis, the sociologist of religion Robert Bellah (1970) started an extensive debate among sociologists, historians, and theologians in 1967. He identified a civil religion in the United States that existed alongside of the religious bodies in the country.

The chief German Enlightenment philosopher, Emmanuel Kant, offered a rational defense of religion. In his *Critique of Pure Reason* he rejected the traditional philosophical proofs for the existence of God. Later, however, in two other works, *Critique of Practical Reason* and *Religion within the Limits of Reason Alone,* he presented arguments for God's existence based on the moral sense in individuals. From this innate sense of duty and obligation to moral laws Kant inferred the existence of God. If God did not exist, he argued, the sense of duty and obligation to achieve the highest good in life would have no object and thus not only sense of duty but also all of human life would be rendered absurd. The existence of God is thus necessary for maintaining the moral order in society. Kant's rationalized faith, however, left little room for piety. The closest he came to expressing religious sentiment are the words that began the *Critique of Practical Reason*:

> Two things fill the mind with ever new and increasing admiration and awe, the oftener and more steadily we reflect on them: the starry heavens above me and the moral law within me. (In Coates, White, and Shapiro, 1966, p. 274)

The Enlightenment and Education

Education was an important concern for all Enlightenment thinkers, who viewed it as the sure way for illuminating the minds of people. It should be noted, however, that the philosophes desired to restrict education to the upper and middle classes. The French philosophes recommended that only a minimal and pragmatic education be given to the lower class (Chisick, 1981, p. 278ff). However, by the nineteenth century the changes in thought introduced by these and later writers did lead to some calls for universal popular education. In any case Enlightenment thinking and practice in education, beginning with Locke and Rousseau, greatly influenced the theory and practice of education in the eighteenth century and became even more influential in the liberal and progressive approaches to education that emerged in the nineteenth and twentieth centuries. In fact, one finds many of these ideals incorporated in the educational philosophy of John Dewey, the fore-most philosopher of education in the United States.

From the earliest years Christian leaders and educators reacted strongly against Enlightenment ideas, especially as these ideas rejected religion outright or excluded religion from education. Over time, how-ever, many educational reforms advocated by Enlightenment educa-tors found a home in Christian education. In the following chapters some examples of Christian rejection and acceptance of these ideas will receive more attention.

The extension of scientific empiricism to aid in understanding human persons and to provide for their education was the main achievement of John Locke (1632–1704). While not strictly speaking a philosophe of the Enlightenment, he is considered one of its princi-pal progenitors (Schouls, 1992, p. 2). Locke's sensationist psychology of learning provides the basis of the Enlightenment theory of educa-tion (Chisik, 1981, p. 39) since it was at the heart of the educational theories of Helvetius and Rousseau. Locke rejected the concept of in-nate ideas advocated by Descartes and argued that all ideas come from reflection on experience. Locke applied his ideas to education in his highly influential *Some Thoughts on Education,* published in 1693. Viewing the child as a *tabula rasa* (a blank slate), Locke assigned crit-ical importance to early educational processes. For him education was mainly a moral affair since its aim was to produce good persons. With regard to moral education, he opposed the doctrine of original sin and argued that virtue could be taught by purely secular means. Locke's trust in the power of education appeared succinctly in his well-known words "Men's happiness or misery is most part of their own making... of all the men we meet with, nine parts of ten are what they are, good or evil, useful or not, by their education" (In Schouls, 1992, p. 187).

Locke's concept of discipline entailed striking a balance between giving reasons to the child for acting in a certain manner and the adults' attempts to correct the child's behavior. In his view, children were to be reasoned with from the earliest years for children "understand it [reasons] as early as they do language... and love to be treated as ra-tional creatures, sooner than is imagined" (Locke, 1968, p. 64). He coupled discipline and self-mastery. The purpose of discipline was in his view to "teach the mind to get a mastery over itself; and to be able, upon choice, to take itself off from the hot pursuit of one thing and set itself on another with facility and delight." For intellectual education Locke stressed literacy, history, and science. He recommended that children be educated at home, warning that parents should not "hazard your son's innocence for a little Greek and Latin" (Locke, 1968, p. 70). What Locke leaves unsettled and unclear is how values can arise if all knowledge results from sensation and reflection.

With regard to religion Locke was not totally in agreement with Enlightenment thinkers. He contended in *The Reasonableness of Christianity* that while reason could in theory confirm the truths of Christian revelation, most people would have to rely on Christian revelation itself because of a general lack of aptitude or patience with reason. Thus while he asserted that reason must be our last judge and guide in everything, he still contended that "the greater part of mankind have not the leisure for learning and logic" (In Schouls, 1992, p. 53). Yet Locke still claimed that all people have the obligation of living by reason. For him humans are born not in a state of original sin but in the state of original neutrality or *tabula rasa,* according to which they are not naturally corrupt. Indeed, they are able to act in conformity with right reason or moral obligation. What Locke proposed then is a rationalized and gentle piety, somewhat similar to that espoused by Erasmus. Religious education should include the Bible, which he viewed as the fountain of morality.

The Enlightenment writer on education par excellence was Jean Jacques Rousseau (1712–1778). In 1792 he published *Emile,* a book that severely disturbed Christian and especially Catholic educators of the time. Yet no book in the history of education, with the possible exception of Plato's *Republic,* has had more influence in educational theorizing and practice. Even some of Rousseau's fellow philosophes were highly critical of this book. The vehemence of the Catholic Church's reaction is well documented. The Archbishop of Paris condemned *Emile,* causing Rousseau to flee to England. The Jesuit Faculty of the University of Paris anathematized this book written by a Jesuit educated scholar who ridiculed and rejected Jesuit colleges as "ludicrous establishments." In 1764 *Emile,* along with Rousseau's *Social Contract,* was put on the Vatican's Index of Forbidden Books and ordered to be burned. In a solemn High Mass in Madrid in 1765 a copy of *Emile* was ceremonially burned, although it turned out that it was only a fake copy of the book.

The strong reaction against *Emile* was caused by Rousseau's intemperate attack on Catholic education. In a notorious chapter he related the fictional story of the Catholic curate of Savoyard who had his eyes opened by his study of French intellectuals. In this tract Rousseau accused the Catholic Church of subverting the quest for truth, natural justice, and social equity through its teaching of narrowly defined dogma and its domination of the schools. He asserted that:

> Such an education leads not to an ennobling vision of the good but to prejudice; nothing, the curate asserts, is more stupid than wasting much of the child's life teaching it the catechism under the delusion that such would lead to the cultivation of human potential for virtue. (In Bowen, 1981, p. 184)

In *Emile,* a romantic and utopian work, Rousseau charged the traditional views on child rearing and education with excessive constraints. In contrast, he proposed that children be allowed to develop according to their natural proclivities, arguing from right reason in an enlightened age. Rousseau contended "that the first inclinations of nature are always right" (Rousseau, 1961, p. 56). Rousseau was dead set against treating children as if they were small adults. His challenge to educators and parents was: "Do precisely the opposite to what is usually done and you will do the right plan." Rousseau rejected such supernatural doctrines as original sin, asserting that individuals were born good but corrupted by society. The famous opening sentence of *Emile* reads: "God makes all things good; man meddles with them and they become evil. He forces one soil to yield the products of another, one tree to bear another's fruit" (Rousseau, 1961, p. 5).

The main thrust of *Emile* argues that education is the principal means of reforming society into a classless society. The book proposed a program of natural education which followed the order of nature, things, and humans. Rousseau prescribed that education should consist of the natural unfolding of the child's latent powers of sensation, memory, and understanding. Learning came naturally through play and observation. The role of the teacher was not to direct or instruct but to aid children to learn from experiences. Rousseau advised teachers:

> Do not command your pupil to do anything... let him from the first feel on his proud neck the hard yoke of necessity, a yoke which is fashioned by the nature of things and not by the caprices of man. (In Castle, 1958, p. 138)

For moral education of children he advised that children should learn from social experiences rather than from religion.

In *Emile* Rousseau also treated the difficult period of adolescence. For this stage of development Rousseau added learning from understanding to learning from experiences. For Rousseau it is at this period that learning from books should be introduced. Adolescence is filled with rising passions as well as emerging rational judgment. Instruction in religion should begin in adolescence since the child has reached the age of reason. For Rousseau youths enter the moral realm around the age of eighteen when they become young adults. (This opinion has been challenged by the research of many scholars, notably Jean Piaget and Lawrence Kohlberg.) Rousseau noted the development of love, sexuality, and friendship during adolescence, suggesting that while stimulating prurient interests should be avoided, questions of curiosity should be honestly answered. About sex education he advised: "Nothing is to be left to chance: if you are not absolutely certain that you can keep Emile in ignorance till sixteen, tell him before he is ten." Educators are urged to guide youth into proper love of self and regard for others. In Rousseau's view moral education should shun preaching and drilling, as was the practice in the schools of the time. Rather, he believed, it would take place naturally in the study of society through reading the biographies of great men of the past. As an integral part of moral education he recommended a Spartan way of life that entailed rigorous physical activity.

In the final chapter of *Emile* Rousseau wrote about the education of girls for whom he proposed a rather sheltered education. Rousseau does recommend some religion to be included in the education of girls since in his view they are more in need of it than boys. He counseled that preferably they should be educated in a convent where they would use only short prayers offered to what appears to be a deistic version of God, who is presented not as a vengeful patriarch but as a divine spirit.

Rousseau's theory of education expounded in *Emile* received additional attention in his *Social Contract.* In the latter, he proposed a utopian vision of the ideal society in which education played an important social role. Rousseau argued that human society needs constitutions and laws to defend valuable human rights and duties. He explained how good laws, which are of divine origin, were to be determined and enacted. Education was assigned the yeoman's service of educating youth into their responsibilities in society. Further, it was given the task of developing the three great powers that God has instilled in humans: reason, conscience, and free will. From an analysis of this treatise it becomes clear that the natural education described in *Emile* is only the first part of the education of youth, something to be supplemented by an education which should attempt to develop the moral and social dimensions of persons. Thus for Rousseau in the ideal society there needs to be some effective check on the natural inclinations of individuals which might impel them to violate the social contract. In a 1772 letter entitled *Considerations on the Government of Poland* he wrote of the advantages of political education for a nation: "It is education that gives to all souls a rational form, so directing their opinions and tastes that they become patriots by conscious affirmation" (In Bowen, 1981, p. 197).

In these three groundbreaking works Rousseau addressed some of the most pressing issues in educational and social theory. What is the nature of the human person and of the good society? How can true freedom and autonomy be attained? How is the individual's right to and need for freedom to be balanced by the necessities of a good society? How are individual and social consciousness to be fostered and balanced? While *Emile* presented a romantic, individualistic, and utopian view of a society of individuals, *Social Contract* and *Considerations* did not fail to deal with the social and political realities of education.

Rousseau's influence on later education has been substantial. While psychologists have challenged the psychological reality upon which his theory depends, his work has been responsible for many educational innovations: the nursery school, the kindergarten, the trade school, physical training, secular education, and even progressive education. Reform-minded educators in the next three centuries have often turned to his writings for alternative approaches to education.

Even in his time many educators took Rousseau to task. A fellow Frenchman Claude Adrien Helvetius (1715–1771) went even further than Rousseau did in presenting an optimistic view of the potential of education in his *De L'Homme*. To a greater extent than Rousseau, he believed in the rational powers of children, understanding them as rational beings whose direction in life is determined by pain and pleasure. Though anticlerical and antireligious in his writings Helvetius still advocated the use of a catechism for moral training and for inculcating a clear concept of justice according to which individuals might reason properly. Accordingly, education was to produce citizens who would bring about the reform of society. Because Helvetius focused on the social environment, believing that it had a great impact on the education and behavior of children, he is considered a social pioneer of sorts. Helvetius recommended that states should mandate education for the masses so that a proper environment might be provided for the natural development of the natural talents of children and youth (Coates, White, and Shapiro, 1966, p. 262).

Another of Rousseau's critics was Madame Necker de Saussure (1766–1841). In her *Education Progressive,* a treatise on rearing children, she was strongly influenced by many of his ideas. However, she did not hesitate to critique what she considered were some of his notable omissions and exaggerations. She pointed out the dangers for the child of Rousseau's negative discipline, contending that parents and teachers should appeal to the rational capacity of children and stimulate in them "a gentle movement towards the good and thus make [them] enter upon life with an inclination in a desirable direction" (In Castle, 1958, p, 147). She believed that children should not be trained in the habit of blind acceptance but in the habit of rational obedience to be inculcated by their parents and teachers. Necker differed from Rousseau in affirming that security and not freedom should be the primary concern of parents and teachers in the education of children. As a mother and a deeply religious woman with strong Calvinist convictions, she placed great value on the religious education of the child, which Rousseau largely ignored. She urged that the religious education of young children be accomplished through affection, childlike prayer, and the awakening of the sentiments of praise and wonder.

A more severe criticism of Rousseau published in 1792 came from the English feminist Mary Wollstonecraft in her *A Vindication of the Rights of Woman* (1992). This work made the persuasive case that the liberal doctrine of inalienable rights extended not only to men but also to women. While Wollstonecraft accepted Rousseau's liberal political ideas, she sharply disagreed with him about the education of women. She felt that he did not repudiate the standard ideas about the inferiority of women and continued to propose a utilitarian education suited only for domestic life. In this work the author, as an Enlightenment philosopher, demonstrated a true commitment to reason:

> Moralists have unanimously agreed, that unless virtue be nursed by liberty, it will never attain due strength — and what they say of man I extend to mankind, insisting that in all cases morals must be fixed on immutable principles; and, that the being cannot be termed rational or virtuous, who obeys any authority, but that of reason. (Wollstonecraft, 1992, p. 316)

In her treatise Wollstonecraft called for equality of educational opportunity for women and for an education that would appeal to their rational abilities and prepare them for a wide range of activities both in the home and in society. Believing that the reform of society depended on the education of women, she proposed that girls be educated with boys at day schools. Presenting her argument for coeducation in moral terms she stated that:

> I principally wish to enforce the necessity of educating the sexes together, to perfect both, and of making children sleep at home that they may learn to love home; yet to make private support, instead of smothering, public affections, they should be sent to school to mix with a number of equals, for only by the jostlings of equality can we form a just opinion of ourselves. (Wollstonecraft, 1992, p. 293)

In a work that has long been neglected by scholars, Wollstonecraft also offered criticisms of the way in which religion was taught in the public schools of England. She believed that a proper and rational belief in God was "the only solid foundation for morality." In her view:

> To love God as the fountain of wisdom, goodness, and power appears to be the only worship useful to a being that wishes to acquire either virtue or knowledge. A blind unsettled affection may, like human passions, occupy the mind and warm the heart, whilst, to do justice, love mercy, and walk humbly with our God is forgotten. (Wollstonecraft, 1992, p. 133)

Wollstonecraft criticized the practice of mandatory chapel in English boarding schools since it fostered in boys a hypocrisy whereby they worshipped only with their lips and not with their hearts and minds. Such a practice, she opined, led eventually to contempt for religion.

Even though many educators, and especially Jesuits, took objection to Rousseau's ideas, his ideas spread through Europe and into the United States. The Jesuits strenuously combated his ideas. In exile from France where they had been expelled in 1764 the Jesuits composed detailed refutations of *Emile,* making use in the writing of lengthy quotations from Rousseau, thus inadvertently further spreading his ideas. A couple of Jesuits even wrote alternative versions of *Emile* from a Catholic standpoint.

Notwithstanding the damaging efforts of church educators, Rousseau's ideas continued to influence educational reform, especially when his ideas were applied in a number of concrete educational alternatives. The philosopher and theologian Johann Bernhard Basedow (1723–1790) established a progressive school in Prussia based on Rousseau's ideas. He called his school "Philanthropinum" a place of human love. Besides the traditional subjects the school included in its curriculum handicrafts, outdoor activities, field trips, games, and camping. The school even introduced pupil government by the students. In accordance with Enlightenment beliefs, Basedow replaced biblical and catechetical instruction with nondoctrinal and heavily ethical teaching that bowed to neither creeds nor revelation. He felt that this natural religion would appeal not only to Christians but also to Jews and Moslems. In sex education his method was to teach through pictures depicting both virtuous and sinful behavior. This frank approach received criticism from many educators (Good and Teller, 1969, pp. 223–237).

In his book *On Education* Emmanuel Kant (1724–1804) attempted to shore up many of Rousseau's ideas on education with a stronger philosophical foundation in German idealism by presenting Rousseau's ideas in logical order. Kant identified a key educational problem which Rousseau had raised: "how to unite submission to restraint with the child's capability of exercising his own free will" (Kant, 1960, p. 21). Accepting Rousseau's theory of natural or organic development of the child but rejecting his theory of negative discipline, Kant argued for a more controlled education of the maturing child. A balanced moral education for him consisted chiefly in achieving freedom through discipline. Children were granted freedom in their early years so long as they did not interfere with the freedom of others. They needed to learn to allow others to use their freedom. Discipline in Kant's view was to be imposed in order that children learn to be independent of others. He wanted children to do the right thing not from habit but for their own reasons. An absolute obedience to parents in early years was supplanted by a voluntary obedience in the years of youth. The goal of moral education for Kant was that youth should accept the call of duty. Within this educational program schools were to create an atmosphere in which the power of reason might develop.

Consistent with his religious deism Kant gave little play to rote learning of the Bible and the catechism. For him religion was no more than "the law in us, in so far as it derives emphasis from a Lawgiver and a Judge above us. It is morality applied to the knowledge of God" (Kant, 1960, p. 111). Religious training was important for Kant insofar as it aided in the formation of moral character. The focus of this training, however, is on sound morality and not otherworldly theology that might result in a superstitious cult. For Kant the teaching of ideas about God should always be constructive ideas about duty to one's conscience. The main task of religious training for him is to attune the child to his or her conscience, that is, the voice of God within. To honor God is to do God's will.

Kant was very interested in various forms of educational experiments believing that "it is useless to expect this salvation of the human race to come from a gradual improvement of the schools. They must be made over if anything good is to come from them" (Kant, 1960, p., 110). He pointed to Basedow's school as a good example of a made-over school. Kant was also keen about making education into a science by finding the proven methods of teaching and the constant patterns of the human mind to which these methods might be adapted.

The most notable attempt to incorporate the Enlightenment ideas of Rousseau and Kant into actual practice came from the Swiss educator Johann Pestalozzi (1746–1827), who established a number of influential experimental schools for poor children. Educators in Germany, England, and the United States visited his schools and were so impressed by his experiments and theories that they used his schools as models for their own experiments. Pestalozzi began with the principle that human nature is inherently good and contains the potential for intellectual and moral development that can best be achieved through the exercise of love and kindness by parents and teachers. He also upheld the truth that individuals have an innate capacity to order into a unified whole various experiences they have gathered through the senses. Believing firmly that education should follow nature, he looked upon education as a natural unfolding of the inner capacities of the person. Through his educational experiments he attempted to devise methods to aid this natural unfolding. For intellectual education Pestalozzi opened wide the doors to sense experience and object experiences. Like Kant he had a great concern for imparting a proper moral education.

In his most famous work, the novel *Leonard and Gertrude* completed in 1800 Pestalozzi contended that the ultimate end of education is a genuine morality that will result in a love for all creation. With regard to religion in education Pestalozzi espoused a form of education that wedded Rousseau's naturalism and Kant's rationalism. By this marriage of ideas, he created a version of Christianity that avoided sectarian doctrine and stressed religion's contribution in acquiring moral experiences and in providing the motivation for the moral life. Pestalozzi wanted a love-centered Christianity to play an important role in moral education:

> For the ultimate destination of Christianity, such as it is revealed in the sacred volume and manifested in the page of history, I cannot find a more appropriate expression than to say that its object is to accomplish the education of mankind. (In Bowen, 1981, p. 231)

In moral education Pestalozzi did not follow Rousseau blindly, but sided with Kant on the importance of direct discipline in education. He commented that:

> The animal is destined by the Creator to follow the instinct of its nature. Man is destined to follow a higher principle. His animal nature must no longer be permitted to rule him, as soon as his spiritual nature has commenced to unfold. (In Bowen, 1980, p. 231)

The German educator Johann Herbert (1776–1841) followed in the footsteps of these Enlightenment educators in his systematization of education. Like them he stressed that education was essentially education for moral living. Through careful instruction children were to be brought into connection with the moral will that controls the world. This fine-tuning was to be done through three steps: first, control or government of the child, if necessary by restraint or coercion on the part of parents and teachers; secondly, the development of inner discipline, a disposition to correct behavior; thirdly, instruction or formation of the will. Herbert placed importance on the humanities and religion in providing students with the social experiences they needed for developing intellectual and moral virtues. He imagined the human soul as composed of various faculties or powers: sensation, intellect, will, memory, and imagination, each of which needed to be cultivated. This faculty theory of psychology has had a long-term influence on educators' approach to thinking about the developing person. Herbart's ideas spread and gained disciples not only in Europe but also in the United States, especially since he stressed a systematic method of instruction by which the areas of knowledge were to be arranged in a logical order and presented to children.

A further systematization of these Enlightenment ideas came from Frederick Froebel's (1782–1852) effort to develop an organic approach to education in his *The Education of Man* (1826). Froebel drew his inspiration not just from Rousseau but from his own teaching of young children in the Pestalozzian Institute of Frankfort. For him education enabled persons to realize their essence by living in tune with the Creator's purposes. In Froebel's mystical philosophy children were to identify with this goal by seeing themselves as part of the unity of the world, developing freedom and self-determination.

Education for Froebel, as for other Enlightenment educators, was accomplished by adapting content and methods to the natural development of the person. Education's highest goal was to enable the child to see God clearly revealed in all his works. Focusing on the education of the child, Froebel compared the child to a plant in a garden whose nature cannot change but who can grow healthily with the aid of a good teacher. (Froebel is considered the founder of the kindergarten, the child's garden.) For him, there existed eternal laws of growth that should guide the activities of parents and teachers. One such law was the law of opposites that entailed giving attention to the good and the bad elements within human nature. Froebel wrote that:

> In all good education, in all real instruction, in all true teaching,
> necessity should evoke freedom, law should induce self-
> determination, external compulsion should develop internal free-will,
> outer hatred should beget inner love. But all education, instruction,
> and teaching fail when hatred gives birth to hatred, law to deceit and
> crime, compulsion to slavery. (In Castle, 1958, p. 215)

In Froebel's view, teachers should recognize both tendencies in children and attempt to find the right and best thing for each child in each situation.

While granting the importance of example and precepts in moral education, Froebel argued that the wholeness of family life and school environment with their components of play, shared activities, and acceptance of life's joys and sorrows was more important than preaching and instruction. Parents and teachers should lead children away from evil and toward the good by assisting them to accept and realize the good that is within them. Froebel did, however, assign some role for punishment when children became youths.

Froebel was among the first who suggested that education should become a science, the cause of which he advanced by his careful ordering of classroom activities:

> Education becomes a science when the educator in and through
> himself practices the science of life—when he recognizes this eternal

order of things and understands its cause and its coherence, when he knows life in its totality. (In Bowen, 1981, pp. 338–339)

What Froebel is most remembered for, however, is his description of the sacredness and wholeness of the educational process. He insisted that parents and teachers allow children to achieve their own identity and meet their own needs.

While many religious educators of the time remained distant from these developments in educational theory and practice, in time they came around to see value in some of the components of the Enlightenment educational theory. The greatest stumbling block for most educators was the Enlightenment's somewhat naïve view of the human person that did not include an adequate recognition of the doctrine of original sin and human inclination to evil. What irked many a moralist was the negative attitude of some of these theorists to the teaching of the Bible and the catechism to young children. Enlightenment theories of education tended to minimize the role of religion in education, especially in the education of the young. In the perspective of many church educators these theories permitted too much freedom to the child and too little control to teachers and parents in moral and religious formation. Many of these same criticisms were leveled against twentieth-century progressive education, which drew in part on the educational ideas and experiments of Enlightenment educators.

Church Education and Emerging National Systems of Education

Enlightenment political and educational ideas, primarily those of Rousseau, paved the way for new political and educational arrangements in Europe and the United States. One of these arrangements led to the development of national systems of education that were to one degree or another free from the control of the churches. The once powerful churches battled the state for control of the educational systems. While the level of conflict differed from nation to nation, significant changes took place in all countries as church leaders accommodated and compromised with emerging national systems of education. In no-win situations church leaders established educational systems of their own outside the national system. State-controlled schools would eventually necessitate the efforts of churches to develop nonschool educational programs in religious education for their children and youth.

The bitterest conflict between church and state over religion took place in France. While leaders in the Catholic Church in France accepted the reality that education had a secular component, they argued vigorously that this component should be subordinated to the religious education of youth and thus remain under church control. This control of education came under attack in France with the publication in 1783 of *Essai d'education nationale* by Louis-René de Caradeuc de la Calotais (d. 1788). His target was the Jesuits who controlled much of secondary and college education in France. In 1764 the Jesuits were expelled from France and their colleges were transferred to other orders or to secular groups.

In the aftermath of the French Revolution Catholic schools came under especially severe attack by the revolutionaries. Religious orders and teaching congregations were disbanded. The reorganization of the schools considerably weakened the power of the church over education. Many Catholic schools, however, did not close but merely went underground. No provisions for religious education were permitted in France until 1803 when Napoleon made with the Vatican a concordat that allowed the return of only two orders, the Brothers of the Christian Schools and the Ursulines. Napoleon even imposed a school catechism, whose authority was revoked when the Emperor died in 1814 (Barnard, 1969).

Napoleon placed all French schools under the control of the Imperial University, making it difficult for church-oriented schools to continue to exist. During the reign of Napoleon's successor, Louis XVIII (d. 1824), the church pressed for control of all education, arguing that religion should permeate all areas of the curriculum. At this time freedom was also granted to Protestants and Jews to establish their own schools.

By the year 1816 much of primary education drifted back under the control of Catholic teaching congregations, though only a fraction of the masses were reached. In their classes of eighty or more students the Christian Brothers used the simultaneous method whereby the teacher taught all students at once. This teacher-centered method was in sharp contrast to the newly adopted monitorial system whereby students were taught in groups by students who were earlier taught by other students.

Although the Jesuits were allowed to return to France in 1814, they were restricted to maintaining only eleven colleges. Their colleges continued to showcase the classical tradition and gave a prominent place to religious studies, prayers, and retreats. Exiled again in 1830 as ultramontanists (extreme loyalists to the papacy) and anti-statists (opposed to the new republic), they revised their *ratio studiorum* to include the vernacular and gave a greater share in the curriculum to history, geography, and mathematics. The Jesuits returned again in 1850 with the emergence of a more favorable climate that allowed them to establish schools and reintroduce their ideal of eloquent piety (Anderson, 1975).

During the Third Republic from 1871 to 1881 the church was again on the defensive and the Jesuits were under renewed attack. Despite the disturbances, they were still able to open new schools at this time. In 1879 with the accession of Jules Ferry, the new ministry of education, Catholic education experienced even greater attack. Jesuit colleges were closed and primary education was made compulsory and secular. In 1904 all religious congregations were prohibited by law to conduct schools, a law that was supposed to be implemented by 1914. The beginning of World War I prevented this from happening. A pattern in France developed in which religious schools were established in rural areas while state schools predominated in cities.

In other Catholic countries the struggles were not so severe as those in France. In the predominantly Catholic country of Spain the Catholic Church through a concordat in 1851 secured the teaching of Catholic doctrine in all schools, both state and church operated. In Italy religious instruction was made optional and religious orders were curbed during the years 1887–1896. Catholics in Belgium refused to cooperate with the education bill of 1879 that established compulsory schooling and set up their own schools. The indignant clergy refused sacraments to parents who sent their children to state schools or who taught in them. At masses the prayer was read, "From Godless schools and faithless teachers, good Lord deliver us." Eventually a state-supported system of education received the support of the church.

Conflicts between Protestants and states did not rise to the same extreme level as happened in Catholic countries. The establishment of a national system of education in Prussia caused no conflict between the state and the churches. Since the time of the Reformation the state had played a major role in education, and the Lutheran faith was virtually an established religion, so the place of religion in the schools was secure. In 1808 education was given the task of regenerating the German people by the philosopher Johann Gottlieb Fichte (1762–1824) who wrote:

> Education has been brought to bear only on the very small minority of classes which are for this reason called educated, whereas the great majority on which in very truth the commonwealth rests, the people have been almost entirely neglected by the system and abandoned to blind chance. By means of the new education we want to mold the Germans into a corporate body, which shall be stimulated and animated in all its individual members by the same interest. (Fichte, 1979, pp. 258–259)

The philosopher Georg Friedrich Hegel (1770–1831) was instrumental in shaping the relationship of education to the emerging German nation. In his philosophy of idealism he outdid the Enlightenment philosophes in arguing that the state is the instrument of divine purpose. In his sweeping philosophy of history he arrived at the conclusion that the main task of the state was to impose order in society. The divinized state can do this because it "is the divine Idea as it exists on earth...the State is the definite object of world history proper" (In Bowen, 1981, p. 265). Thus since the state is prior to the individual, the individual must be subordinated to the state. The major task of education is to train people for their roles within the state. In turn, the school is subordinate to the community and the state is "the will and requirement of these towards the child" (In Mackenzie, 1908, p. 94). Within this rarified context education becomes the process by which individuals are liberated from the bonds of nature. Hegel wrote:

> Pedagogy is the art of making man moral: it regards man as one with nature and points the way in which he may be born again, in which the first nature may be changed into a second—a spiritual nature—in such a way that the spiritual nature may become habitual to him. (In Mackenzie, 1908, p. 63)

Inculcating good moral habits in childhood demands absolute obedience to parents. But schooling has as its purpose to fit youth for public life by enlisting the free cooperation of young people. The moral education Hegel proposed was considerably intellectual or rational; it consisted in the study of justice, rights, community, family, and the state. A religious dimension was included: a study of conscience, faith, the nature of God, and the meaning of sin. The philosophical goal of moral education is stated by Hegel: "we must make the conscious mind acquainted with moral ends, strengthen it in moral resolutions and lead it to reflection upon them" (Mackenzie, 1908, p. 168).

While Enlightenment political ideas did not succeed in establishing a republic in regal England, they did serve to loosen education from the control of the Anglican Church and the middle classes and to extend education to poor children throughout the country. Education in early nineteenth-century England was caught in crossfire between the defense of ecclesiastical and bourgeois privilege and the liberal, Enlightenment-inspired programs for mass schooling.

Nineteenth-century British educational reformers carried on in the empirical tradition of Bacon and Locke. Empiricism served as the basis for the distinctive English philosophy of utilitarianism that proclaimed that the highest ethical goal for a society is to attempt to achieve the greatest good and happiness of the greatest number of people. In the hands of Jeremy Bentham (d. 1832) this philosophy became the platform of a moral system which greatly impacted the direction of education. What utilitarianism needed was a greater vision of the common good. Education was saddled with the task of articulating this vision.

The Scottish philosopher James Mill (d. 1836) capitalized on this philosophy of utilitarianism by opposing bourgeois privilege and the established Anglican Church. In a pamphlet entitled *Schools for All, in Preference to Schools for Churchmen Only* Mill defended the charity schools against Anglican attacks. The charity schools were established by the Quaker educator Joseph Lancaster for poor children in London. Mill accented that education was the means furnished to individuals for moving out of poverty, believing as he did that "all the differences which exist, or can ever be made to exist, between one class of men, and another, is wholly owing to education" (In Bowen, 1981, p. 289).

The charity school movement provoked the Anglican Church to assert its exclusive right over education. In a sermon preached in 1811 in St. Paul's Cathedral, London, Herbert Marsh, Professor of Divinity at Cambridge, declared that "national education must be conducted on the principles of the national religion" (In Bowen, 1981, p. 296). Alarmists argued that educating the lower classes would make them unwilling to perform the servile work that needed to be done if society were to continue to function smoothly. Mill countered these specious assertions by arguing that the Anglican Church did not have exclusive rights in education and that it would be for the betterment of the common good to educate the lower classes. By the 1840s, the Anglican Church supported the establishment of a national society for the education of the poor. Further, Quakers and Methodists provided a basic education for children of the lower classes.

The Enlightenment and Education in the United States

Enlightenment ideas were highly influential in shaping education in the United States in the early national period. Many of the main players in the American drama had breathed in and became addicted to Enlightenment thought: Benjamin Rush, Noah Webster, Thomas Jefferson, Benjamin Franklin, and Horace Mann. However, a national system of education such as developed in Europe did not emerge even though there were concerted efforts by federalist-minded educators such as Rush and Webster to establish one. In the end education remained the province of local communities and states and received no attention in the federal Constitution adopted in 1781. Religious differences among Protestant sects, regional loyalties across the original states, and the fear of federal control were among the main reasons for the rejection of a national system of education.

Most of the schools that were established in colonial times came by way of Protestant churches and remained under their control. Puritans established schools in New England. Quakers and Presbyterians started schools in the middle colonies. Anglicans founded a few schools in the south. Even though these schools received some form of public financing, they were, in fact, sites where assimilation and indoctrination into the church life of particular denominations happened. Many of the teachers were ministers; the curriculum included the teaching of the Bible and the catechism and a heavy hand in piety and morality.

Motivated by Christianity and Enlightenment liberalism Benjamin Rush (1746–1813), a Pennsylvania physician, campaigned and worked for social and educational reform. Having studied medicine in Scotland he was influenced by the more moderate Scottish Enlightenment of Adam Smith and David Hume. Rush interested himself in all forms of education from elementary schools to medical education. Tirelessly, he proposed plans for elementary schools, approved of the German-speaking schools in Pennsylvania which Franklin strenuously and successfully opposed, fostered the development of Sunday Schools, and was the principal founder of Dickinson College in Pennsylvania. In his religious faith he turned from a strict Calvinism to a more universalist, antisectarian, and antidoctrinaire faith which was compatible with his moderate Enlightenment views (Sloan, 1971).

In his extensive writings Rush proposed a threefold task for education: political, social, and religious. The political purpose of schools was to inculcate civic virtues in the young members of the republic, to train future leaders for the republic, and to provide a unified culture devoid of sectarian strife. To the new republican schools he mapped out, he gave the task of making young citizens into republican machines which would take their places in government:

> It is plain that I consider it is possible to convert men into republican machines. This must be done, if we expect them to perform their parts properly, in the great machine of the government of the state. (In Rudolph, 1965, p. 17)

This new republican education was also to "render the people more homogenous, and thereby fit them more easily for uniform and peaceable government" (In Rudolph, 1965, p. 11).

The social purpose of education for Rush was, as it was for Franklin, to spread and promote useful knowledge, specifically modern languages, the science of government, commerce, agriculture, industry, chemistry, natural history, and practical mathematics. The new nation needed to turn out individuals who could make a positive and practical contribution to its well being. Rush adamantly opposed the teaching of the classical or dead languages, which he viewed as vapid adornments of aristocratic societies.

The religious purpose of education for Rush was to instill religious convictions in the young. For in his view, without such principles, that is, the universal principles of Christianity, the new republic could not succeed. Rush favored the teaching of the Bible in schools since it was a powerful reinforcement of the teaching of equality among mankind, respect for laws, and the acquiring of the civic virtues necessary for republicanism to flourish. Rush also advocated public financing of denominational schools. In calling for the establishment of public schools in Pennsylvania in which Christianity was to be taught Rush contended that "without this [teaching] there can be no virtue, and without virtue there can be no liberty, and liberty is the object and life of all republican governments" (In Cremin, 1980, p. 118).

Patriotic Rush advocated a single state philosophy that would permeate the schools and offer support of a federal university to which students would go after college to prepare themselves for political careers. He was strongly committed to the education of women, being influenced by the writings of Bishop Fenelon. It was his contention that such education should prepare women not only for family life but also

for their civic responsibilities. Rush also denounced slavery and contended that blacks should be given equal opportunities in education as
well as in other areas of society. Cremin commented on the unifying
principle in all Rush's endeavors:

> At the bottom of all these opinions, plans, and campaigns was a vision
> of human beings as perfectible through education, of social
> institutions capable of perfecting them, and of a society dedicated to
> the enhancement of their dignity. (Cremin, 1980, p. 121)

The Connecticut lexicographer Noah Webster (1758–1843) was
also a strong voice in the call for a national system of education. He
proposed the teaching of religion as a means for instilling a patriotic
and national spirit. He wrote that:

> It is an object of vast magnitude that systems of education should be
> adopted and pursued which may not only diffuse a knowledge of
> science but may implant in the minds of the American youth the
> principles of virtue and liberty and inspire them with just and liberal
> ideas of government and with an inviolable attachment to their own
> country. (In Cremin, 1980, p. 264)

While Webster favored the teaching of religion in schools, he rejected
the direct teaching of the Bible, arguing that too much familiarity with
the Bible would lessen respect for it. Webster did, however, propose
teaching the history and morality of the Bible through selected passages. Ever the wordsmith, he also developed a federal catechism and
a moral catechism that he included in his famous spelling books. On
the one hand, Webster considered science an important subject in the
curriculum. On the other hand, he argued on republican principles
against the study of the classics, which he viewed as more appropriate
for an aristocratic nation. Webster was also a strong advocate of the
education of women. He argued that education would implant in their
tender minds "such sentiments of virtue, propriety, and dignity as are
suited to the freedom of our governments" (In Rudolph, 1965, p. 68).

The Enlightenment figure par excellence among the founders of
the nation was certainly Thomas Jefferson (1743–1826). The Declaration of Independence for which he is largely responsible was indebted
to Enlightenment ideas on human nature, rights, and duties. Jefferson
considered Bacon, Newton, and Locke the greatest influences on his
thinking. It was his belief that human nature was changeable and that

education in all forms represented the chief means of accomplishing this. Jefferson's proposals for state-controlled and free public education in Virginia ran into strong opposition from the Anglican Church, which had establishment status in the state. However, his *Bill on Establishing Religious Freedom* was passed and became a model for other states as they decided to disestablish their state churches.

With regard to the teaching of religion, Jefferson found the Bible unsuitable for children due to the immaturity of their ideas of religion. Since he believed that the imposition of one religion in education was a form of tyranny, Jefferson held that moral instruction should be based on reason and should make appropriate use of the lessons of history. With regard to religion, his educational program was based on these principles: rational persons need education to arrive at religious truths and political wisdom; this education should be given in state-sponsored schools rather than state-sponsored churches; the cause of religion is best served if churches educate their members in a private capacity (Cremin, 1970, p. 442). By the time of his death only a portion of his educational program was in place, the chief accomplishment of which was the establishment of the University of Virginia where he had become president after leaving the Presidency. While religion was not part of the curriculum of the college, Jefferson encouraged local churches to offer within it denominational instruction to students.

For most Europeans Benjamin Franklin (1706–1793) embodied the principal ideals of the Enlightenment as realized in the new republic. He was committed to Enlightenment ideas about science, politics, and religion. Religion had less influence on him, however, as he moved from Puritan New England to Quaker Pennsylvania. For the development of character he favored not religious education but moral education. Franklin praised self-education and a utilitarian education, both of which he described in detail in his autobiography. He helped shape the charity schools set up for educating poor children in Pennsylvania. His desire for a unified nature and culture led him to oppose German-speaking schools in Pennsylvania. In his view children of German immigrants should go to school with English-speaking children so that:

> They may contract such early friendships with each other as may in time lead to those intermarriages, and create that sameness of interests, and conformity of manners, which is absolutely necessary to the forming them into one people, and bringing them to love, and peaceably submit to the same laws and government. (In Carlson, 1975, p. 35)

In 1750 Franklin published proposals for the education of youth in Pennsylvania in which he stated that students be taught:

> Everything that is useful, and everything that is ornamental: but art is long, and their time is short. It is therefore proposed that they learn those things that are likely to be most useful and most ornamental, regard being had to the several professions for which they are intended. (In Cremin, 1970, pp. 375–376)

Practical subjects had the lion's share of the curriculum in which little of the classical curriculum remained. This education was to prepare youth for the professions and for practical affairs.

Despite the secularizing tendencies of educators influenced by the Enlightenment, in the early republic religious groups still had great power in the control and maintenance of schools. Religious denominations were involved in all levels of education from primary schools to colleges. In the early nineteenth century they established charity schools for poor boys. All of these schools benefited from public financial support. The situation changed greatly, however, when in the first part of the nineteenth century large number of Irish Catholics immigrated into the urban areas of the East Coast. When states such as New York and Massachusetts refused financial support to Catholic schools, a series of changes were set in motion that resulted in the common school supported by public funding and under public control. The curriculum, which included a nondenominational Protestantism symbolized by a daily reading from the King James Version of the Bible, so offended Catholics that they established a separate school system of their own, without public support.

The architect of the common schools was Horace Mann (1796–1859), the secretary of the Board of Education in the state of Massachusetts. Mann was motivated by many of the Enlightenment values: human freedom, equality, reason, environmentalism, and democracy. Like many European liberals of the time he believed that these values could be best promoted through universal public schooling. In his view only common or public schools could provide the common value system that would give unity and solidarity to the nation. It was his singular accomplishment that he convinced a majority of religious, political, and industrial leaders in Massachusetts that the common school was the best way to achieve national unity. Once the common school was established in Massachusetts, other states adopted the same system of education.

One of Mann's most difficult problems was to convince the various Protestant groups in Massachusetts that they should support the common school movement and cease funding schools of their own. While he was not able to convince conservative churchmen, he did appease many church leaders by infusing the schools with a curriculum that included a common piety rooted in Scripture and a common civility grounded in the history of the Christian republic. He also proposed that the schools teach the moral doctrines of Christianity among which he included piety, justice, love of country, benevolence, sobriety, frugality, chastity, moderation, and temperance.

Mann argued against what he considered the four alternatives to this nonsectarian religious and moral education. He rejected the position that the schools give no religious instruction since this benign neglect would make the schools un-Christian and would not satisfy the general population. He also vetoed the alternative that the state should define or prescribe a particular religious system. For him this would amount to government establishment of religion and be offensive to the religious freedom of children. The third alternative was that each religious sect would define the religion to be taught in the schools to their children. In his estimation, resulting sectarian religious rivalries in the school would destroy its common and unifying character. Finally, he rejected the position that the state should not in any way be involved in the education of the young, since he found many good reasons to support establishment of common schools. The form of Christian teaching which Mann proposed for these schools he termed nondenominational. It has been noted that this form of Christianity bears many similarities to Mann's Unitarian faith, which he had embraced about spending a painful youth under the severity of Calvinist beliefs (Messerli, 1972).

In conclusion, Enlightenment ideas have had a profound influence on the direction of politics and education in the nineteenth and twentieth centuries. Political liberals in the nineteenth century used Enlightenment principles in arguing for the creation of states in which citizens participated in electing governments. Economic liberals appealed to its principles in arguing for markets freed from government control. Religious freedom in the form of separation of church and state and freedom of the press were among the important legacies of Enlightenment thought. The dedication to science and technology was a continuation of the empiricism that characterized Enlightenment commitments.

In the past two centuries Enlightenment thought has also come under severe criticism. Conservatives thinkers have decried the rejection of authorities that this thought has encouraged. Those committed to a more romantic view of life, centering on feeling, intuition, imagination, and spirit, have criticized it for its excessive rationalism. Marxism, which owes so much to Enlightenment views on history, science, and religion, has joined the ranks of romantic critics in identifying Enlightenment with the emergence of the bourgeois class.

In the twentieth century, the Enlightenment's overly optimistic belief in reason and progress has been severely damaged by the experience of wars and the horror of the Holocaust. Freudian psychoanalysis has questioned the primacy given to reason in individual and social life. Critical social theorists such as Adorno, Horkeimer, and Marcuse followed Marx in connecting the Enlightenment movement with the rise of the bourgeois mentality. However, while some postmodernist theorists, notably Lyotard and Foucault, have taken the Enlightenment as the starting point of their critique of modern society, the German philosopher Jurgen Habermas has defended the Enlightenment as an unfinished project. Enlightenment thought is also under attack by communitarian social philosophers for it overemphasis on the individual at the expense of community, society, tradition, and history.

Although there is now much criticism of Enlightenment thinking among some scholars who wish to go beyond Enlightenment thinking into Post-Enlightenment or postmodernism, the achievement of the Enlightenment and the poor record of the churches' grappling with Enlightenment thought must be noted. Scholars such as Hans Kung, the German Catholic theologian, contend that the Christian church was on the wrong side of the argument when it vehemently opposed Enlightenment thinking. He boldly states:

> It was not the Christian Churches—not even those of the Reformation—but the "Enlightenment," often apostrophized by Church and secular historians as "superficial," "dry" or "insipid" which finally brought about the recognition of human rights: freedom of conscience and freedom of religion, the abolition of torture, the ending of the persecution of witches, and other humane achievements. It was the Enlightenment moreover which demanded intelligible religious services, more effective preaching and more up-to-date pastoral and administrative methods for the churches—reforms widely extended in the Catholic Church only from the time of Vatican II. (Kung, 1968, p. 29)

Kung goes so far as to contend that those periods in which the churches dominated were marked by reactions against human freedom. He concludes that "it was a Church therefore in the rear guard of mankind, compelled by its fear of anything new always to drag its heels, without providing any creative stimulus of its own to modern developments" (Kung, 1968, p. 29).

Summary

In the West the Enlightenment offered a serious challenge to religion and education in religion. Philosophes directed their criticisms at the authoritarianism and supernaturalism of both Catholicism and Protestantism. They also laid out radical plans for education based on Enlightenment rationalism, naturalism, and supernaturalism. It was the ideas of these critics that motivated many political leaders in establishing school systems in which the churches had less influence and in which religious education played a smaller role. This period was marked by often-bitter conflicts between church and state as well as among various religious groups. Both Catholic and Protestant religious education in the last two centuries has dealt with the power influence of the Enlightenment and the ideas and movements which it has spawned or with which it is associated. In recent years Orthodox educators have also grappled with the legacy of the Enlightenment.

Chapter 6

Protestant Education in the United States: Nineteenth and Twentieth Centuries

> I answer in the following proposition, which it will be the aim of my argument to establish, viz.: That the child is to grow up a Christian. In other words, the aim, effort, and expectation should be, not, as is commonly assumed, that the child is to grow up in sin, to be converted after he comes to a mature age; but that he is to open on the world as one that is spiritually renewed, not remembering the time when he went through a technical experience, but seeming rather to have loved what is good from his earliest years. (Horace Bushnell, 1967, 1847, p. 6)

> The clue to Christian education is the rediscovery of a relevant theology which will bridge the gap between content and method, providing the background and perspective of Christian truth by which the best methods and content will be used as tools to bring the learners into the right relationship with the living God who is revealed to us in Jesus Christ, using the guidance of parents and the fellowship of life in the Church as the environment in which Christian nurture will take place. (Randolph C. Miller, 1950, p. 15)

The sheer diversity of Protestantism in the United States makes it difficult to review all of the efforts that Protestant Churches have made to educate their members. Protestants in the United States have engaged in some unique movements and established distinctive institutions for conducting Christian education. Churches of the Protestant Reformation have utilized schools, colleges, revivals, Sunday schools, and campus ministries in their educational efforts. These forms of education are each rooted in different cultural situations and are related to different theological movements.

In this chapter my intention is to present some chief forms of Protestant religious education, but especially to review the theological underpinnings for the prominent modes of Protestant education. The history of these educational efforts is closely linked with the theological and educational changes of the past two centuries. Since the focus of this book is on the intellectual rather than the social or institutional history of Christian education, more attention will be given in this chapter to the theories of religious education that have been identified with religious movements within Protestantism in the United States. The chapter will treat the evangelicalism that inspired the revivals and the Sunday school, the liberal and social theology of the religious education movement and the revitalized Sunday school, the neoorthodoxy which called for a restoration of a biblically based Christian education, contemporary theologies of liberation and faith which reconceptualize Christian education, and the neoevangelicalism of the modern day Christian school and college. Within each have emerged scholars and educators who have tied the movement's spirit and aims to the enterprise of Christian education.

Very few Protestant groups today maintain all-day schools as a principal means for providing Christian education for their members. The situation was different in the first half of the nineteenth century when Protestants relied on denominational schools and colleges to hand on the Reformation faith. By the beginning of the twentieth century the situation was greatly changed. Presently, full-time day schools are prevalent to a significant degree only among Lutherans and certain evangelical denominations. Protestants have also accepted nominal relationships with the colleges and universities that they established earlier in the nation's history. To replace these early nineteenth century institutions Protestants have developed other approaches to education.

The decline of Protestant influence in schooling has led to the secularization of American education (Nord, 1995, p. 63). While colonial schools and colleges were maintained under the auspices of Protestant churches, this control did not continue throughout the nineteenth century. The purposes and curricula of these early schools were clearly religious and moral. The chief goal of education then was biblical literacy. Also, the first colleges established in the colonies were directed primarily at the training of men for the ministry. In the early part of the nineteenth century Protestant churches added charity schools to deal with the education of poor children. Sunday schools and infant schools also became part of the Protestant educational effort.

The establishment of the common school radically altered the Protestant approach to the education of children. Horace Mann and other educational reformers persuaded and convinced many Protestant leaders as well as political and business leaders that they should support free public schooling for children of all classes and religions. Protestant support for the common schools was largely due to the desire to deny public support to schools sponsored by the Roman Catholic Church.

The common schools established in Massachusetts and elsewhere retained enough aura of Protestant religious and moral influence to satisfy many Protestant leaders that the basics of Protestant religious education of their children was provided for in these schools. Reading from the King James Version of the Bible and the inclusion of Protestant history and piety in readers and textbooks also increased Protestant confidence that the common schools were doing their religious duties. The Sunday school added elements of religious education. Those religious groups, notably the Lutherans in the Midwest, who were not satisfied with this arrangement built their own schools.

Evangelical Christian Education in the Great Awakenings

In the eighteenth and nineteenth centuries there occurred a number of religious revivals or awakenings in the United States that left their stamp on the form of religious life and education among American Protestants. Viewed as religious events, religious revivals featured charismatic evangelists calling persons to religious rebirth, conversion, and regeneration through dramatic and emotional preaching. Viewed as social phenomena, these awakenings broadcast charged religious responses to dramatic changes in the culture. The revivals have been interpreted as:

> Periods of fundamental ideological transformation necessary to the dynamic growth of the nation in adapting to basic social, ecological, psychological, and economic changes . . . , periods when the cultural system has had to be revitalized in order to overcome jarring disjunctions between norms and experience, old beliefs and new realities, dying patterns and emerging patterns of behavior. (McLoughlin, 1978, pp. 8, 10)

These early religious awakenings had a major impact in the development of Christian education in Protestant churches. The awakenings themselves were educational experiences for adults and to a lesser degree for children. In their tent meetings religious awakenings took to task not only the quality of religious observance but also the existing educational methods of producing so-called committed Christians. In addition, the revivals led to the establishment of new educational institutions for maintaining and fostering the spirit of the religious revival. Revivals eventually brought about changes in family patterns, reformed school curricula and methods, and enacted new laws in the churches and society (McLoughlin, 1978, p. 22).

The first awakening occurred in the years 1730–1760. The towering figure in this awakening was Jonathan Edwards (1703–1758). This revival had a profound effect in the colonies, reaching almost every community. It left many educational institutions. To the spirited leaders of the revival, people did not appear as committed to the practice of religion as they had been in previous years. Many preachers joined Jonathan Edwards in calling Protestants to repentance and to religious renewal.

The first awakening raised and struggled with the issue of the relative importance of conversion and nurture in Christian education. Those who advocated revivalist methods for regenerating religious life favored emotional conversion experiences over a gradual nurturing in the faith. In contrast, those who tended to be critical of the revivalists' stress on the conversion experience in religious growth were supportive of the processes of education. From another perspective, the struggle over the revivals was between advocates of the importance of feelings in religious growth and the proponents of a more reasoned approach to nurture and education.

This first awakening also singled out the issue of who had the right to preach and to teach within church communities. Those committed to revivalist methods claimed that only those who themselves had been regenerated by conversion experiences had the right to preach and teach. Skeptical critics of revivals did not demand conversion experiences in their ministers. The first awakening also drew the line in the sand on the issue of how one proceeds in the Christian education of children. The zealots among the revivalists wanted children to be included among those who were in sin and needed to be converted.

It would not be entirely correct to cast the revivalists against education as such. The case has been made that revivalists were dead set against the educational approaches and methods currently used in the churches. Actually, the revivalists introduced new institutions that fostered education such as private associations of families, societies of converted youth, and neighborhood groups for prayer and self-examination. Revivalists created many new academies, seminaries, and colleges, one of which was Queens College in New Brunswick, which later became Rutgers College. In truth, it can be said that the revivalists revivified teaching and extended it to households, communities, and colleges. In the view of one historian:

> In the last analysis, it was less that the revivalists downgraded
> religious education than that they changed its pedagogy. As in earlier
> dissenter revolutions, prophecy replaced edification as the central
> technique of churches once again awakened to their mission in the
> world. (Cremin, 1970, p. 321)

Another religious awakening occurred in America between the years 1800 and 1830. Leaders in this revival included Lyman Beecher, Charles Finney, and George Whitfield. Beecher assigned an important role to education in solidifying the new American republic. In *A Plea for the West* (1835) he called for a renewal of faith that would settle the fate of the expansion into the western part of the United States. He felt that it would be through schools, churches, colleges, seminaries, and missions that the West would be won to Protestantism. In *A Plea for Colleges* he thumped anew that it would be through educational institutions that Protestantism would triumph over Roman Catholicism in dominating the religious life of the new frontier. His revivalist preaching was similar to that of Charles Finney, who in his lectures on *Revivals of Religion* (1835) described the various histrionic techniques that he used in achieving the many conversions which came about through his preaching. In this work he also detailed tactics that preachers could use at prayer meetings in their revivals. Finney left his brand on Christian education for "when Finney died in 1875, evangelism had become the characteristic form of Protestant Christianity in America, and surely the most pervasive version of the Protestant American *paideia*" (Cremin 1980, p. 43).

As mentioned earlier, the most important educational issue surfaced during the power struggle between evangelists and their critics was that of the relative value of education through conversion experiences versus education through nurture in home and church. More succinctly, the question is how one weighs the place of feelings and reason in religious education. One way of understanding this issue is to examine two classic theological treatises from this period: Jonathan

Edwards's *A Treatise Concerning Religious Affections* written in 1746 and Horace Bushnell's *Christian Nurture* written in 1847.

Jonathan Edwards was the principal evangelist during the eighteenth century awakening. Edwards made a strong case for the respectability of the religion of the heart. He accused New England Unitarians of extolling reason and ignoring the heart. In his view the religious affections were very important in one's spiritual life. He stated that:

> There was never any considerable change wrought in the mind or conversation of any person by anything of a religious nature, that ever he read, heard or saw, that had not his affections moved. . . . There never was any thing considerable brought to pass in the life of any man living, by the things of religion, that had not his heart deeply affected by those things. (Edwards, 1959, p. 16)

Believing that these affections were tendencies toward sainthood, Edwards advocated that they be stirred up by a style of preaching which stressed the sinfulness of humanity and the sovereign grace of God. Through God's freely given grace sinners were saved and they turned away from sin.

Though he stressed the affections, Edwards did not deny the benefits of knowledge and understanding in the religious life. For Edwards "holy affections are not heat without light; but evermore arise from some information of the understanding, some spiritual instruction that the mind receives, some light or actual knowledge" (Edwards, 1959, p. 266). Although Edwards recognized the value of knowledge and understanding, he declared that rational knowledge alone was not inspiring enough to produce the saints that Christians were called to be. To bring about religious conversion he interjected in his preaching images of hell, judgment, and damnation. However, while he preached an angry and stern God, he also preached a God who showed mercy and peace to those who repented of their sins.

Horace Bushnell (d. 1876), a New England pastor, raised objections against the revivalist approach to preaching, especially when children became the objects of conversion. In his *Christian Nurture* (1967, 1847), which is considered a classic work in Christian and religious education, he argued for the careful nurturing of children in the faith by families and churches. While Bushnell praised religious revivals for providing supernatural experiences, he criticized them for making so little use of the home and the church as instruments of God's grace. Bushnell opposed the view that, given the depravity of humans and the sovereignty of God, pathetic and passive parents could only mouth and explain Christian beliefs and urge their children to seek salvation through a conversion experience. Bushnell also rejected the views of New England Unitarians who held to the innate goodness of persons.

Bushnell's (1967) focus on the essence of Christian education is found in the answer to the question he posed: "What is the true idea of Christian education?"

> I answer in the following proposition, which it will be the aim of my argument to establish, viz.: That the child is to grow up a Christian. In other words, the aim, effort, and expectation should be, not, as is commonly assumed, that the child is to grow up in sin, to be converted after he comes to a mature age; but that he is to open on the world as one that is spiritually renewed, not remembering the time when he went through a technical experience, but seeming rather to have loved what is good from his earliest years. (p. 6)

Bushnell placed emphasis on the home as the proper center of religious education. This education was to take place through a process of growth and not through artificially induced conversion experiences in childhood. Bushnell contended that the child's character was largely formed by early experiences within the home. Building upon that religious teaching parents and teachers should adapt instruction to the age of the child. He contended that experience, not the transmission of doctrine, was the best foundation for teaching religion. Of parents he said that:

> They should rather seek to teach a feeling than a doctrine; to bathe the child in their own feeling of love of God and dependence on him and contrition of wrong before him, bearing up their child's heart in their own, not fearing to encourage every good motion they can call into exercise; to make what is good, happy and attractive; what is wrong, odious and hateful; then as the understanding advances, to give it food suited to its capacity, opening upon it gradually the more difficult views of Christian doctrine and experience. (Bushnell, 1967, p. 39)

Bushnell argued strenuously for the baptism of infants against those who made baptism a sacrament of conversion for older adolescents. He railed against parents who pressured their children to have religious experiences; he urged them to be patient with their children as they went through a period of doubt.

The contrasting views of Edwards and Bushnell about the role of knowledge and affections, as well as of conversion and nurture, have been constant challenges to Christian educators. One hears in them echoes of arguments between Augustinians and Thomists, Bernard and Abelard, pietists and rationalists. While present-day Christian educators try to do justice to all facets of education, questions still break out about how the differing components are to be organized and where the emphasis should be placed. Greater understanding of the processes of human and faith development and knowledge of differences among individuals give contemporary educators more information and insight on how to provide for the religious education of children and youth.

While the Bushnell approach to Christian education eventually won wide acceptance by Protestants, for most of the nineteenth century the Sunday school was an evangelical institution. As mentioned in Chapter 4, this institution originated in the Church of England in the latter part of the eighteenth century. From its founding in Gloucester by the layman Robert Raikes (d. 1811) it remained a lay organization throughout its history.

The Episcopal Church first established Sunday schools in the United States for underprivileged children. Early on these schools taught basic literacy, but in time as more children went to charity schools and then to the public schools, the Sunday schools became instruments of inculcating in the young the principles of evangelical Protestantism. The focus in these schools was on the study of the Bible while their objective was the conversion of students.

In 1824 the Sunday school movement in the United States came under the control of The American Sunday School Union, a voluntary, lay run, and nondenominational organization that developed Sunday school curriculum for forty years. In its early years tensions existed between the clergy and the lay Sunday school workers. One of the conflicts was the prominent role that women played in the Sunday school movement. The Union established thousands of schools, including many schools on the frontier. By the time of the Civil War many Protestant denominations had started their own Sunday schools. When the Sunday school movement became international in the second half of the nineteenth century, the Sunday School Union produced uniform lessons for all children; it also sponsored teacher-training institutes. Eventually graded lessons were published for all grades. The curricu-

lum of the Sunday school, once it focused exclusively on Christian education, was largely devoted to the Bible, a book used as a reader for
children of all ages (Lynn and Wright, 1971).

The Sunday school has evolved considerably over the years. It
went from being a school for the poor and working classes to an instrument of evangelical or revivalist Protestantism to what it is today,
a school for the education of Protestant believers of all ages. While the
achievements of the Sunday school movement have been considerable,
it has not been without its critics. At the 1837 meeting of the Sunday
School Society William Ellery Channing, a Unitarian minister, criticized the Sunday schools for their mechanical teaching and lifeless
way they handed on the faith. In criticizing the Sunday school Channing offered what have clearly come to be recognized as liberal goals
for religious education. He criticized the schools "for stamping our
minds on the young, making them see with our eyes, giving them information, burdening their memories, imposing outward behavior,
rules, and our prejudices." The goals of religious education for Channing were to stir up the minds of the young, to invite them to see with
their own eyes, to inspire in them a fervent love of the truth, to quicken
the powers of their mind, to prepare them to judge for themselves, and
to awaken their consciences to discern what is good. Religious educators were

> Not to tell [the young] that God is good, but to help them see and feel
> him live in all that he does within and round them; not to tell them of
> the dignity of Christ, but to open their eye to the beauty and greatness
> of his character, and to enkindle aspirations after a kindred virtue.
> (Channing, 1838, p. 10)

While the Sunday school came under criticism by Channing and
many others, the significance of this institution cannot be minimized.
The Sunday school has had immense power in educating millions of
children and a large number of adults in the Protestant faith. The movement encouraged all denominations to take seriously the religious education of their members. One of its historic achievements is that it
prepared the way for the public school by presenting a model of a
school with teachers, students, curricula, and buildings. Very often the
same group that sponsored the Sunday school moved on to become the
strongest advocates for the common schools. The Sunday school has
been called the big little school since while:

Compared to public education, Sunday school is marginal to American society, yet it is an important *little* school in the rearing of the whole nation. The Sunday school is the big little school of the United States. (Lynn and Wright, 1971, p. xi)

The Rise of Religious Education: Liberal Protestantism

The perceived inadequacies of the Sunday school in dealing with the modern world led in the early twentieth century to the emergence of the religious education movement. Rejecting the theology of evangelical theology and embracing both Protestant liberal theology and many of the features of progressive education, the religious education movement attacked the revivalist piety and education provided by the traditional Sunday school. The religious education movement did not try to replace the Sunday school but rather attempted to bring to it a new approach to the teaching of religion. The movement also added other educational efforts to traditional Protestant religious education: adult education, religion in public schools, research in religious education, and the religious education of the public.

The religious education movement embraced the chief themes of Protestant liberal theology, which included the attempt to reconcile Christianity with the intellectual world that emerged after Darwin's *Origin of Species.* Liberal theology disagreed with the negative assessment of modernity found in evangelical churches. Instead, it took an evolutionary viewpoint on the world, accepted the application of modern historical methods to the study of the Bible, and agreed with the positive assessment of human nature bequeathed by the Enlightenment. Liberal theology elevated ethics over dogmatics in the Christian life, arguing that Christians were not just to be absorbed with the salvation of individuals but also were to struggle for a more just world. Liberal theology viewed Christian doctrines as historically conditioned attempts to understand the mystery of human life. Theological liberals tended to give humanistic and social interpretation to the traditional Christian teachings on God, humanity, salvation and redemption, Jesus Christ, ethics, the church, revelation, and Scripture. Finally, this form of theology preached a tolerance for different religious views and discouraged evangelistic and proselytizing efforts.

While the founders of liberal theology were European, especially Friedreich Schleiermacher and Adolph Harnack, it had influential proponents in the United States, including the Social Gospel preachers

Washington Gladden and Walter Rauschenbush. The American theologian who applied this theology to the task of religious education was George Coe (d. 1951), a professor at Union Theological Seminary and one of the leading intellectuals in the religious education movement.

What Coe and others in the religious education movement did was to wed Protestant liberal theology to elements of the progressive educational theory of John Dewey. Coe synthesized in his approach to religious education the main thrusts of progressive education: utilization of the new disciplines of psychology and sociology, emphasis on the child's growth and learning through active experiences, stress on adapting education to the interests of learners, and forging a close connection between education and social change and reform.

Coe in his highly influential *A Social Theory of Religious Education* (1917) bestowed on religious education the challenging goal of social reconstruction. He was critical of the revivalist approach to Christian education for its individualism, emotionalism, and antiintellectualism. In formulating his theory of religious education Coe attempted to blend the science of religion, a local and global sense of responsibility, and a philosophy of personalist idealism.

Coe moved religious education toward the goal of "growth of the young towards and into mature and efficient devotion to the democracy of God and happy self realization" (1917, p. 55). For him education came alive and realistic through social interaction in which both the Bible and contemporary social issues comprised the curriculum. What Coe meant by democracy of God, a term he preferred over the biblical "kingdom of God," was a social order in which the principles of Jesus would be realized. In using this expression Coe made clear that the goal of religious education went beyond individual salvation and the well-being of the church to encompass the reconstruction of society through social welfare, social justice, and a world society. Working for the democracy of God was Coe's way of expressing the traditional doctrine of redemption:

> Our generation has come to see that the redemptive mission of the
> Christ is nothing less than that of transforming the social order itself
> into a brotherhood or family of God. We are not saved each by
> himself, and then added to one another like marbles in a bag. . . . (p. 8)

Like the advocates of the Social Gospel Coe gave a social interpretation to sin and redemption. For him conversion had to be not just an individual experience but a social reconstruction of society.

In a later work, *What Is Christian Education?* (1929), Coe pointed out the limitations of forms of religious education in which the transmission of religious stories and truths predominated. He pointed out that the transmission approach to religious education runs the danger of indoctrination and irrelevance. Coe proposed that religious education become a process of creative discovery in which students dealt with both their individual and social experiences. The task of creative religious education for him was to help students evoke "the unprecedented by their thinking, experimenting, daring and suffering. Reconstruction, continuous reconstruction, is of the essence of the divine work in and through the human" (p. 33). For Coe the chief content of religious education flowed from the lives and experiences of students as these were illuminated by the religious tradition of the church. The influence of both liberal theology and progressive education is seen in his definition of religious education:

> It is the systematic, critical examination and reconstruction of relations between persons, guided by Jesus' assumption that persons are of infinite worth, and by the hypothesis of the existence of God, the Great Valuer of Persons. (p. 296)

While Coe was the principal proponent of what has been called the social-cultural approach to religious education, he was joined by other prominent theorists. William Clayton Bower's *The Curriculum of Religious Education* (1925) was influential in spelling out the social goals of religious education. Religious education for him entailed initiating the young into creative experiences of both a personal and a social nature. A special concern of his was the relation between religious education and public education.

Also, Sophia Lyon Fahs gave special attention to the curriculum of religious education for children. In her *Today's Children and Yesterday's Heritage* (1952) she spelled out the various dimensions of a curriculum that would foster creativity, freedom, and discovery. Fahs utilized the social-cultural approach in developing a liberal approach to religious education in the curriculum of the Unitarian Church. Her liberal design to religious education included the following dimensions: human phenomenon as the starting point of religious education; the Bible as a book for adults, not children; emphasis on the present and future, not the past; the study of history and world religions; learning about human relationships; importance of self-understanding; dealing with sex education and death education; and openness to children's spiritual or mystical experiences (Boys, 1989, p. 55).

Ernest Chave, in weaving the social aim of religious education
with its more traditional aim, further enhanced the definition of religious education:

> By religious education we mean the development of the ideas and
> habits that are of the highest social character. We mean a growth in a
> vital conception of God, an increasing valuation of life itself, and an
> enlarging capacity and responsibility for all social relationships. It
> involves the study of the best religious experiences and traditions of
> the race, including a particular study of the records in the Bible, with
> the current beliefs and practices of religion in the world today. It also
> means helping each person to get a working philosophy of life, and to
> put into practice the ideals inspired by an evolving religious
> experience. (In Schmidt, 1983, p. 74)

In the opinion of some interpreters Chave went even further than Coe
and others in carrying the liberal approach along naturalistic lines in
his attempt to avoid the sectarianism and supernaturalism of traditional
Protestant forms of religious education (Burgess, 1975, pp. 65–66).

Where the advocates of religious education differed most from
the evangelical religious educators was in their treatment of the Bible
as God's revelation. Their approach to the Bible was also the main issue raised by later critics within the neoorthodox theology movement.
For the evangelicals, the Bible as the Word of God alone was the exclusive content and subject matter for religious education. For Coe and
other social-cultural theorists the Bible was one of a number of resources for religious education. For them the Bible had a prominent
place in religious education not because it was the authoritative Word
of God but because it narrated valuable social experiences. They advised religious educators to foster the divine life in students by making use of the experiences recounted in the Bible, so long as they related these biblical experiences to the present experience of learners.

Liberal religious educators such as Coe, Brower, and Fahs were
the driving forces in establishing in 1903 the Religious Education Association (REA). Growing out of dissatisfaction with the Sunday
school the REA mobilized academics and parish educators to profes-
sionalize the field of religious education. This transformation they accomplished through yearly meetings, conferences, and the journal *Religious Education.* The liberalism of the religious education movement
received its most serious challenge between the World Wars with the
emergence of Protestant neoorthodoxy (Schmidt, 1983).

The Challenge of Protestant Neoorthodoxy:
Christian Education

Between the World Wars a theological movement arose in Europe under the leadership of Karl Barth which radically challenged the Protestant liberal theology. Neoorthodox theology also had a great impact on Protestant religious education in the United States. Neoorthodoxy distanced itself from Protestant orthodoxy by its acceptance of modern critical approaches to the study of the Bible. It criticized liberal theology for ignoring fundamental biblical doctrines in its attempt to make Christianity relevant in the modern world. The inspiration of this theology was the letters of Paul and the theologies of Martin Luther and Søren Kierkegaard. The principal theological thrusts of this movement include the appeal to Biblical revelation, an emphasis on the transcendence of God, a greater awareness of human sin, a restatement of the doctrine of justification by grace through faith, the recognition of Jesus as the revelation and deed of God, the recognition of the tragic elements in human existence, and an appeal to eschatological hope. In the United States the neoorthodox approach to theology appeared prominently in the work of H. Richard Niebuhr, Reinhold Niebuhr, and Paul Tillich.

The challenge of neoorthodox theology to Protestant religious education can be seen in a comparison between two influential books written in 1940. Harrison Elliot, a professor at Union Theological Seminary, defended religious education based on liberal theological principles in his *Can Religious Education Be Christian?* In this critique of neoorthodoxy he argued that if its theological viewpoint prevailed in religious education, the result would be indoctrination. He rejected the appeal to the Bible as a transcendent authority, contending that for religious education to be truly Christian it had to rest intrinsically on human experience and not on an appeal to the extrinsic authority of divine revelation. For him religious education was:

> An enterprise in which historical experiences and conceptions are utilized in a process by which individuals and groups come to experiences and convictions which are meaningful for them today. (Elliot, 1940, p. 310)

The case for reformulating religious education according to neoorthodox theology was made in H. Shelton Smith's *Faith and Nur-*

ture (1940). Smith averred that religious education as proposed by Coe and Elliot was based on philosophical principles rather than on Biblical or theological roots. Smith raised the question:

> Shall Protestant nurture realign its theological foundations with the newer currents of Christian thought, or shall it resist those currents and merely reaffirm its faith in traditional liberalism? (p. vii)

Smith called for a reformulation of Christian education along neoorthodox lines. (The term *Christian education* became the label for writing and speaking about religious education for those who proposed a more theologically oriented religious education.) Smith made the Bible and not the life situations proposed by liberal religious educators the heart of religious education. He saw the need for balancing the liberals' optimism about human potential with an awareness of human sinfulness. Human autonomy in education had to gives way to the authority of God as revealed in the Scriptures. In his view education should serve the power of God's Word influencing individuals. Smith criticized liberal education for its overreliance on the social sciences at the expense of Christian theology. He charged liberal educators with a failure to give prominence to God's transcendence. Smith, like the neoorthodox theologians he relied on, tried to broker a middle way between the old orthodoxy that placed emphasis on a one-time conversion experience and liberal theology that identified religious education with normal growth. In his view liberals such as Coe and Elliot had reduced the Kingdom of God to the particular social order prevailing in the United States. Smith even ventured to argue that liberal religious education had rejected the true Christian faith:

> For Christian faith . . . envisages human society within a framework that is theocentric. It sees man from a perspective that includes the empirical natural order, but also transcends it. It expressly denies that human values can be adequately understood as to their origin, worth, or destiny within the frame of a purely empirical democracy. With equal conviction it rejects the idea that the source of deliverance from sin, meaninglessness, and frustration had its center in humanity. (p. 201)

Smith's *Faith and Nurture* was a watershed book in the history of Protestant religious education. The work was more a criticism of the liberal or progressive approach to religious education than it was a detailed description of what neoorthodox religious education would be.

In the ensuing years some Protestant religious educators continued to advocate the progressive approach championed by Coe, while other Protestant religious educators attempted to assign the newer approaches to theology a more central role in religious education than had been given by the liberals (Cully, 1965, pp. 22–24).

In 1947 the movement for a more theologically oriented religious education received strong impetus from a report entitled *The Church and Christian Education,* which defined the aims and objectives of Christian education. Based on an examination of the writings of prominent Protestant educators, this document essayed to reconcile the social-cultural approach of the liberals with neoorthodox theology. With regard to the curriculum of religious education it stated that:

> The purpose of the curriculum of Christian education is to confront individuals with the eternal gospel and to nurture within them a life of faith, hope, and love, in keeping with the gospel. The organizing principle of the curriculum from the viewpoint of the Christian gospel, is to be found in the changing needs and experiences of the individual as these include his relation to (1) God, as revealed in Jesus Christ; (2) his fellow men and human society; (3) his place in the work of the world; (4) the Christian fellowship, the church; (5) the continuous process of history, viewed as a carrier of the divine purpose and revealer of the moral law; (6) the universe in all its wonder and complexity. (Vieth, 1947, pp. 145–147)

In the 1950s many Protestant religious educators espoused a more theologically oriented religious education. Randolph Crump Miller's *The Clue to Religious Education* (1950) held sway during this period. At the time Miller was an Episcopal priest on the faculty of Yale Divinity School. For him:

> The clue to Christian education is the rediscovery of a relevant theology which will bridge the gap between content and method, providing the background and perspective of Christian truth by which the best methods and content will be used as tools to bring the learners into the right relationship with the living God who is revealed to us in Jesus Christ, using the guidance of parents and the fellowship of life in the Church as the environment in which Christian nurture will take place. (1950, p. 15)

For Miller the task of Christian education was not to teach theology but to make theological truth relevant through the interpretation of experience. Miller called his theology a relationship theology since in his view the truth of theology is best expressed in terms of relationships between God and humans and between men and women. Thus theology for him could be instrumental in bringing learners into a right relationship with God through the church. Miller fine-tuned his theology in two additional works, *Biblical Theology and Christian Education* (1956) where he applied his theory for different age levels and *Christian Nurture and the Church* (1961) which describes the task of the local church in Christian nurture. Miller's writings had great influence on the theory and practice of Christian education. His early work has been criticized for an overuse of the term relationships and for a failure to deal with the existential situation in which Christian education occurs. Miller has continued his lifelong effort to relate religious education to theology by exploring theologies that make use of conceptual analysis and process philosophy.

The neoorthodox position also found expression in James D. Smart's *The Teaching Ministry of the Church* (1954). Smart, a Presbyterian pastor and later a member of the faculty of Union Theological Seminary, attempted to bring theology to bear on educational practice. His advocacy of theology went further than Miller's approach. He warned against a too great dependence on educational psychology and the techniques of progressive education. Smart sharply criticized the social theory of George Coe, finding in his writings "a rather thin doctrine of divine immanence, a belief in the naturalness of Christian growth, a blissful confidence in the goodness of man, and a Unitarian conception of Jesus Christ" (p. 58). Smart sought greater theological education for Christian teachers. He favored a stronger emphasis on the transmission of the theology and tradition of the church. In summarizing the goals of Christian education he stated that:

> Christian education exists because the life that comes into the world in Jesus Christ demands a human channel of communication that it may reach an ever-widening circle of men, women, and children, and become their life. The aim of Christian teaching is to widen and deepen that human challenge, to help forward the growth and enrichment of the human fellowship, through which Jesus Christ moves ever afresh into the life of the world to redeem mankind. (p. 108)

Criticizing the liberal religious educators for naively ignoring sin, repentance, and conversion, Smart advocated that conversion play

a much more pivotal role in Christian education. He opposed, however, the moralistic and revivalist approaches to conversion. For him
conversion, which included religious and moral growth, is the work of
God. The task of the teacher is to sow the seeds for conversion by
teaching the truths of God's revelation and by helping learners grow
and develop in the faith. At the end of his work Smart explained the
advantages for Christian education if a more theological approach
were to be implemented. He asked for a thorough rethinking of the
place of Christian education in theological schools and schools of education, a recognition of the role of teachers in Christian ministry, a
more theological education for church teachers, and more emphasis on
the congregation's role in teaching. He summed up his arguments:

> Set a new aim for education, one that is significant for a Church that is
> interested in regaining its evangelizing power. The call we hear is
> simply the call to be the Church for which Jesus Christ lived and died,
> a royal priesthood, daring to put itself at his service to be used by him
> for his conquest of the world. (pp. 206–207)

The neoorthodox approach to Christian education was also advanced through the writings of Lewis Sherrill, D. Campbell Wyckoff,
Sara Little, Iris Cully, and Howard Grimes. Many of these theologically oriented writers were influential in working with denominations
in developing curricula for Christian education. Smart's influence is
seen in the Presbyterian *Christian Faith and Life* curriculum; Miller's
ideas are reflected in *The Seabury Series* of the Episcopal Church.
Sherrill's signature is evident in the development of the curriculum of
the United Church of Christ (Cully, 1965, pp. 157–158).

Theological Pluralism and Protestant Religious Education

The dominance of theological neoorthodoxy came to an end during the
1960s. What has replaced this movement is pluralism of theologies.
The same can be said of approaches to Protestant religious education.
The changing of the guard has been marked by a number of competing approaches, some of which have been limned by Seymour and
Miller (1982; 1990) and Seymour (1997). The period since the mid-
1960s has been also described by Little (1993) as time of critical reflection in Protestant religious education, a time in which "there is no
one clue, no dominant theory . . . but a spectrum of theories and di-
vergent interests" (p. 20). For the purposes of this historical study a

number of approaches can be highlighted: faith community approaches, faith development approaches, liberation theories, evangelical religious education, and feminist approaches. While in all of these approaches theology is the dominant factor, integration occurs with the social sciences, psychology, and educational theory.

Since the 1960s there has been a marked convergence of views between Protestant and Catholic religious educators. The ecumenical movement in theology also had its effects in religious education. Roman Catholics joined the Religious Education Association in large numbers as well as the Association of Professors and Researchers in Religious Education. A commonality of interests developed among Protestant and Catholic religious educators. The approaches that are described here as Protestant resonate in Roman Catholic circles. The same can be said, but in a lesser degree of Orthodox Christian religious educators.

What these approaches have in common is that they are part of the effort to carve out an approach to religious education that is a distinct part of practical theology. In this way contemporary approaches are indebted to the legacy of neoorthodox theology and Christian education. The case for Christian education has been made forcibly by Richard Osmer (1990) who continues the work of James Smart in discovering and recovering the teaching office of the church. For him "the single most important task before the mainline Protestant churches today is the reestablishment of a vital teaching ministry at every level of church life" (p. x). Osmer does this by steering a middle ground between rampant individualism and counter modern authoritarianism. In his approach to practical theology Osmer and other Protestant religious educators while maintaining theology's critical role in religious education move beyond neoorthodoxy to incorporate elements of praxis, other academic disciplines, and various contexts for theological and educational reflect.

Faith Community or Socialization Approaches

While most Protestant Christian educators in the neoorthodox tradition focused their attention on schools, some influential educators in the 1960s and 1970s returned to the insights of Horace Bushnell in their development of socialization or enculturation models of Christian education. C. Ellis Nelson in his groundbreaking work *Where Faith Begins* (1967) utilized biblical studies, theology, communications, and social psychology. He argued for less attention to schooling and more attention to home, church, and community as enculturating environments for Christian education. He strongly suggested a greater commitment by the churches to the Christian education of adults. Nelson propounded the view that religious faith is profoundly situated within a person's sentiments and results from the way in which a person is socialized by significant adults. For him:

> Faith is communicated by a community of believers and . . . the meaning of faith is developed by its members out of their history, by their interaction with each other, and in relation to the events that take place in their lives. (p. 10)

While the theological basis for Nelson's s theory of religious education is certainly influenced by neoorthodoxy, the same cannot be confidently said of Westerhoff's more radical espousal of socialization-enculturation theory. His approach was influenced by the emerging theologies of liberation in Latin American and elsewhere. In a number of works but especially in *Will Our Children Have Faith?* (1976), echoing the radical educator Ivan Illich, Westerhoff advocated the de-schooling of the Protestant Sunday school. In his view the Protestant "church's educational problem rests not in its educational program, but in the paradigm or model which undergirds its educational ministry—the agreed-upon frame of reference which guides its education" (1975, p, 6). He wanted a fundamental shift away from the schooling-instructional paradigm to an enculturation-socialization model. This model housed all the formal and informal ways in which individuals learn. It included schooling but was not restricted to it. In later writings he preferred the term *catechesis* for this new paradigm since it placed emphasis on the way persons are initiated and grow in a Christian faith community. Catechesis for him is not an educational activity but rather a pastoral activity of transmitting the faith. The goal of this catechesis is not knowledge per se but a conversion in which persons take ownership of their faith and commit themselves to a Christian way of life.

This approach to religious education thus focuses primarily on the faith community itself and less on its particular educational programs. It stresses "the essentially corporate and communal character of the church's efforts to incorporate ever-new generations of children and youth into its life and mission" (Foster, 1982, p. 59). The community attempts to hand on its identity, history, stories, lifestyles, and rituals. Education takes place in formal and informal settings. The Roman Catholic religious educators Berard Marthaler (1979; 1980) and Robert O'Gorman (1997) have also stressed a faith community approach to religious education.

Foster (1994) has given a full-length treatment of this approach, including practical applications for congregations. After pointing out some flaws in church education relating to communal memory, ineffective teaching, unclear goals, failure to deal with contemporary culture, and the lack of an overall strategy, Foster describes how events in the life of the church can be truly educational. The proper tasks of church education are described as community building, meaning making, and discerning vocation.

Mary Elizabeth Moore (1983) has offered a slightly different approach to education for faith community. In her traditioning model she combines the elements of religious socialization in a community with a reconstructionist model of religious education. For her, education must focus on methods that promote both the continuity of the community as well as the ability to change through the critique of various aspects of community life. For Moore:

> Both continuity and change are essential to the life of the Christian community. The phenomenon of continuity makes it possible for persons to enter the life of the community, and the phenomenon of change provides for the community's openness to present experience and future possibility. (p. 18)

In a later work (1998) Moore makes use of concepts from process theology and phenomenology to examine various methods in religious education (case study, gestalt, phenomenological, narrative, and conscientizing). Her task in this foundational book is to engender "a passion for organic theology and organic teaching for the sake of a healthy body" (p. 198).

Faith Development Theory

A second significant factor in contemporary Protestant religious education has been the influence on religious education of theories of human development, especially the faith developmental theory of James Fowler (1982). Developmental theory posits a sequential and ordered movement of individuals through clearly defined stages that become increasingly complex. Individuals move toward a particular goal or full maturity through their interaction with the environment. Cognitive development, as described by Jean Piaget, is a movement from sensori-motor activity through thinking of a very concrete nature to processes of abstract thought. Moral development, as studied by Lawrence Kohlberg, proceeds through stages where reward and punishment provide moral motivation through stages where one's moral thinking is influenced by accepted moral standards to moral thinking based on self-chosen moral principles. The faith development theory of Fowler posits an ordered process of growth in individuals from a mythical and literal form of faith in childhood to an acceptance of church doctrine in adolescence to the development of a personal and mature faith in adulthood.

Fowler (1983) drew some implications of this theory for religious education. He pointed out that since faith development is a lifelong process, religious education should continue throughout life. He further observed that the very process of getting individuals to reflect on their faith development is a valuable learning experience. Fowler, however, cautioned educators against viewing stage theory as a test of achievement. His research also indicated that the language, rituals, and teachings of particular faiths were of great importance in faith development. Fowler also admonished religious educators not to overreach themselves but to work within the limits of an individual's faith development. Since faith development is closely related to other aspects of human development, education in other domains can aid growth in faith. Finally, faith development theory makes clear that transitions in faith often involve disruption, pain, confusion, and a sense of loss.

Since its introduction into the field faith development theory has generated much discussion among religious educators. The theory has come under a great deal of fire. Critics question whether the theory has a cultural bias, whether the stages are universal, and whether the sequence is a necessary one. The theory does not appear to deal adequately with the issues of regressing in faith or repudiation of faith. Many observers and practitioners have commented that the concept of development does not do justice to the Christian concept of conversion. Notwithstanding these and other criticisms the theory has attuned many religious educators to the developmental nature of religious faith (Dykstra and Parks, 1986).

Liberation Approaches

Another development in Protestant religious education is the focus by many educators on the role that religious education might play in so-

cial liberation and the struggle for social justice. Educators such as Allan Moore, William Kennedy, Malcolm Warford, Grant Schockley,
Letty Russell, and Daniel Schipani have identified with and utilized
theology of liberation and the pedagogy of the oppressed of Paulo
Freire. Accordingly, they have argued for a more explicit social and
political role for religious education (Moore, 1982). In some ways
these writers hearken back to Coe's social-cultural approach to religious education. This educational approach aligns and couples the social experiences of learners and social analysis of oppressive structures
to liberation theology and appropriate learning strategies. In doing this
proponents desire to raise learners' consciousness of social injustices
and to motivate them to participate in the struggle for justice and social transformation. Warford described this model of education as "the
continuing praxis of evoking the church's growth as a liberating community and encouraging the development of critical consciousness"
(Warford, 1976, p. 54).

Allan Moore (1982) has proposed a liberating education appropriate for churches in North America. He grounds this education
in a reflection on the actual experiences of oppression that people
have endured. Liberation supplies the theological vision that moti-
vates his approach to religious education. Liberating or prophetic
education beckons persons to develop a critical awareness of their
experience of injustice. For him this education entails a critical reflection on praxis that is sensitive to forms of human injustice, dis-
crimination, sexism, and racism. This approach should involve not
only programs but also changes in lifestyles, that is, the beliefs, values, and attitudes of individuals and communities. A Christian vision
of a just society should be the basis of any reflection on social
situations.

William Kennedy (1986) has made an analysis of ideologies the
focus of his approach to a liberating education. His venue begins with
an understanding of others and ourselves as human beings in order to
make us sensitive to and critical of the dominant ideologies of the culture. He then moves to an analysis of our pedagogical action to see how
dominant ideologies are reflected in the content of courses. As particular means for accomplishing this he calls for the following: the use of
aesthetic and creative modes of learning, special attention to the
knowledge and experiences of oppressed groups, a problem-posing
form of education, the use of conflict as a tool for reflection and action,
and an analysis of contradictions in society. Lastly, Kennedy recom-

mends that teachers of religious education be involved in political action themselves.

Letty Russell has consistently used the language and themes of liberation as well as partnership to integrate hermeneutics, theology, and education in her corpus of work. In reviewing her work she has noted:

> I have constantly returned to a description of education as liberation: a process of action-reflection on the meaning of oppression in the light of our participation in God's creation of a fully human society. The perpetuation of structures of oppression such as racism, sexism, and classism became a key issue of critique, and the emphasis on participatory education as a process of action/reflection was a continuing theme. (Russell, 1984, p. 6)

While remaining true to the biblical foundations she laid in early works—mission, tradition, and building up community—she has added the themes of liberation, partnership, and diakonia as well as exodus, nurture, and empowerment to present a rich theological and educational approach to religious education.

Daniel Schipani (1988) has made the most sustained attempt to relate liberation theology of religious education in his profound probing of the relevance of Freire's work for religious educators. He has examined the philosophical roots of Freire's theory of conscientization in an attempt to fashion a theory. He has made a persuasive argument that religious education in the church should be grounded in a biblical-theological foundation concerned with liberation, justice, and peace.

While the liberation approach to religious education has held a privileged place for the past twenty-five years, it has not escaped the sort of criticisms once leveled against the social-cultural approach. Boldly, the approach runs the risk of political indoctrination. There is the danger of subordinating education to political ends and blurring the distinction between education and political action. It may depend on a selective reading of the Christian tradition. This approach may rely on a simplistic social analysis of complex problems. Finally, the approach tends to ignore other legitimate functions of religious education.

Evangelical Christian Education

The twentieth century began with the dominance of evangelical and revivalist approaches to Protestant religious education. At the end of the twentieth century this approach had a resurgence with the remarkable growth of evangelical Protestantism. The strength of the evangelical wing of Protestantism is seen not only in membership numbers but also in the establishment of Christian schools, Bible colleges, and theological seminaries. Concern with Christian education has been a major preoccupation in evangelical Protestantism. While evangelical religious educators have been opposed to the approaches recommended by liberal religious educators, they have not done battle with neoorthodox theologians and educators, presumably because of the latter's acceptance of the findings of modern research on the Scriptures. A number of prominent educators have offered rationales for Christian education based on evangelical theology.

Christian education for Frank E. Gaebelein, a prominent evangelical educator, is the communication of biblical or supernatural truths in the classroom and the pulpit. If faith comes by hearing, then students hearing these truths taught and preached well will live by these truths. While Christian education is directed toward bettering human lives in this world, its primary and ultimate purpose is participation in God's kingdom. The content of Christian education is God's revelation written in the Scriptures. Gaebelein (1967a) made in strong terms the evangelical case for the centrality of the Bible in Christian education:

> No other book can compare in educating power with the Bible. Let no Christian educator ever apologize to the sophisticated of the educational world for giving the Bible the highest place. To take as the center of the curriculum the one book among all other great books to which alone the superlative "greatest" can without challenge be uniquely applied—this is neither narrow nor naive. Rather it is simply good judgment to center on the best rather than the second best. (p. 41)

Gaebelein enthrones the acceptance of Christ through a conversion experience as an essential task of Christian education and as the foundation for Christian living. He contended that:

> The pupil must be guided toward a crisis in his education that involves his repentance, his not withholding acceptance of Christ as his personal Lord and Savior, his obedience, and his infilling by the Holy Spirit. (1967b, p. 229)

For Gaebelein only those who have had conversion experiences should become Christian educators.

Another evangelical educator Kenneth O. Gangel (1978) has outlined the basic principles of evangelical Christian education:

> (1) A commitment to the authority of the Bible. (2) A recognition of the contemporaneity of the Bible and the Holy Spirit. (3) A clear understanding of the nature, source, discovery, and dissemination of truth. (4) The integrative process based on designing a curriculum which is totally constructed on the centrality of special revelation. (5) A demand for the development of a Christian world and life view. (6) Bibliocentric education to extend to all areas of student life. (pp. 100–105)

While most evangelical religious educators place a priority on the transmission of a biblical content as primary in Christian education, Lawrence Richards has introduced a broader theory, which comes closer to the socialization theory described above. In his *Theology of Christian Education* (1975), while he contends that theology and not educational philosophy that should control Christian education, he states with subtlety that:

> Theology points us to the landmark truths that are to be taught, warns us against a transmissive approach that would treat Scripture as information, and suggests that learning processes must be found to communicate the Christian revelation as an unveiling of reality (p. 211).

Feminist Religious Education

A final voice heard in contemporary Protestant religious education has come from feminist religious educators who have pioneered approaches to religious education that spotlight themes and issues from feminist scholars, especially those in theology, history, and education. Catholic, Protestant, and Jewish scholars have been involved in this enterprise. Prominent Protestant feminist religious educators include Letty Russell, Nelle Morton, Mary Elizabeth Moore, and Carol Lakey Hess.

Prominent themes in feminist approaches to religious education have been described by Keely (1997). These scholars argue for the integration of life and experience into one educational event and attempt to achieve the integration of theory and practice. They stress the community aspect of education and its liberating nature. For these educators issues of power within the church are critical in achieving recognition of the gifts and talents of all members, clergy and laity. Feminist religious education attempts to extend the immediate contexts of learning to include broader historical and social settings. Many feminist educator are especially sensitive to the importance of religious language, especially language about God, the ultimate Christian symbol. Learning for such scholars is connected to and respects the partnership of teacher and learning.

The richness of contemporary Protestant religious education can be interpreted as the striving to maintain a balance between competing values: traditional and modern, biblical and secular, theological and human, God and world. The same tensions can be found in the history of Protestant higher education in this country.

Protestantism and American Higher Education

Protestantism has had a longtime relationship with American higher education. It has already been noted how religious denominations were powerful forces in the establishment of the colonial colleges in the seventeenth century, notably the Congregationists at Harvard and Yale, the Presbyterians at Princeton, the Baptists at Brown, the Dutch Reformed at Queens (Rutgers), the Anglicans and Presbyterians at Kings (Columbia) and the College of Philadelphia (later the University of Pennsylvania), and the Anglicans at William and Mary. In the early years of their existence these colleges focused primarily on the training of clergy for the various denominations. The curriculum of these colleges included both secular and religious learning. In the passage of time the ties of these colonial colleges with their founding religious bodies have been almost totally severed (Marsden, 1994, Part I).

The religious revival in the early nineteenth century had a profound effect on the development of higher education in the United States. The revival spawned many academies, colleges, and seminaries for the education of Christians and the training of their ministers. The colleges that were established often became centers of religious revival where direct efforts were made to evangelize students, something that was not permitted in the common schools.

The Protestant churches also played a significant role in the establishment of state universities in the middle of the nineteenth century. These universities, which rested on the foundation of the colleges established by evangelical Protestants, had clergymen as their first presidents, included biblical Christianity in their curriculum, and sponsored religious revivals on their campuses. Issues relating to faith and knowledge as well as science and religion amicably shared space in the curriculum. In these colleges strenuous efforts were made to evangelize students and to compel them to attend religious services.

The new public universities had the enthusiastic support of evangelical Protestants with Protestants of every denomination attending these institutions. It has been argued that it was a misguided zeal that led evangelical Protestants to support these more utilitarian colleges, a situation that backfired and caused the decline of the distinctively denominational colleges. The evangelicals:

> Were determined that their sons and daughters would receive the technical training they needed in order to make their way in the world and equally determined that they should not be exposed to the hazards of classical and liberal learning. (Littell, 1971, pp. 126–127)

The process of secularization of American higher education began in the middle of the nineteenth century. The education of clergy was no longer a defining concern since students were now being prepared for various professions and occupations. Many colleges decided to embrace a nonsectarian Protestantism in order to accommodate students from different denominations. Colleges began to serve the needs of rapidly growing business and industry more than the needs of churches. Furthermore, the ideals of the Enlightenment took a strong hold in the colleges with the result that the study of theology gave way to the course in moral philosophy. Although wary of the new science and its often negative attitude toward religion, many Protestant educators within the universities shared the optimism of Charles Eliot, president of Harvard, who contended that modern science:

> Has proved that the development of the universe has been a progress from good to better, a progress not without reactions and catastrophes, but still a benign advance toward ever higher forms of life with ever-greater capacities for ever finer enjoyments. It has laid a firm foundation for man's instinctive faith in his own future. . . . It has thus exalted the idea of God—the greatest service which can be rendered to humanity. (In Sloan, 1994, p. 3)

The unqualified acceptance of science by many Christian educators was even further enhanced when scholars such as William James, Stanley Hall, and others applied science to the study of religion.

In the second half of the nineteenth century Protestant colleges began to face the issue of the nature and identity of the Christian college within a more secularized higher education. The presence and influence of clergy on the faculties of these schools waned. While many religious leaders believed that there should be no conflict between Protestantism and a secular culture that favored openness and free inquiry, they also realized that colleges ran the risk of losing their distinctiveness as Christian institutions if they totally embraced all aspects of secular creed and culture. Many American colleges had already embraced the scientific and philosophical positivism that virtually ruled out religious considerations in academic inquiry. The chief question for Protestants concerned what role doctrinal orthodoxy should play in Christian colleges. Should there be religious tests for teachers at these colleges? The soul-searching issue became even more complex as some colleges added graduate and professional schools where the academic ethos demanded even more free inquiry and secularized studies. The establishment of The Johns Hopkins University in 1876 provided a model of a university committed to a value-free scientific method.

While Protestant influence was still considerable at the public universities established as land grant colleges, a more secular approach to higher education emerged with the establishment of the University of California in 1867. The university began its history committed to a Protestant but nonsectarian approach; it was broadly but vaguely Protestant. The criterion of religious orthodoxy had no role in the choice of administrators and professors. The school benignly neglected to include the voluntary chapel services held at other state universities. It became the most secular college in the nation and was criticized by many Protestants for being irreligious and even antireligious. According to one historian the university set the trend for the coming years wherein:

> The universities could be practically Unitarian with lots of room for liberal Christian opinion, religious indifference, or skepticism. The specifics of traditional Christianity could also flourish, but as an encouraged voluntary activity. From the dominant Protestant perspective, the university then should hardly look subversive to Christian interests. (Marsden, 1994, p. 146)

Liberal Protestantism with its commitment to the social gospel supplied the rationale for rethinking the influence of Protestantism at many colleges and universities. It was a liberal theology that motivated the state senate of Michigan in 1873 when in an investigation of the presence of Christianity on the campus of the University of Michigan it declared that:

> The teachings of the university are those of a liberal and enlightened Christianity, in the general, highest and best use of the term. This is not in our opinion sectarian. If it is, we would not have it changed. A school, a society, a nation devoid of Christianity, is not a pleasant spectacle to contemplate. We cannot believe the people of Michigan would denude this great university of its fair, liberal and honorable Christian character. (In Marsden, 1994, p. 170)

The University of Michigan made a strenuous effort to make Christianity present on campus through lectures and voluntary chapel. A large number of the faculty were Protestant church members. A prominent member of the faculty at that time was John Dewey. He expressed the sentiments of this liberal Christianity when he stated that because the scientific method of discerning truth could have no limits, it was necessary "for the church to reconstruct its doctrine of revelation and inspiration, and for the individual to reconstruct within his own religious life, his conception of what spiritual truth is and the nature of its authority over him" (In Marsden, 1994, p. 178).

While many universities easily accommodated themselves to the spirit of liberal Protestantism, the Presbyterians at Princeton University offered strong resistance to the liberal theology which they viewed as a dangerous Trojan horse to the survival of Protestantism in the university and the churches. President McCord of Princeton attempted to forge a stronger Christian and Presbyterian identity for the university by avoiding the broad nonsectarianism that prevailed at Harvard and other New England universities. The theologians at the university maintained a more evangelical Christianity which did not endorse the higher criticism then being applied to the Scriptures (Marsden, 1994, p. 209). Under the presidency of Woodrow Wilson the university made strenuous efforts to maintain a distinctive Christian identity.

The establishment of the University of Chicago in 1892 as a Baptist university with support from John D. Rockefeller and the Baptist Church introduced elements of Low-Church Protestantism into the American university scene. The polity of the Baptist Church and the ties of the university to industrial interests introduced a curious mix of Christian and business ethos to the American university. Its academic spirit was marked by pragmatism, less emphasis on tradition, competitiveness, emphasis on individual freedom, openness to the scientific spirit and business interests, and the tendency to identify Christianity with democracy (Marsden, 1994, p. 259). Liberal Christianity prevailed at the university not only in its biblical studies but also in the new field of sociology which was viewed as both a scientific and a moral discipline.

Early in the twentieth century Protestant ties to universities became considerably weakened. When a college reached for university status and began to serve a broader public than one particular denomination, and when its support from sources other than the denomination increased, it was difficult for it to maintain ties with its denominational tradition. Early in the century these factors were operative at both Vanderbilt University and Syracuse University, both of which were established by Methodists.

The ties of universities to Protestant Christianity were further weakened with the emergence of the American Association of University Professors. The ideals of academic freedom, which the association promoted, found no quarter in institutions established to promote particular religious, economic, or political views. In 1915 John Dewey, the first president of the association, explained that the goals of the university were:

> To investigate truth; critically to verify fact; to reach conclusions by
> means of the best methods at command, untrammeled by external fear
> or favor, to communicate this truth to the student; to interpret to him
> its bearing on the questions he will have to face in life—this is
> precisely the aim and object of the university. (In Metzger, 1977, p. 8)

Schools that wanted to be accepted as universities thus could not maintain that their academic policies were shaped in a normative manner by religious doctrines or traditions. The fierce debate over the teaching of evolution in schools and universities further convinced academics that religious denominations should have little say over academic decisions relating to hiring of professors and the freedom of academics to teach.

The secularization of Protestant colleges was furthered in 1906 when the Carnegie Pension Fund was established for college teachers. The fund was made available only to those private institutions which were not owned or controlled in any way by denominations and in which there was no denominational teaching of religion. Many colleges severed their ties to denominations in order to take advantage of the fund (Langemann, 1983)

In the 1920s the influence of Christianity in education further declined when some states began to ban the reading of the Bible and the reciting of morning prayers in public schools. In other states, however, religious exercises were still required. At the state universities, which had begun to educate an increasingly larger part of the college population, Protestant leaders tried to find ways in which to minister to the religious needs of students. Campus ministries were established, Bible chairs were endowed, chapels were built, and attempts were made to establish schools of religion.

The Protestant neoorthodox movement in theology, which greatly influenced writing in religious education for youth and adults, did not seem to have much influence on what was happening on campuses with regard to the teaching of religion and religious practices (Marsden, 1994, p. 349, 374).

In the 1930s the most prominent spokesperson for American universities, Robert Hutchins of the University of Chicago, attempted to revolutionize college curriculum by going against the national trend of vocationalism by introducing a strictly liberal arts curriculum that focused on the Great Books of western civilization. In his highly influential *The Higher Learning in America* (1936) Hutchins asserted that the heart of the enterprise of higher education was the medieval metaphysics of Thomas Aquinas and not theology. In his view while theology had served as the organizing principle in the past it could no longer do so for a generation that took no stock in revelation. For Hutchins "theology implies orthodoxy and an orthodox church. We have neither. To look to theology to unify the modern university is futile and vain" (Hutchins, 1936, p. 119).

The role of religion in the undergraduate curriculum deteriorated further in the Harvard Report of 1945, *General Education in a Free Society,* which set the tone for post–Second World War college education. The report noted that Protestant colleges no longer found unity through sectarian teaching. It concluded that with the varieties of faith and unfaith that existed in America it could not find a justification for religious instruction in the undergraduate curriculum. The report did recommend, however, that the great religious classics be taught in a humanities program. The report contended that the goal of education is not in conflict with but largely lines up with the goals of religious education, education in the Western tradition, and education in modern democracy.

A serious effort within Protestantism to engage American higher education began in 1953 with the first issue of *The Christian Scholar,* a journal that attempted to explore the meaning of Christian faith for contemporary higher education and from that engagement to seek new and deeper meanings of the Christian Gospel. The collapse of this effort has been ascribed to a failure to deal with deep issues relating to faith and knowledge and the place of religion in modern culture (Sloan, 1994). In Sloan's view the theological renaissance ushered in by Protestant neoorthodoxy (as well as Roman Catholic neo-Thomism and the Jewish Renaissance of Buber, Heschel, and Herberg) did not seriously engage American higher education. He is also skeptical of efforts of Protestant neoevangelical scholars such as Marsden who have described the secularization of American higher education in their call for a more explicit Christian scholarship on American campuses. The search for the religious identity of religious colleges and universities besets all American denominations.

Summary

The past two centuries have seen richness in Protestant approaches to religious education. The great evangelical awakenings placed emphasis on conversion and individual experience. Sermons by enthusiastic evangelists and Sunday schools were the principal forms of Christian education. Voices were soon heard that advocated the slower process of Christian nurture through educational experiences in families and churches. At the beginning of the twentieth century the religious education movement made use of educational theory as well as the psychological and social sciences to reform the way both children and adults learned. The theological challenge mounted by neoorthodoxy strove to place theology at the center of the Protestant educational enterprise. While theology has maintained a dominant role in thinking about and implementing Protestant education, a pluralism of theologies is utilized. Futhermore, most educators find a significant role for other dialogue partners such psychology and the social sciences. Significant changes in higher education have noticeably weakened Protestant influence in institutions of higher education.

Chapter 7

Catholic Education in the United States: Nineteenth and Twentieth Centuries

> In a Catholic university, therefore, Catholic ideals, attitudes, and
> principles penetrate and inform university activities in accordance
> with the proper nature and autonomy of these activities. In a word,
> being both a University and Catholic, it must be both a community of
> scholars representing various branches of human knowledge, and an
> academic institution in which Catholicism is vitally present and
> operative. (John Paul II, 1991, p. 37)

Catholic educational theory in the past two centuries has developed in
relation to three educational theories of the past. First and foremost, it
has been grounded in the Christian humanist tradition that incorporates
biblical, monastic, medieval, and Renaissance elements. A second
grounding, at least until the past thirty years, has been its development
in opposition to theological views of Protestant reformers. Third,
Catholic education has had to come to terms with modernity, that is the
combination of ideas ushered in by the Enlightenment, continued in
liberalism, and found most prominently in progressive education in the
United States. While in the nineteenth century Catholic theology and
education were mainly on the defensive vis-à-vis the modern world,
the seminal event of the Second Vatican Council (1962–1965) was a
serious attempt to deal with both Catholic heritage and modern ideas.
What was mainly a philosophical and cultural confrontation has had
dramatic effects on the nature and direction of contemporary Catholic
education.

Catholic education has maintained its commitment to the humanist or liberal arts tradition in education. Major educational theo-

rists such as John Cardinal Newman and the French scholars Jacques Maritain and Etienne Gilson were strong advocates of this humanism. The major educational encyclical *Divini Illius Magistri* published in 1931 by Pope Pius XI gave prominent place to the humanist tradition. For the most part Catholic schools, colleges and universities, and seminaries have upheld a humanistic curriculum that many consider their strongest contribution to education. These institutions have, however, considerably expanded their curricula to include sciences and professional studies.

Catholic education since the Reformation took on a Counter Reformation character. This facet is seen particularly but not exclusively in the teaching of religion and theology in its educational institutions. For many years a defensive or apologetic approach was taken in these studies. Those elements of theology were emphasized which had come under question by the sixteenth-century Protestant Reformers. Catholic opposition to state schooling in the United States and other countries was motivated by elements of Protestantism that held sway in state or public schools. In the past thirty years, however, the Counter Reformational character of Catholic education has considerably diminished as Catholic theology and education came under the influence of positive and irenic changes introduced at the Second Vatican Council.

Finally, Catholic education has also been shaped by its criticism of and dialogue with educational theories inspired by Enlightenment educators of the eighteenth century, liberal philosophers of the nineteenth century, and progressive educators of the twentieth century. A major challenge to Catholic philosophy and theology, and consequently to Catholic educational theory, arose from new philosophies of rationalism and empiricism, as well as from the rise of science and the historical method in the eighteenth and nineteenth centuries. New theories of knowledge such as rationalism on the Continent and empiricism in England challenged the very bases on which the traditional education was conducted. The initial response of the Catholic Church to these challenges was a defensive and dismissive posture toward all modern ideas, viewing them as intrinsically destructive to Christian faith and education. Errors were pointed out and modern thought, especially liberalism and modernism, was condemned (McCool, 1981). In more recent years more positive attitudes have largely prevailed.

This chapter treats the rather defensive forms of Catholic education that developed in the nineteenth and twentieth century rejection of modernity. Principal examples of this combative stance are found in

Newman's idea of a Catholic University, Pius XI's encyclical on Catholic education, and the neo-Thomistic philosophy of Catholic education. A latter part of this chapter presents an understanding of the influence of the Second Vatican Council and its aftermath on Catholic education. It looks particularly at the educational theory of Vatican II, the catechetical or religious education movement within the Catholic Church, and the overriding issue of the religious identity of Catholic schools. Roman Catholic education is examined from both official church sources and the analytical and critical work of scholars.

Catholic Responses to Enlightenment and Liberalism

The initial nineteenth century Catholic response to the ideas of Enlightenment thinkers was largely negative. For Catholic thinkers this movement minimized tradition and authority and replaced them with the authority of reason or feeling. Catholic opposition was based on the fact that Enlightenment thinkers rejected the authority of the Church and the Scriptures as valid resources for arriving at truth. Enlightenment thinkers were also condemned because they denied the supernatural, the notion of revelation, and any form of extrinsic authority. While some Protestant theologians made overtures to Enlightenment thinking by developing a liberal Christianity (e.g., Adolph Harnack and Friedrich Schleiermacher), Catholic theologians for the most part rejected Enlightenment thought. Those Catholic scholars who attempted to deal creatively with Enlightenment thinking were often condemned by the Catholic Church (McCool, 1977).

The reaction against Enlightenment and its offspring liberalism reached its high point in 1864 when Pope Pius IX promulgated the *Syllabus of Errors* in which all modern developments were condemned. Leo XIII in his encyclical letter *Aeterni Patris* called Catholic theologians and educators to return to the tradition of Thomas Aquinas. Unfortunately in the hands of many Catholic scholars of the time their approach to Aquinas was often defensive and hostile to modern thought (McBrien, 1981, p. 54). This negative attitude continued in the pontificate of Pius X who condemned modernist heresies.

In the early twentieth century Catholic thinkers opened a new dialogue with Enlightenment thought in what has come to be called modernism. There are many elements within modernist thought. Alfred Loisy applied modern historical methods to understanding the Bible. He contended that the Bible should be read as any other historical doc-

ument, without doctrinal presuppositions. George Tyrell argued that church dogma was merely an intellectual effort to come to terms with the divine force acting in all individuals. Furthermore, modernism in Italy favored the establishment of states freed from church control.

The papacy reacted strongly to the modernist crisis in the church. Biblical scholars were forbidden to apply modern historical methods to understanding the Scriptures. In 1907 Pius X condemned modernism in the Holy Office Decree *Lamentabili* and the encyclical *Pascendi.* Catholic clergy worldwide were required to take an oath against modernism, the one exception being for Catholic university professors in Germany.

One of the effects of modernism was to put off a serious confrontation of Catholicism with modern thought. It was not until Vatican II that this theological effort began in earnest. Notwithstanding the basically negative attitude toward modern thought at this time, there were some creative Catholic efforts among theologians in Germany (e.g., Scheeben and Mohler) and Newman in England. Newman's work is especially valuable in the area of university education. For the most part these men operated outside the Thomist and Scholastic tradition, emphasizing historical theology. In this way they came to grips with one aspect of Enlightenment thinking, the new historical understandings.

Newman's Idea of a Catholic University

The best ideals of Catholic education for university and college education were expressed by John Cardinal Newman, especially in his *The Idea of a University* (1982, 1852). Newman's effort bore fruit in his Oratory School but failed at the university level since the university was short-lived. In 1851 Newman was invited by the bishops of Ireland to become rector of a new Catholic university, modeled after Louvain University established by the Belgium bishops. He accepted the invitation and prepared lectures to win support for the project and to explain what his idea of a Catholic university was. These lectures in their published form have become a classic statement of the nature and aims of a Catholic or religious university as well as of the nature of liberal education. The ideals expressed in them are adaptable in many ways to all Catholic and religious schools.

In the lectures Newman argued first of all that the study and teaching of theology has a prominent role in a university. He combated the new view being proposed by the English government and accepted by some Irish bishops that purely secular universities should be established where the teaching of theology was restricted to the efforts of particular churches in extracurricular situations. Newman countered, first of all, that a university that professes to teach all knowledge could not exclude theology, since theology is an integral part of human knowledge. Secondly, contending that there was a unity of all knowledge, he averred that other subjects would be taught deficiently if their connections with theology were severed since theology complements and corrects other disciplines. Thirdly, he pointed out that if theology were not taught, other subjects would usurp its role and intrude into its domain to the detriment of these disciplines and the students who studied them.

Newman then proceeded in his work to a defense of the nature and usefulness of a liberal education. At that time charges were being made that the classical university education given at Oxford and Cambridge lacked usefulness either in producing virtuous persons or in preparing persons to enter the professions. For Newman a liberal education views all branches of knowledge as constituting a unity, an integral system in which they mutually complement one another. Each academic discipline gives knowledge that is trustworthy.

By no stretch of the imagination was Newman a maverick. He was in agreement with general Catholic thought of this period and its opposition to liberalism in religious thought. Newman opposed early developments in liberal Protestantism, which he judged gave too much power to human reason at the expense of divine revelation and church traditions. Thus his educational philosophy remained within the humanist tradition and did not take a turn toward the more radical and liberal elements in religious thought.

In the ensuing century and a half Newman's writings on university education have had a significant influence in shaping the goals of higher education. The issues that he raised—the role of religion and values in education, the competing claims of liberal and professional education, the nature of the academic community, the broader role of literature, and the conflict between religion and science—have been widely discussed, often with reference to his work. Contemporary university scholars still find his thought provoking (Turner, 1996).

Encyclical Letter of Pius XI

In the realm of education the Catholic Church eventually took cognizance of the Enlightenment's effects on education systems throughout the world. State systems of education developed in Europe apart from the Catholic Church. Also, a philosophy of education emerged that was based on purely naturalistic principles, giving little room to a serious study of religion and morality. It was in this context that Pope Pius XI promulgated in 1929 the only major encyclical letter of the church (*Divini Illius Magistri*) on education.

The encyclical presented the educational theory for Catholic schools of its time. The fact that the document was almost exclusively about the education of youth in schools was instrumental in restricting the term "Catholic education" to the education of young people. The papal document presented a powerful rationale for the thousands of Catholic schools that had emerged worldwide from the middle of the nineteenth century. While Vatican II and later documents have modified some of the teachings in the encyclical, much of its spirit continues to constitute Catholic educational theory. Recent authoritative statements still make reference to it, including the *Declaration on Christian Education* issued by Vatican II.

The 1929 encyclical did two main things: it made the case for the teaching mission of the church through traditional Catholic education and it attacked certain aspects of the new education in Europe and progressive education in the United States. Its main quarrel with the new and progressive education was the latter's rejection of the overriding importance of religion in education and its denial of the doctrine of original sin. In condemning particular forms of natural or progressive education the pope declared that:

> Every method of education founded, wholly or in part, on the denial
> or forgetfulness of original sin and grace, and relying solely on the
> powers of human nature, is unsound. Such, generally speaking, are
> those modern systems bearing various names which appeal to a
> pretended self-government and unrestrained freedom on the part of
> the child, and which diminish or even suppress the teacher's authority
> and action, attributing to the child an exclusive primacy of initiative,
> and an activity independent of any higher law, natural or divine, in the
> work of his education. (Pius XI, 1929, p. 34)

A primary purpose of the encyclical was to defend the rights of the church in education and to spell out what it considered to be the roles of the major players in education. The church asserted its rights to maintain schools and to exercise continued vigilance over the education of Catholics even in state schools. However, the papal letter bowed to the rights of civil authorities to supervise education in church schools. From its vantage point the document saw no reason for conflicts among the rights of the church, the state, and the family even with regard to the freedom to pursue knowledge in science and profane subjects.

The document asserted the inalienable rights of the family in the sphere of education, a right that comes from nature. It condemned the view, then prevalent in socialist countries, that the child belongs to the state before it belongs to the family, thus giving the state absolute right over education. It recognized, however, that the family's right is not absolute for it must be exercised in accordance with divine and human law. Parents are obliged to provide for the moral and religious education of their children, as well as for their physical and civic education. In its pages the Roman document did not miss the opportunity to praise the United States Supreme Court's decision in the Oregon school case (*Pierce v. Sisters of the Holy Names of Jesus and Mary,* 1925) that asserted the rights of children and parents over the state.

The document then moved into the difficult area of the rights of the state and how these interact with the rights of the church and the family. Acknowledging that God has conferred rights on the state in education in order to promote the general welfare, the document specified some of these responsibilities of the state. The state has the function of protecting the rights of the family and the individual to a secure peace and stability in which they can freely exercise their rights. Furthermore, the state also has the function of respecting the rights of the church. The state, along with the church, should protect the rights of children when their parents are found wanting physically or morally. The state should promote the religious and moral education of children by removing public impediments to their conduct. Finally, the state should use its resources to assist families and the church in their educational tasks.

The encyclical recognized rights of the state in the sphere of education. It has the right to provide a civic education as well as suitable physical intellectual and moral education. Other positive rights of the state include the right to establish schools for the administration of public affairs and for the protection of civic peace, such as military schools. The document warned against any state monopoly in education that forces families to make use of state schools and thereby go against their consciences or legitimate preferences.

The encyclical then ventured into the thorny area of church-state tensions in education. It contends that whatever in education relates to the sacred, the salvation of souls, and the worship of God pertains to the church. Whatever relates to the civic and political order pertains to the authority of the state. The state, however, is subject to God and the divine and natural law, because all legitimate authority and law come from God. The encyclical claimed that the church in fostering spiritual betterment simultaneously fosters the well-being of the state. The papal document scored as erroneous the opinion that good citizens and a moral and just society could be produced without Christian education.

The second main purpose of the encyclical was to state the Catholic view of education in opposition to the naturalistic or progressive view of education then being propounded in both Europe and the United States. In clear terms it depicted the Catholic view of the person as consisting of soul and body, reason and faith, possessing the effects of original sin in weakness of the will and disorderly tendencies, and in need of grace through the sacraments. The encyclical took aim at theories of education that deny or minimize these truths. While it affirmed that pupils could cooperate in their own education, it still asserted learners' dependence upon the teacher's authority and ultimately on the authority of God as manifested in the universal moral code. Arguing against excessive self-directed learning the pope contended that education whose purpose is to emancipate children by making them self-governing only makes them slaves to their blind pride and disorderly affections.

The encyclical set forth the basic philosophy or purpose and objective of the Catholic school:

> It is necessary that all the teaching and the whole organization of the school, and its teachers, syllabus and textbooks in every branch, be regulated by the Christian spirit, under the direction and maternal supervision of the Church; so that religion may be in very truth the foundation and crown of the youth's entire training; and this in every grade of school, not only the elementary, but the intermediate and the higher institutions of learning as well. (p. 44)

The pope described the ultimate purpose of Catholic education as the formation of the supernatural person "who thinks, judges and acts constantly and consistently in accordance with right reason illumined by the supernatural light of the example of Christ; in other words, to use the current term, the true and finished man of character" (p. 51). This education is neither an abstraction nor a suppression of natural abilities, nor a rejection of contemporary life, nor harmful to social life and prosperity in the world. Rather it is a full development and a perfection of all that is human by the power of the supernatural.

The encyclical recognized the changing role of the church in education in Europe. No longer in control of education as in the days of Christendom, the pope accepted the legitimate role of the national state in developing and maintaining educational systems. Yet he still attempted to protect the church's rights over its own schools and to influence the direction of education in states where it still had power, for example in Italy, Spain, France, and Portugal. The document gave encouragement to Catholic educational movements in countries where no state support was forthcoming, as in the United States, where the church had to settle for noninterference by the state in their schools. The entire discussion on church-state relationships in education assumes an older theological view which was superceded by Vatican II's declaration on religious liberty in the secular sphere. This breakthrough document accepted the view that the state can be neutral with regard to the religions existing within state, neither directly supporting any nor discriminating against any.

Although many educators shared the encyclical's reservations about progressive education during the early years of the twentieth century, eventually Catholic educators came to accept valuable elements of progressive education. Catholic educators were able to cut through the antireligious biases of many of its proponents. Eventually the encyclical's strictures against coeducation were largely abandoned partly for economic reasons and partly because of the emergence of psychological and pedagogical theories supporting coeducation.

The excessively dualistic theological approach of the encyclical—nature and supernature, body and spirit, faith and reason, sin and grace—has been superceded by a Vatican II theology which grapples more realistically with the polarities and tensions of human life. The Thomistic philosophy and theology of the encyclical no longer dominate thinking among Catholic scholars. More recent church documents have modified a number of its teachings in taking a more positive attitude toward human culture and the human person, a more integrated approach to faith and knowledge, and a less rigid supernaturalism (Kelty, 1999).

The Montessori Method

The Catholic Church looked favorably on one mode of progressive thought, the system of education developed by Maria Montessori (d. 1952). Montessori developed an approach to education while working with mentally retarded children in Italy. Trained as a medical doctor and knowledgeable about Enlightenment educators she took practical steps to embody these ideas within an orthodox Catholicism. She avoided however the philosophical debates around Enlightenment theories and Catholic theology.

Montessori developed a quasiscientific pedagogy, which placed the experiences of the child at the center of education. Viewing children as absorbent beings of human experiences from the environment, she devised methods for their ordered education in a prepared environment. She accepted the assumptions that children naturally wanted to learn and that learning should proceed through processes of growth, development, and maturation. The teacher in her view was not an instructor but a director of learning who was attuned to the sensitive or growth periods in children's development. The ultimate goal of education was to move beyond utilitarian knowledge to a spiritual awareness of the profound truths of life.

Although American progressives, notably William Kilpatrick, criticized the method, it appealed to many educators around the world as an alternative to the rigid methods associated with the dominant Herbartianism, which stressed the directive role of the teachers. In 1918 Pope Benedict XV wrote a commendation as a foreword to an edition of *Scientific Pedagogy* helping the approach to gain acceptance in Catholic countries. When the Vatican officially approved the method in 1929, it was adopted in even more Catholic schools and teachers colleges (Kramer, 1978).

Neo-Thomistic Educational Theory

The Pius XI encyclical on education was instrumental in the development of a distinctive Catholic philosophy of education that prevailed in the Catholic world between 1930 and 1960. This philosophy was prepared for by the resurgence of interest among Catholic philosophers and theologians in bringing up to date the medieval synthesis of Thomas Aquinas. This effort called neo-Thomism or neo-Scholasticism had strong support from the popes of the period and resulted in extensive scholarship in theology and philosophy, including philosophy of education. This revival of Thomistic philosophy, advocated by Pope Leo XIII in an encyclical *Aeterni Patris* in 1879, attempted to bring the philosophy of Thomas Aquinas into dialogue with modern thought. The fundamental ideal presented in this philosophy was the integration of the arts and sciences by the believing mind under the guidance of theology. This ideal, while recognizing the distinction and independence of the arts and sciences, tried to integrate the cultivation of both faith and culture. The recognized intellectual leader in this movement was the French philosopher Jacques Maritain. Many other scholars, however, contributed to this version of Catholic philosophy of education, including Etienne Gilson, Christopher Dawson, many Jesuit educators, and the Anglican Bishop George Beck. The one enduring work in this philosophical tradition is Jacques Maritain's *Education at the Crossroads* (1943), a book based on his Terry Lectures at Yale University.

Neo-Thomistic philosophy draws its principles both from religious and philosophic sources. Neo-Thomists agreed with neo-rationalists such as Robert Hutchins and Mortimer Adler in much of their educational theory. However, the neo-Thomists argued that the latter do not go far enough in their metaphysics to include the existence of God and the supernatural realm. Gilson (1957) agreed with this position when he argued that persons, especially the young, could not arrive at metaphysical and moral philosophical truths without the help of religious faith and revelation. In sharp contrast, others hold that the system of neo-Thomism in no way derives its principles from religious faith or from the authority of the Catholic Church but from experience (Beck, 1964).

Neo-Thomistic philosophy, based on metaphysics, the science of being itself, is a form of knowledge that enunciates the general principles underlying all reality and knowledge. This metaphysics entails a system of unchanged and unchanging absolute truth. Its proponents contend that it is possible for persons with the help of God's grace to arrive at absolute metaphysical truths. Because of this absolutism, Catholic philosophy was trumpeted as the one true philosophy, since there is but one origin of all wisdom, namely God.

The starting point of neo-Thomistic philosophy of education is a view of the human person. Only when we know what human persons are can we decide what sort of society they should live in and what kinds of institutions they need. The neo-Thomist believes that persons have rational spiritual natures, are destined for immortality, and transcend every other element in the universe. Such a supernatural view of the person weaves together the Greek concept of persons as rational animals whose highest dignity is in the intellect, the Jewish conception of persons as free individuals in personal relationship with God whom they are to obey voluntarily, and the Christian view of the person as "a sinful and wounded creature called to divine life and to the freedom of grace, whose supreme perfection consists of love" (Maritain, 1943, p. 7). This overarching view of persons entails the existence of God as creator, the sinfulness of human persons, the gift of grace by means of which persons can overcome their sinfulness, and the supernatural destiny of all persons. Human beings consist of material bodies and spiritual souls which are destined for life eternal. Though grace has been provided through the redeeming activity of Jesus, humans are free and personally responsible for their own salvation. The grace of God enlightens the mind and strengthens the will and thus enables persons to achieve knowledge and perform the actions necessary for salvation. In neo-Thomistic philosophy the chief goal of Catholic education is to enable persons to achieve the power of mind and will necessary to achieve eternal salvation.

With regards to the aims of education neo-Thomists make a clear distinction between the primary and secondary aims of education. The primary aim seeks the formation of the person as a spiritual being. Secondary aims focus on the transmission of a heritage or a culture, preparation for life in society and good citizenship, and training for family life. Progressive or pragmatic educators often present these aims as primary. Neo-Thomistic theory asserts that the primary aim of education remains the same in all cultures and societies while secondary aims change according to needs of society (Maritain, 1955, p. 64).

As stated above, the essential aim of education for the neo-Thomist is to help persons to make their way on earth by loving God and neighbor, and thus work out their eternal salvation by striving for the glory of God both on earth and hereafter in heaven. This task faces roadblocks because of the sinfulness of human persons. For neo-Thomists it is essential that education accept the sinfulness of persons and the need for grace. This human sinfulness often expresses itself in uncontrolled emotions. It was recognition of this tendency toward sinfulness that led many Catholic educators at one time to oppose both co-education and sex education in schools.

Neo-Thomists insist on a hierarchy of values in educational aims. While charity is the supreme virtue, in the intellectual realm wisdom is the highest value. Maritain argues that contemplation is thus the highest educational value. The goal of education is to produce truly contemplative persons from whom proper actions will flow. According to his view, pragmatic and progressive values are subordinate to intellectual virtues such as contemplation and wisdom. Maritain recognizes that in education, especially that of children, action must come first but only in order to awaken contemplative processes. He considers education from praxis to knowledge the normal method, especially in the first steps. But for him this is a matter of methodology rather than philosophy (Maritain, 1955).

Education for the neo-Thomist also has a social aim, albeit an indirect one. Although the essential aim of the human person is the perfection of the individual, perfected persons will have an influence on the common good of society. An education that produces intelligent persons, persons with strong moral consciences and a respect for law, will make a valuable contribution to society. Thus the influence of education is indirect on society. Education appears to have no direct aim with regard to society.

Maritain maintains that the primary aims of the school are defined in terms of intelligence and not in relation to society and social work. He contends that teachers do not have to make the school into a stronghold of the established order or to make it into a weapon to change society. For him education is "neither for conservative nor for revolutionary purposes but for the general purpose of teaching how to think." He argues that the schools "have to foster in the pupils the principles of the democratic charter" (1955, p. 70).

The study of religion and theology is at the center of the neo-Thomistic philosophy of education. The curriculum must include both secular and religious truth. Religious truth is explored not only because it leads to salvation but also because it prevents the narrow concern with this world which may lead to a dehumanized life.

Moral formation in virtues should also be cultivated. This should take place through both the inspiration of teachers and the study of humanities. Moral education is to be founded on religious principles since the moral life is linked, at least unconsciously, with religious belief and experience. Maritain (1955) asserts that "if the existence of the One who is the Absolute Being and the Absolute Good is not recognized and believed in, no certitude in the unconditional and obligatory values of moral law and ethical standards can be validly established and efficaciously adhered to" (p. 83).

Maritain does not sidestep the practical difficulties with this principle about the place of religion in public education, especially in pluralistic states. He argues that religious training should be available on a voluntary basis according to the desires of students and parents. He contends that this education should be given in connection with the life of the school. For him God as a truly existing being has as much right to a place in the school as the electron and Bertrand Russell. Religious truth demands a rightful place alongside all of truth. Practical arrangements and compromises should be made in this area. Echoing Newman, Maritain maintains that theology also should have a major place in colleges for a college or university that claims to deal with universal knowledge must include theology. The teaching of theology in secular and nondenominational institutions should recognize the implications of the principles of pluralism.

Neo-Thomists emphasize that learning is coming to know the objective reality, the truth. For them truth is the correspondence of the mind with reality. Learning takes place when individuals with intelligence and free will come to knowledge of objective reality. Fundamental truths concern God, the nature of persons, and the nature of the world. Learning fundamentally means acquiring intellectual virtues. According to neo-Thomists the process of learning begins in the senses, moves to the intellect, and activates the will. The relativity of truth is not accepted in this theory. With God's grace and a helpful teacher there is a confidence that persons will arrive at the truth.

Neo-Thomistic philosophy of education does not prescribe appropriate methods for learning. The philosophy, however, acts as a negative norm in eliminating methods that are manipulative or dishonest. Neo-Thomists adapt and even adopt many of the methods of progressive education when these lead to more self-activity on the part of students. Maritain gave special praise to the method of silence used by Montessori since it fostered the contemplative spirit. He also saw some value in problem-solving methods as a means for fostering the activity of the child (Maritain, 1955, p. 68).

Following Thomas Aquinas, neo-Thomists analyze of the role of the teacher via the notions of act and potency and a theory of causality. The teacher draws out the potentiality of students to perfection and activity. The student is the material cause in that the teacher works the mold. Student's activity is the efficient cause of learning in that it is responsible for bringing learning about. The formal cause or the aim of learning is the integrated and liberated human person. The final cause of learning, or its ultimate goal, is the ideal which the educational achievement offers, that is the vision of God. In the process of learning the teacher acts as an instrumental cause to stimulate the activity of the learner. Thus the teacher has a ministerial or secondary role. In

Aquinas's analogy teachers are like physicians in that they cooperate with God and nature in assisting student learning. As the physician works through nature in ministering to the sick person, so the teacher administers to the mind of students, contributing judgment, intellectual skill, and understanding (Beck, 1964, p. 126).

In the 1960s neo-Thomism declined as a dominant force in Catholic theology and consequently in Catholic educational theory. A respected Thomistic philosopher conjectures that the coup de grâce of neo-Thomism was the "radically different approach to culture, theology and philosophy in the Catholic community since the Second Vatican Council" (McCool, 1981, p. 33). It has been suggested that the reason for its "rapid and precipitous decline" is not entirely clear but such things as the "authoritative aura" and "dogmatic attitude" of neo-Thomists "alongside the freedom and openness purported to the hallmarks of the new philosophies of existentialism, personalism, phenomenology, and existential phenomenology, proved to be too great a strain on the would-be followers of St. Thomas" (Clarke, 1979, p. 12). The pluralism which marks Catholic theology today is matched by the pluralism in approaches to Catholic educational theory which has developed in the post Second Vatican Council era.

While many Catholic theologians and educators have totally abandoned neo-Thomism for modern philosophies, others theologians such as Bernard Lonergan and Karl Rahner have attempted to retrieve elements of the philosophy in an effort to deal with contemporary thought (Elias, 1999). However, it can be noted that:

> The more characteristic response was simply a loss of enthusiasm for making Thomism appear forward-looking. For many, the Thomistic synthesis died from weariness. The constant struggle to adapt it to new insights and new worlds absorbed too much energy. It seemed better to just accept the new world (Halsey, 1980, p. 176)

Contemporary Catholic Education

The present-day educational scene in Roman Catholicism is marked by a pluralism of viewpoints and by a struggle between traditionalists and reformers. The watershed event was the Second Vatican Council, which in its educational document focused primarily on Catholic schools. Around the time of the council there also emerged a vibrant catechetical movement in which the aims and methods of teaching religion received extensive treatment from religious educators. Finally, the identity of Catholic colleges and universities as well as that of all Catholic institutions has become a subject of widespread debate and discussion.

Vatican II and Catholic Education

Vatican II marked a watershed in all aspects of Catholic life, including education. Although education as such was not a central focus of the council, much that it decreed has had widespread implications for the educational work of the church. The council's efforts to renew the life of the church by vivifying the inner structures of the church and the church's relationship to the broader human community created a new framework in which the post–Vatican II church has attempted to educate.

Educationally relevant principles from the council have been identified (Donohoe, 1973). First, the council gave a strong endorsement to the positive values of secular culture, that is, the arts, sciences, technology, and politics of the human community. This principle honored the work of Catholic educators who have for centuries attempted to combine an education in the faith with an education for life in society. Furthermore, the principle also forms the basis for the contemporary urgency of the continuing education of Catholic adults and how Catholic teaching relates to contemporary issues and problems in society.

A second conciliar principle affirmed the role and the responsibility of the laity, not only in human society but also in the very life and structures of the church. By this affirmation the church signaled that the laity's entrance into such a field as education was due neither to default nor to declining numbers of clergy and religious but was their right and responsibility as members of the church. A corollary to this emphasis was the need for Catholic communities and institutions to provide the education requisite for assuming such roles.

A third principle underscored human freedom as the basis for personal worth and dignity. This principle of freedom governs many aspects of education: rights of teachers and students, proper modes of instruction, elimination of indoctrination and manipulation, and the rights of parents. The freedom of individuals with regard to religious education found this support in the council's Declaration on Religious Liberty (Abbott, 1966):

> In spreading religious belief and in introducing religious practices
> everybody must at all times avoid any action which seems to suggest

coercion or dishonest or unworthy persuasion especially when dealing
with the uneducated or the poor. Such a manner of acting must be
considered an abuse of one's own right and an infringement of the
rights of others. (Section 4)

A fourth principle focused on the value of community in bringing about the unity of the human family and the common bond of humankind. Education is seen not as an individualistic enterprise but as
an activity that takes place within a group that shares common values
and aspirations. This principle nested in many educational documents
written after the council.

While Vatican II's declaration on education *Gravissimum edu-
cationis* (Abbott, 1966) is not considered one of the council's great
achievements, it did enunciate a number of important principles for
Catholic education and urged further work by Vatican commissions
and bishops conferences. The declaration showed an interest in all
forms of education, not only Catholic education. It affirmed the rights
of all individuals to an education to prepare them for life in the world
and for their ultimate end. This education should utilize the advances
of psychology and pedagogy in order to promote a proper sense of responsibility and freedom. In addressing the social goal of education the
statement broadened the goals of Catholic education to include not
only that students worship God properly as mature persons in the faith,
but also that they help in the Christian formation of the world and work
for the good of the whole society. The inclusion of a broader social
goal for Christian education is in keeping with the Council's thrust in
showing interest in and concern not just for the life of the Church but
also for all of society.

The declaration spelled out the goals of Catholic education as
both individual and social. It stated that the church should educate its
members for the fullness of life in the hereafter and the goodness of the
earthly community. Specifically the church carries out its religious
mission through catechetical instruction, the enlightening and
strengthening of faith for more active and intelligent participation in
the liturgy and for involvement in apostolic activity. Besides this instruction, the church has the duty of penetrating and ennobling other
forms of education including communications, groups for mental and
physical development, youth associations, and schools.

While previous church documents focused only on Catholic
schools and disparaged secular schools, this document maintained a
positive tone in its treatment of secular or state schools. The importance

of schools lies, it stated, in promotion of intellectual development, social development, and professional development. The school as a center of work and progress encompasses families, teachers, and various associations. The teacher's work is extolled as a vocation demanding "special qualities of mind and heart, very careful preparation and a continuing readiness to renew and to adapt." (p. 5)

The document emphasized the distinctive religious function of Catholic schools in addition to their cultural and human formation goals:

> To create for the school community a special atmosphere animated by
> the Gospel spirit of freedom and charity, to help youth grow
> according to the new creatures they were made through Baptism as
> they develop their own personalities, and finally to order the whole of
> human culture to the news of salvation so that the knowledge the
> students gradually acquire of the world, life and man is illumined by
> faith. (p. 8)

The goals of the schools are thus both religious and secular. Through its right to establish schools the church also protects the rights of parents and fosters the development of human culture. Teachers in these schools, whose work is part of the apostolate, should prepare themselves in secular and religious knowledge, work with parents as partners, and form lasting friendships with students. Parents have the duty of sending their children to these schools wherever and whenever it is possible and of supporting and cooperating with their work

Significantly, the declaration broadened the concept of Catholic education. It praised the efforts to establish different forms of Catholic education: "professional and technical schools, centers for educating adults and promoting social welfare, or for the retarded in need of special care, and also schools for preparing teachers for religious instruction and other types of education" (p. 9). Again, the inclusion of these schools broadens the concept of the Catholic school and Catholic education beyond the primary and secondary schools. This wider vision makes it clear that adult education and special education are integral parts of Catholic education. The document also advised that pastors and laity should through their schools care "for the needs of those who are poor in the goods of the world or who are deprived of the assistance and affection of a family or who are strangers to the gift of faith" (p. 9). This expression of an option for the poor has become a new and growing element in official discussions of Catholic education.

The declaration addressed the functions of theological faculties where priests are trained, teachers are prepared, and research is conducted. The research task of these faculties is:

> To make more penetrating inquiry into the various aspects of the sacred sciences so that an ever deepening understanding of sacred Revelation is obtained, the legacy of Christian wisdom handed down by our forefathers is more fully developed, the dialogue with our separated brethren and with non-Christians is fostered, and answers are given to questions arising from the development of doctrine. (p. 11)

What is new here, in keeping with a dominant conciliar concern, is encouragement for active presence and pursuit of the ecumenical aspect of theological work.

The Vatican II document on bishops contains a number of general guidelines for catechetics. A sound catechesis is to be based on a contemporary understanding of Scripture. The aim of all catechesis is to aid persons to participate more fully in the life of the church. The doctrinal component of catechesis is to come not from catechism formulas of the past but from the more contemporary theology of the council. The full impact of catechesis is to be judged by the witness of Christians to the faith within them as they attempt to bring salvation both to themselves and to the world. The educational impact of the council on religious education or catechesis was felt in the *General Catechetical Directory* (1971), the documents of the worldwide synod on catechesis, and the directories and catechisms prepared in many countries. These conciliar principles gave added impetus to the newly emerging catechetical movement in Catholicism.

The Catechetical Movement

Vatican II galvanized many movements within the Catholic Church, one of which was the catechetical or religious education movement. The beginnings of this movement were in Europe where church educators in the late 1950s began to import into religious education recent developments in biblical studies, theology, liturgy, and pedagogy. The most creative of these efforts took place in France, Belgium, and Germany. A number of Catholic educators received their catechetical education at European centers and introduced the movement into the United States through lectures, courses, and textbooks.

In general terms the catechetical movement in the United States has gone through at least three stages. In the first period instruction in the catechism and doctrines of the church was replaced by a kerygmatic catechetics with emphasis on the Bible and liturgy. The second phase witnessed the introduction of experiential approaches that attempted to meet psychological and developmental needs of students. A third phase ushered in a pluralism of approaches including peace and justice issues, feminism, spirituality, culture and multiculturalism. Within the movement there are also persons who reject these approaches in favor of a strong doctrinal approach.

The 1950s and 1960s catechetical movement in the church revitalized the teaching of religion in Catholic schools and parishes. Previous efforts at change in religious education had focused on introducing new methods in the teaching of religion such as the German Munich method, which advocated a three-step approach to teaching religion. The catechetical movement infused new life into the Confraternity of Christian Doctrine whose task was the education of children who did not attend Catholic schools and also adult members of the church. Increased attention to religious education led to the hiring of parish directors of religious education (DREs), diocesan offices of religious education, religious education materials and textbooks, catechetical journals such as *The Living Light* and *Religion Teachers Journal,* increased emphasis on adult education, and graduate programs in religious education at colleges, universities, and seminaries.

Early pioneers in the Catholic educational revival in the United States were Gerard Sloyan and Johannes Hofinger. Through his writings and his position at Catholic University Sloyan (1958, 1960) made known to American educators the rich catechetical tradition of the church, the most recent developments in catechetics in Europe, and the writings of theologians, biblical scholars, and liturgists. Sloyan was also a keen critic of the Baltimore Catechism's approach to teaching religion on educational, theological, and biblical grounds.

Hofinger's chief contribution to religious education in the United States may lie in his introducing Joseph Jungmann's seminal work *The Good News Yesterday and Today* (1962). Written in 1936 but published in English in 1962 this work argued that the catechism be replaced by a clear proclamation of the person and teachings of Christ. His main effort was to revive the spirit of the early church when its central activity was proclaiming the central teaching of Christianity, the mystery of the life, death, and resurrection of Jesus. He also wanted students introduced to the riches of a vibrant liturgy.

Hofinger utilized this approach in a series of international study weeks. In a number of works including *Art of Teaching Christian Doctrine* (1957) Hofinger introduced into the United States the kerygmatic method of teaching. This method moved beyond what had been the traditional doctrinal approach to teaching Catholicism found in all schools and colleges, namely, authoritative teaching of the church as presented through catechisms and textbook. The kerygmatic method placed an emphasis on proclaiming the Bible as salvation history, initiating students into the mystery of Christ through the liturgy, engaging students intellectually in the study of theology, and challenging students to witness to their Christian faith in their individual and communal lives.

At the heart of the kerygmatic approach was an interpretation of the Bible as containing a unified plan of God for the salvation of humankind. The concept of salvation history became the central concept in liturgical, biblical, and catechetical renewal. This concept borrowed heavily from Protestant biblical theology that lay at the foundation of neoorthodox theology and its approaches to religious education. It constituted one of the bases on which Protestants and Catholics engaged in ecumenical dialogue.

Maturity came to the catechetical movement when the kerygmatic approach received a full-scale criticism from Gabriel Moran (1966a, 1966b). Moran pointed out the weakness of the theological underpinnings of the approach, focusing especially on the theology of revelation. Moran viewed religious education as a process that invited students to reflect on God's present revelation in their lives. He also exposed the kerygmatic approach's weak educational theory, characterizing it as merely a recounting of events from the past. In sum, Moran found the kerygmatic approach wanting on many fronts, but especially in dealing with the religious experience of students.

On a more positive note, Moran had a hand in introducing progressive and experiential elements into Roman Catholic textbooks in the 1970s and was a key leader in an anthropological or experiential religious education. Moran's alternative theory bore many similarities to Protestant liberal theology and Deweyan progressive education. His lasting contribution to the field of religious education was his broader vision of religious education, including not only the activity of schools but also education within parishes, families, the workplace, and all of life itself.

This broader vision has been enunciated in many works in the past thirty years. Furthermore, together with James Schaefer (1972) he made the education of adults in the faith a major focus for church educators.

More recent writings of Moran are not directly connected with Catholic education but are rather attempts to develop a broadly ecumenical field of religious education (1993) and present a theory of adult religious education (1979). In all of these works Moran amasses a penetrating analysis of language, concepts, assumptions, and arguments situated in the intersection of religion, culture, and education.

Moran has also been resistant to the effort of some Roman Catholic religious educators to describe their field as a ministry or a form of practical theology. He favors a broader vision of religious education that would include Jewish and Muslim education as well as religious education in public or state schools where such is the practice. While Moran admits that some forms of religious education among Catholics might be considered ministry, he thinks that religion teachers in Catholic high schools would describe their work as the academic study of religion rather than as a form of church ministry. Moran argues for a concept of religious educator as distinct from the pastoral or priestly role contained in the concept of ministry.

The attempt to separate religious education from too close a connection with theology is also a driving force in James M. Lee's (1971, 1973, 1985) social science approach to religious education. In his theory it is the social sciences that give religious education its foundation and essential structure. Religious education is a branch of education, which is in turn an offshoot of the social sciences. In three scholarly works Lee has offered a comprehensive and systematic theory of religious education from which he contends effective practices flow. In this theory religious education is "the structuring of the learning situation to most effectively facilitate the modification of behavior along religious lines" (1971, p, 56). It is his contention that only the social sciences can provide the explanations, prediction, and verification of desired behavioral outcomes.

The kerygmatic approach also received criticism from Mary Boys (1980) from both a biblical and educational perspective. She challenged the biblical theology that was at the basis of the approach. In her view this approach, in assuming a Christocentric theology, did not do justice to the relationship between the Hebrew Scriptures and the Christian Gospel. Boys (1989) has developed an approach to religious education which attempts to do justice to the Christian tradition and to attend to the need for this tradition to become accessible to Christians in such a way that it promotes personal and social transformation. She has stated succinctly the general goals of religious education:

> If religious education is to avoid the pitfalls of fossilization and an uncritical pursuit of relevance, then it must both conserve and change, continue ancient symbols and explore new possibilities, hand on tradition and transform the world. Traditions, like roots, are lifelines to vital sources from which new entities develop. Transformation exists to make transformation possible. (Boys, 1979, p. 14)

Making accessible the tradition entails processes of explaining, introducing, commenting, translating, and making maps as well as processes or removing obstacles to learning.

Berard Marthaler, Sloyan's successor at Catholic University, has made catechesis and not kerygma the central concept in his socialization theory of religious education. The term *catechesis* is an ancient one and is used in official Catholic documents such as the *General Catechetical Directory* (1971), Pope Paul VI's *Evangelii Nuntiandi* (1974) and Pope John Paul II's *Catechesi Tradendae* (1980). This term does not imply the use of a catechism but refers to an education in which the faith and communal life forms the context for learning. It is Marthaler's (1997) contention that catechesis is not adequately understood and that United States seminaries have not taken seriously enough the preparation of clergy.

Marthaler (1978) has infused catechesis with deeper meaning by utilizing concepts from sociology of knowledge and cultural anthropology to explain the process of Christian learning. Marthaler's focus has been on an education into the faith of a particular community by participation in the symbols, rites, values, and lifestyles of members. Religious education takes place in the interaction between learners and all activities and persons in their environment.

The concept of catechesis underlies the Church's initiation of individuals in the rites of the church. This is especially true for initiation of individuals into the adult catechumenate, a rite restored in 1972 for aiding potential members through liturgical rites and catechetical instructions. The catechumenate is both an experiential experience through prayer and celebration as well as an educational process. In many Catholic Churches it has become a primary form of adult education (Dunning, 1979; Morgan, 1990).

Michael Warren (1982) has also made catechesis a key concept in his approach to religious education, focusing primarily on youth and young adult catechesis. In a recent book Warren (1997) has enriched the field of religious education with a cultural criticism of media. Earlier, Warren was also a leading figure in the youth ministry movement in the Catholic Church that crystallized in the statement of the United States Catholic Conference on Youth Ministry. The document included the following components: outreach or ministries of welcome, evangelization in youth fellowship meetings, systematic catechesis, service projects, and peer ministry (United States Catholic Conference, 1976).

An attempt to construct a synthetic approach to religious education is found in Thomas Groome's theory of Christian religious education (1980, 1993). Groome has given a strong theoretical rationale from Christian and philosophical sources for a shared praxis approach to religious education. He has used the Christian symbols of Kingdom of God, salvation, liberation, and a critical theory of praxis as major elements in his theoretical approach to Christian religious education. The heart of Groome's theory of education is a theological and educational insight (similar to that found in Paul Tillich's correlational theology or David Tracy's revisionist theology) that the normative Christian story and vision is in dialectical interaction with an individual's personal story and a community's contemporary story.

Groome's (1980) shared praxis approach is indebted to the praxis pedagogy of Paulo Freire. This approach attempts to move religious education beyond a focus on individual experience to challenge learners to name and express actions in the world. Through this approach learners are encouraged to utilize reason, memory, and imagination to relate their lives to the Christian story and call. Groome (1993) has considerably expanded this approach by extending it to other forms of pastoral ministry besides religious education.

Some Catholic religious educators have paid special attention to the role of aesthetics in religious education. They have pointed out that Catholic religious education has tended to focus on rational and intellectual goals and methods. Utilizing research on the two hemispheres of the brain and the nature of symbolic or metaphoric thinking, Durka (1990) has contended that religious educators should include the nurturing of experiences of artistic enrichment, interpretation of a wide variety of artwork, and art forming through the use of many artistic media. Harris (1987) has explored theories of imagination and the ways in which religious educators can attend more creatively to the imagination of students. Sawicki (1988) in presenting a highly original interpretation of the origins of Christian education has explained how liturgical symbols foster religious understanding.

Education for peace and justice has become a principal focus for a number of Roman Catholic religious educators. This work has been inspired by developments in liberation theology and the social teachings of the church, especially the pastoral letters of the United States bishops on peace and the economy. The educational component of these approaches is largely indebted to the educational theory of Paulo Freire, a Brazilian educator who has included church education as one of his major concerns. Freire's pedagogy of the oppressed (1970, 1973) was based on the premise that education is not a neutral process but rather a tool for liberation or domestication. The task of educators is to humanize individuals by engaging them in processes of analysis, confrontation, and transformation. In this dialogical and problem-posing education students and teachers seek conscientization, that is reflective engagement and action for liberation.

Toton (1982) has made the most sustained effort to relate religious education to justice issues. In a groundbreaking work she showed how religious educators could deal with world hunger. Using the methods of liberation theology and the educational work of Paulo Freire she probed how ideology, social class, the world of work, and technology as well as social and economic systems are involved in world hunger. O'Hare (1983) collected essays by Catholic religious educators who examined the foundations for justice and peace education and dealt with a wide range of issues in both religious education and pastoral ministry.

A number of Catholic religious educators have brought feminist critique to bear on religious education. Durka (1984) has analyzed the structural situation of women in religious organizations and in religious education, especially as this relates to power. She has called for them "to make a conscious effort to direct their energies [from the personal-interpersonal levels] towards the structural levels of reality" (p. 176). Boys (1989) has synthesized the principles of feminist theories on knowledge, sources, overlooked information, methodology, and new theories. Drawing on these theories as well as on the work of feminist theologians, she argues for the importance of a feminist perspective in religious education. She contends that feminist religious educators can contribute the feminist commitment to process and collaboration as well as other aspects of feminist pedagogy. Harris (1988, 1989) has written perceptively and movingly about the connections among religious education, feminism, aesthetics, and spirituality.

Identity and Mission of Catholic Colleges

The previous chapter showed how in the past two centuries Protestant colleges gradually became secularized, that is, they freed themselves from the control and influence of religious denominations. A similar process has taken place in Catholic colleges since 1960. As Catholic colleges struggle to maintain their distinctive Catholic identity, a debate rages over the teaching of theology or religious studies. The Catholic debate on institutional autonomy and academic freedom is complicated by the nature of teaching authority in the church, which rests ultimately with the pope and bishops. For some the very future of Catholic colleges depends on some resolution to this debate and the acceptance of an agreed-upon ideology (Gleason, 1995).

Before the 1960s most Catholic colleges were owned and operated by religious orders of men and women, and in a few cases by particular dioceses. The Catholic identity of these institutions was unquestioned. Neo-Thomism or neo-Scholasticism, as taught in philosophy departments, provided the philosophy of education and the ideological basis for Catholic higher education institutions. In just about every Catholic college and university students took eighteen credits or more in neo-Scholastic philosophy. Courses in religion were few in number. Theology as such was not taught in these colleges, being a subject that future priests studied in seminaries. Courses in religion often took on a catechetical and apologetic or defensive nature. Furthermore, courses in the humanities stressed the existence of a distinctive Catholic culture, which developed between the two World Wars (Halsey, 1980). Almost all of the teachers were Catholics, many of them priests and sisters. The lay men and women that taught in these institutions had generally attended Catholic institutions themselves. Most colleges had enforced attendance of students at religious services. Students were also involved in a multiplicity of Catholic activities under the umbrella of Catholic Action.

The contemporary higher education scene is vastly different. Radical changes began in the 1960s as social, political, and cultural upheavals in American society had their effect on Catholic higher education as they did on other American institutions. At this time Catholics achieved a higher degree of acceptability in the general culture with the presidency of John F. Kennedy. A larger number of Catholic men and women attended college.

During the sixties Catholic campuses were rocketed with many crises and disputes. Theological influences from Europe, especially after the Second Vatican Council, brought new ideas and radical interpretations of Catholic teachings. Controversial theologians were barred from speaking at Catholic University. A large number of Catholic scholars dissented from papal condemnation of artificial methods of birth control. These conflicts have continued to the present time.

Today many colleges are owned and governed by boards consisting of laity, priests, and members of religious orders. Neo-Thomism or neo-Scholasticism no longer rules philosophy and theology departments. Requirements in philosophy and theology, which replaced religion courses, have been significantly lowered. The numbers of clergy and religious have decreased while lay men and women constitute the majority of the faculty in almost all institutions. Many of these received their education in secular universities. Many non-Catholics attend these institutions and attendance at religious services is optional. A study of changes in religious colleges in New York from 1962 to 1972 found these and other changes evidence of a revolutionary change (Maloney, 1973). Maloney's appraisal is that these institutions had become ecumenical colleges and should declare themselves as such.

The first serious challenge to Catholic intellectual complacency came from Monsignor John Tracy Ellis's critique of American Catholic intellectual life. He indited Catholic intellectuals for their failures in the realm of ideas, culture, and influence on American society (Ellis, 1955). He challenged Catholic scholars to present the distinctive Catholic tradition in a more effective manner. Ellis's critique set off a debate and coincided with increased Catholic efforts to expand graduate work and improve Catholic scholarship (Gleason, 1995). But as Catholic colleges and universities strengthened their curriculum in many new disciplines and fields of study, fewer courses remained to treat the Catholic tradition. The irony of the situation did not escape critics: the more Catholic institutions were committed to greater professionalization, the weaker became their distinctive Catholic identity.

In general terms, changes in Catholic higher education have generated a number of responses. A few institutions have adopted an almost exclusive or sectarian Catholic identity. A small number of col-

leges have abandoned their Catholic affiliation and have become totally secular. The vast majority of Catholic institutions, however, have
attempted to remain committed both to Catholicism and to secular academic values. Nevertheless, some influential voices within Catholic
higher education have contended that these institutions are no longer
Catholic in any real sense (Burtchaell, 1998). At the present time these
institutions struggle valiantly to maintain their Catholic identity and
religious mission. These struggles carry over into the teaching of theology or religious studies.

In 1967 a group of influential bishops, universities presidents,
and intellectuals, led by Fr. Theodore Hesburgh, president of Notre
Dame, gathered at Land O' Lakes, Wisconsin, to hammer out a statement on the Catholic university in the United States. It dealt with such
issues as institutional autonomy, academic freedom, and the teaching
of theology. This statement contended that:

> The Catholic University today must be a university in the full modern
> sense of the word, with a strong commitment to and concern for
> academic excellence. . . . It must have true autonomy and academic
> freedom in the face of authority of whatever kind, lay or clerical,
> external to the academic community itself. . . . Institutional autonomy
> and academic freedom are essential conditions of life and growth and
> indeed of survival for Catholic universities, as they are for all
> universities. (Gallin, 1992, pp. 7–12)

While rejecting hierarchical control or interference over the university,
the signers of this declaration assured that the university would remain
Catholic because Catholicism would be "perceptively present and effectively operative" in the work of scholars who engage directly in exploring the depths of Christian tradition. The document made the oft-
quoted statement that while the university is not of the church, the
church is in the university. The Land O' Lakes statement made a strong
case that it is principally through the teaching of theology that the
church would be present in the university: "In the Catholic university
this operative presence is effectively achieved first of all and distinctively by the presence of a group of scholars in all branches of theology" (Gallin, 1992, pp. 7–8).

While Catholics in higher education continued to debate the identity and mission of their institutions, the Vatican became concerned
about what was happening to Catholic universities throughout the
world. In 1985 Roman officials issued a draft constitution on Catholic

higher education institutions. Influential presidents at universities in the United States criticized the draft as contrary to the democratic and pluralistic situation in which institutions are chartered in the United States. They especially reacted to the Vatican's efforts to control the teaching of Catholic theology, which they saw as contrary to academic freedom in the United States.

After many debates the apostolic constitution finally appeared in 1990 as *Ex Corde Ecclesiae,* proclaimed by Pope John Paul II. In many ways this document is positive in describing the role and mission of the Catholic university in the Church:

> In a Catholic university, therefore, Catholic ideals, attitudes, and principles penetrate and inform university activities in accordance with the proper nature and autonomy of these activities. In a word, being both a University and Catholic, it must be both a community of scholars representing various branches of human knowledge, and an academic institution in which Catholicism is vitally present and operative. (John Paul II, 1991, p. 7)

According to *Ex Corde Ecclesiae* the Catholic university is the place where the dialogue between reason and revelation, faith and culture takes place. While the pope enunciates the principles of institutional autonomy and academic freedom, these norms are limited by the authority of bishops when it comes to the teaching of Catholic theology. The document also suggests that a majority of the faculty at these institutions should be Catholic. A committee of American bishops and university presidents engaged in drawing up ordinances to implement the recommendations of *Ex Corde Ecclesiae* (O'Brien, 1994, pp. 61–68). The Vatican rejected a first set of recommendations drawn up by American bishops. At issue were proposals that theologians receive a mandate for teaching from the local bishop, that efforts be made to have more Catholic faculty members, and that presidents of colleges take an oath to uphold Catholic doctrine. Guidelines were finalized in 2001.

While there has been great turmoil at the hierarchical and institutional levels in the church, there have also been developments within the universities themselves to deal with issues of identity and mission. Although the teaching of theology occupies a central focus in these efforts, the controversies are not limited to theology. Also included as important factors in Catholic identity are campus ministry programs, commitments to peace and justice, clear mission statements, clerical or religious leadership in key administrative positions, and efforts to engage faculty in conversations over the identity and mission of Catholic institutions. Some have argued that a commitment to peace and justice is the distinguishing mark of Catholic higher education, citing church documents from Vatican II to the present. Jesuit colleges and universities have made a special commitment in this area as has the Association of Catholic Colleges and Universities. This social Catholicism rationale has also been adopted by many Catholic secondary schools (Bryk, Lee, and Holland, 1993).

Theology has long replaced philosophy as the key department carrying on the Catholic mission of these institutions. Many have characterized theology departments as being in a state of disarray. Theological pluralism reigns in methods, sources, and approaches, as has often been the case in the church. Even neo-Scholasticism was not the monolith many thought it was, since within it were varying points of view. Theologians are often torn by competing commitments to the church, the academy, and the wider community and culture.

In debates within theology some favor almost exclusive concentration on Catholic theology, while others propose an ecumenical theology. Still others opt for a religious studies approaches. At times a department has representatives of all three views. Some influential Catholic theologians contend that theology should be taught in higher education institutions through a faith-centered approach that does not seem to allow for serious questioning of Catholic theology or for an ecumenical stance. Dulles (1997) cautions that:

> If the professors challenge and undermine the settled doctrine of the Church, it begins to be doubtful whether the department of theology is serving the purposes for which it was erected and whether it is meeting the legitimate expectations of those who make financial sacrifices to attend a Catholic college or university. Students who sign up for courses in Catholic theology normally and, I think legitimately expect to hear it presented from the perspective of faith. The bishops and the religious who have established most of the Catholic institutions of higher education, and the benefactors who support those institutions, presumably intend that theology be taught from a recognizably Catholic perspective point of view. (pp. 15–16)

For Dulles and theologians who take his view theology is the proper subject in Catholic institutions of higher education, a theology that presumes a faith commitment within a tradition of worshippers and believers. *Ex Corde Ecclesiae* explicitly states that courses in Catholic doctrine be made available to all students (John Paul II, 1991, pp. 4, 5). While this approach seems to entail a serious limitation on academic freedom, its advocates contend it is justified to protect and ensure the integrity of Catholic higher education institutions.

Other theologians consider this faith-oriented approach unrealistic given the multifaith makeup of classes in Catholic institutions and the faith condition of many Catholic students. Hellwig (1997) notes that:

> There seems to be underlying assumption that a course on the subject matter of the student's own faith tradition ipso facto presumes the student's faith and adherence in his tradition. As one who regularly offers a course entitled Introduction to Catholic Theology to an undergraduate class which frequently contains Protestants, Jews, Muslims, Hindus, and others, I find the link between Catholic subject matter and the assumption of Catholic faith in the student out of touch with the present reality in our classrooms. (p. 72, fn. 6)

In light of the problems presented by Hellwig and others, some departments have decided to organize themselves as religious studies departments, which include studies in Christian and Catholic theology. Religious studies take the approach that subjects are taught by assuming a scientific detachment, standing outside the phenomena it observes and analyzes. Thus theology operates within a particular religious tradition while religious studies takes a stance outside particular religious traditions. The tension between the two becomes less if theology is seen in an ecumenical context that takes interreligious dialogue seriously and religious studies gives serious attention to the Catholic theological tradition.

One thing is clear from these debates among theologians: while theology is important it cannot carry the full weight of maintaining the Catholic identity of institutions. O' Brien (1994) may be correct in his insight that the problem of the Catholic mission of colleges and universities is pastoral, that it "has something to do with living the faith, and speaking about it, in such a way that the church and its traditions and ideas seem worth considering" (p. 213). He contends that these institutions will maintain their identity more by "inviting the people who give their lives to Catholic higher education to join in the great work of enriching human life and culture . . . . than complaints about selling out to secular goods" (p. 214).

Summary

Catholic education in the past two centuries began in a defensive mode in reaction to Enlightenment thought and liberalism. In the nineteenth century a milestone work was John Cardinal Newman's intellectual blueprint for Catholic higher education institutions. The charter document for Catholic education was the encyclical letter of Pope Pius XI. This document was buttressed by the influential neo-Thomism of scholars who spelled out in philosophical terms the bases for Catholic education. The contemporary renewal in Catholic education began with the Second Vatican Council, which made a serious attempt to correlate Catholic tradition with modern thought. The vibrancy of contemporary Catholic thinking on education is found in the writings of many scholars who have made religious education or catechetics their main focus. The future of Catholic education may well be at stake in the current debates over the identity and mission of Catholic institutions of higher learning, especially as they relate to the teaching of theology.

Chapter 8

Orthodox Christian Education

> Even after the fall of Byzantium, when Eastern Christians were
> deprived of schools, books and all intellectual leadership, the liturgy
> remained the chief teacher and guide of orthodoxy. Translated into the
> various vernacular languages of the Byzantine world—Slavic,
> Georgian, Arabic, and dozens of others—the liturgy was also a
> powerful expression of unity in faith and sacramental life.
> (Meyendorff, 1979, p. 7)

Eastern Orthodox Churches trace their traditions and practices back to
the early days of the Christian church. The Orthodox churches originated in the Middle East, spread to the countries of Eastern Europe,
and are now found also in the West, including North and South America. These churches take their doctrinal lead from the Scriptures, the
fathers of the early church, especially the Greek fathers, and the first
seven ecumenical or worldwide councils of the Christian church.
While the various national churches that form Orthodoxy are independent from one another, they are united and possess a unity in faith
through their acceptance of the patriarch of Constantinople as a first
among equals of the bishops of the Orthodox Church.

The Orthodox Church today consists of a family of churches that
are self-governing but joined together by a common faith and communion through the sacraments and episcopacy of the church. First,
there are the churches of the East that date from the fifth and sixth centuries. These include the Assyrian Church, the Syrian Church of Antioch, the Syrian Church of India, the Coptic Church of Egypt, the Ar-
menian Church, and the Ethiopian Church. A second group of
Orthodox churches emerged in the eleventh century as a result of the
splitting off of Eastern churches from the Western churches. Orthodox

churches were established in Constantinople, Greece, Russia, and other Eastern European countries of Serbia, Romania, Bulgaria, and Cyprus. In the past two centuries Eastern Orthodoxy has spread into the countries of Western Europe, North America, and South America.

Presenting the history of education in the Orthodox Church is not an easy task. Education in Orthodox churches has traditionally been a holistic endeavor centered more in the liturgy, prayer, and spiritual guidance than in formal educational practices. Although Orthodoxy has a rich theological tradition, until very recently, there has not existed within this tradition a body of writings that explicitly treats the aims and processes of Christian education. Thus one does not find in Orthodoxy writings on education comparable to those of Augustine, Alcuin, Thomas Aquinas, Martin Luther, and Erasmus. Christian education in much of Orthodoxy's history might more appropriately be termed Christian formation and spiritual development. In recent years, however, there has been an effort among some Orthodox Christians to present a more systematic approach to religious education, drawing on the riches of Orthodox theology and spirituality as well as contemporary theories in social sciences and education.

This chapter explores the history of Orthodox education in a number of phases. First, it focuses on those teachings and practices that were formed in the pre-Constantinian Church. Orthodoxy shares this history with the other branches of Christianity: Roman Catholicism and Protestantism. Second, the chapter examines the emergence of a distinctive theological and educational tradition in the Byzantine Empire, dating from the fourth to the fifteenth century. Third, the chapter treats the period in which Orthodox Christianity was greatly influenced by theological and educational developments in the West. The fourth period begins with the reform or renewal of Orthodoxy that occurred in the middle of the nineteenth century and continues to this day. The final section period describes Orthodox education in North America and contemporary theories in Orthodox religious education.

Beginnings of Orthodox Education: Pre-Constantinian Era

The Orthodox Church shares a common apostolic and postapostolic history with Roman Catholicism and Protestantism: the formative biblical period, the early spread of the church throughout the Roman Empire, the era of church apologists and early fathers, and the age of persecutions. The first chapter of this book detailed this history with special emphasis on the educational efforts of the first Christian communities.

The Orthodox Church considers itself the church that is most faithful to the traditions developed in the first three centuries of Christian history. It notes that most of this early history took place in the eastern part of the Roman Empire. Jesus lived his life in the East. For the most part his apostles confined their ministry of evangelization to the peoples of the East. The East gave to the church the culture and the language of the New Testament. Of the first patriarchates or dioceses established in the Christian church three were in the East: Jerusalem, Alexandria, and Antioch. From the church in Jerusalem, the first church in Christendom, apostles and disciples went out to the east and west. It was in eastern city of Antioch, in Syria, that the followers of Jesus were first called Christians. The city of Alexandria in North Africa witnessed the development of the prominent catechetical school of Clement and Origen, whose brilliant theologies were described earlier.

The Orthodox Church considers these early centuries of Christianity as providing valuable insights and examples for its contemporary spiritual and educational life. The earliest preaching of the Gospel called people to conversion experiences and to full membership in a Christian community. Once individuals were converted they continued their education in the faith through the fellowship of prayer, the learning of doctrines, and the breaking of the bread. Many early Christians were asked to make a total commitment to Christianity as the way of life, the way to God's kingdom. For many Christians in the East their commitment to Christianity entailed the giving up of their lives through the shedding of blood or martyrdom. The ways of persecution and martyrdom have long been viewed by Eastern Christians as promoting and leading to the education and salvation of all of its members.

The church that developed in the East was a body whose religious life centered essentially in the liturgy of the Eucharist. Ignatius, bishop of Antioch, placed special importance on the gathering of people around the bishop to celebrate the Eucharist, the medicine of immortality and the center of learning about the faith. He wrote: "Let no one do any of the things which concern the Church without the bishop. . . . Wherever the bishop appears, there let the people be, just as wherever Jesus Christ is, there is the Catholic Church" (In Ware, 1993, p. 13). The importance of the local community of faith is also seen in Cyprian of Carthage's admonitions about the unity that Christians in local communities possess through communion with their bishops. In Cyprian the

Orthodox Church finds the basis for its esteemed conciliar principle
which affirms that the highest authority in the church rests not in a single individual but in a united episcopacy.

The Orthodox Church prides itself on its continuing commitment
to the traditions of early Christianity. Being Orthodox entails for its ad-
herents a legitimate commitment to "changelessness" and a loyalty to
maintaining the teachings of the church as they have been received. The
Orthodox tradition of faith includes the Bible and the early Christian
creeds. In later years the church expanded this tradition to include the
decrees of the first seven ecumenical councils, the writings of the fathers, the canons, service books, and holy icons, and "in fact the whole
system of doctrine, Church government, worship, spirituality and art
which Orthodoxy has articulated over the ages" (Ware, 1993, p. 196).

The Christian faith was transmitted to new believers through the
various forms of education that were described in chapter 1: preaching
and teaching by apostles, evangelists, prophets, and teachers; the living witness of the Christian community; and the service of love that
Christians manifested to one another. However, the form of education
from this early period that has been greatly stressed for the entire history of Orthodoxy was the community's gathering to break bread in
imitation of Jesus, what Orthodox Christians call the Holy Liturgy.

Education in the Byzantine Empire

The Orthodox Church created its distinctive form within the Byzantine
Empire, which was established in the East when Constantine embraced
the Christian faith and moved the capital of the Roman Empire to the
city of Byzantium, on the Bosphoros. This city, whose name was
changed to Constantinople, had a dominant influence in the development of the Orthodox Church until the middle of the fifteenth century.
The city grew even more important when the Christian churches in
Jerusalem, Antioch, and Alexandria were considerably weakened because of the dramatic spread of Islam beginning in the seventh century.

The history of education in Byzantium reveals two distinct but
related forms of education. The inner education was largely confined
to the monasteries of men and women and consisted in a study of the
spiritual traditions of Orthodoxy: the Scriptures, church fathers, and
ecumenical councils. An outer education, provided in the state schools,
academies, and universities, introduced students into the liberal arts
and then to the study of philosophy or law.

Inner Learning: Theological and Mystical

The Orthodox Church has always placed great emphasis in its theology and education on the theological doctrines that were clarified at the councils of bishops in the first eight centuries of Christian history. The first council, which took place in the eastern city of Nicea in the fourth century, was called by the Emperor Constantine to deal with the heretical doctrines of Arianism. It was in these earliest councils, all held in the East, that the fundamental doctrines of the church were defined: the Blessed Trinity, the dual natures of Jesus as divine and human, the dignity of Mary as Mother of God, and the propriety of venerating icons. Each of these doctrines was defined in the face of what were declared to be heretical and unacceptable views held and propagated by some members of the Christian church. It was these doctrines that formed the foundation for the theological and mystical education that took place in Orthodox monasteries.

The Orthodox Church thus is a conciliar church in that it places ultimate teaching authority in the councils or meetings of bishops that made decisions on matters of Christian faith and life. In asserting this principle of authority the Orthodox Church differs from the Roman Catholic Church which assigns a special role to the bishop of Rome and Protestant churches whose ultimate authority rests in the Scriptures.

Next to the teachings of the early councils Orthodox churches honor the writings of the fathers of the church, especially the Greek fathers of the fourth century. Chapters 1 and 2 treat some of the theological and educational writings of the prominent Greek fathers: Clement, Origen, Basil, John Chrysostom, Gregory Nazianzan, and Gregory of Nyssa. The theological works of these writers and of later Eastern leaders like Cyril of Alexandria, John Damascene, and Gregory Palamas are considered the mainstream of Orthodox theology. As a corpus, these writings are considered by many to convey the essence of the Orthodox experience. Their ideas and words contributed greatly to the renewal in Orthodoxy that took place in the middle of the nineteenth century.

Many of the Greek fathers lived in the numerous monasteries of the East, found not only in the countryside but also in cities. Monasteries for both men and women grew in number as the church moved from the age of persecution to a time of acceptance and power. Monasticism has been described as a white martyrdom of asceticism and self-sacrifice in contrast to the red martyrdom undergone during the years of bloody persecutions. For the most part Eastern monasteries were not the places of formal education and learning like their counterparts in the western part of the Roman Empire. The copying of manuscripts was deemed more a work of manual labor than a work of scholarship. While Eastern monasteries were noted for their social and charitable works in serving the needs of the poor, their main role in Orthodoxy was the praise of God in daily prayer, the provision of living examples of holiness, and the offering of spiritual guidance to all Orthodox Christians. All these aspects of life in a monastery constituted the inner learning that is characteristic of Orthodoxy.

For good reason the theology that emerged in the Byzantine Empire has been characterized as a monastic theology since it was the monks who were the great proponents and defenders of Orthodox teachings. The theology of the East did not undergo the experience of the West where in the Middle Ages theology became a university faculty and an area of academic study. This pivotal fact accounts for the rather spiritual, mystical, and unsystematic nature of Byzantine theology. The type of Christian education that grew in this period also had the marks of monasticism on it: liturgical, spiritual, mystical, and formative. Finally, it was from the monastic liturgies that the moving and elaborate cathedral and parish liturgies flowed. These celebrations formed and educated the masses of people. These liturgies became critical in the preservation of Orthodoxy in that:

> Even after the fall of Byzantium, when Eastern Christians were
> deprived of schools, books and all intellectual leadership, the liturgy
> remained the chief teacher and guide of orthodoxy. Translated into the
> various vernacular languages of the Byzantine world—Slavic,
> Georgian, Arabic, and dozens of others—the liturgy was also a
> powerful expression of unity in faith and sacramental life.
> (Meyendorff, 1979, p. 7)

It is hard to overstate the central importance of the liturgy in Orthodox education. The liturgies constituted the main sources of learning and inspiration in Orthodoxy.

Within the rich Orthodox liturgical heritage arose like incense to the heavenly realm the spiritual hymns and religious poetry that were composed for Orthodox liturgies in the fifth and sixth centuries. While the monks at first resisted the introduction of such hymns, they eventually became leaders in creating liturgical hymns, which were sung to the accompaniment of beautiful music. These hymns contain many elements of the theology of the Orthodox Church. They have been called "a poetic encyclopedia of patristic spirituality and theology" (Meyendorff, 1979, p. 123). The singing of hymns bonded the laity together in voice when liturgies began to be celebrated for thousands of people in large basilicas, with veils and barriers erected that practically excluded the people from active participation. A prominent Orthodox historian and theologian has written that:

> In the darkest ages, when traditions were broken and education became rare, people in the Church would rediscover again and again the universal, all-embracing and inexhaustibly profound Orthodoxy in its golden age. . . . There were no seminaries, academies, or theological faculties; but devout monks and Christians drank the living waters of divine knowledge from hymnology. (Schmemann, 1963, p. 228)

Intimately connected with the liturgy were liturgical catecheses or instructions in which bishops and monks delved into the deeper meaning of the liturgical rites. Theodore the Studite (759–826), a major figure in the monastic contribution to liturgical hymns and catechesis, was also a vigorous defender of the use of icons in worship and prayer.

Noteworthy personages in Orthodox monasticism were the "elders" or "old men," monks of great spiritual discernment and sagacity. From such men, and also some women, other monks and laypersons sought spiritual guidance. It was the function of the elders to point out the concrete ways in which people could respond to the will of God in their lives. The elders gave truth to the statement that monks withdrew from the world in order to return to it, spiritually nourished and religiously wise, to aid their fellow men and women in their journey through this life into the heavenly life. This form of guidance and the writings that contain much of this wisdom are a rich educational resource in Orthodoxy.

Eastern monks played an important role in one of the most controversial issues in Orthodox Christianity, the debate over the validity and role of icons in Orthodox worship, spirituality, and education. Icons are material representations or images of Jesus, Mary, the saints, or angels. Attacks were made on the use of icons periodically from the eighth through the ninth centuries. The severest attacks often came from some of the emperors. The iconoclasts who opposed the use of icons appealed to the Old Testament condemnations of the use of images of God. They charged that the veneration of icons was actually a form of idolatry or superstition. Those who favored the use of icons, at times called iconodules, while recognizing some dangers and real abuses in the use of icons, considered them essential for the profession and expression of the Orthodox Christian faith.

John of Damascus (675–749), a principal defender of icons in the eighth century, gave a number of arguments for the legitimacy of venerating icons. He made a distinction between the adoration that was due to God alone and the substantially lesser veneration or honor that was given to icons. John also defended the use of icons by pointing out that material things such as wood, stone, and paint had the power of bearing spiritual realities. In his view icons could be sources of divine grace and sanctification. In upholding the spiritual nature of matter John offered a powerful defense for the Incarnation and divinity of Jesus. Eventually the defenders of icons received the support of bishops gathered in the Second Council of Nicea in 787.

In defending the use of icons John of Damascus also attested to the educational value of icons, which they have retained throughout the entire history of Orthodoxy. John called them "open books to remind us of God" and wrote that "What the written word is to those who know letters the icon is to the unlettered; what speech is to the ear, the icon is to the eye" (In Ware, 1990, p. 149). In the mind of defenders of the icons one can learn about the teachings of the Church not only through studying books of theology but also through contemplating the mysteries of faith depicted in icons.

For many interpreters the real heart of Orthodox theology, spirituality, and religious education lies in the mystical experience to which Orthodox Christians are called. In the period after the seven councils a mystical theology emerged that has remained an integral part of the Orthodox tradition. Symeon the Theologian (949–1022), a religious poet in the latter part of the tenth century, was a chief figure in this movement. It was his claim that all baptized Christians could attain an immediate and conscious experience of the Holy Spirit. The purpose of this experience is the gradual *theosis* or deification of each Christian, an experience which is considered the heart of Orthodoxy (Hussey, 1986, p. 3). Through union with the Holy Spirit the Christian comes into contact with Jesus in a vision of divine light that transforms those that contemplate it. Symeon addressed this divine light with these poetic words:

> O power of the divine fire, O strange energy!
> You who dwell, Christ my God, in light wholly unapproachable,

> How in your essence totally divine do you mingle yourself
>   with grass?
> You, the light, are joined to the grass in a union without confusion,
> And the grass becomes light; it is transfigured yet unchanged. (In
> Ware, 1990, pp. 155–156)

The most influential mystical movement in Orthodoxy began in the fourteenth century in connection with the Hesychast controversy. A Hesychast is a person who seeks inner stillness or silence through the constant repetition of the Jesus Prayer, "Lord Jesus Christ, Son of God, have mercy on me." This "prayer of the heart" is made with the accompaniment of physical techniques (head bowed, chin resting on the chest, eyes fixed on the place of the heart), and controlled breathing. The famous controversy over Hesychast mysticism is presented in the next section.

Outer Learning: Classical Liberal Education

Throughout the course of the Byzantine Empire the classical Greek education, the outer learning, continued in schools, academies and universities. Rather early in the history of Byzantium there developed a conflict between this classical education and the newer inner learning in the churches and monasteries. Throughout the sixth, seventh, and eighth centuries some Christian leaders followed the example of Basil in assigning an important value to classical studies in the full intellectual education of Christians. Other spiritual leaders, especially those in monastic communities, did not advocate such studies and even viewed them as dangerous for the formation of Christians. While in the universities the study of the classical literature prevailed, the monasteries were largely dedicated to the study of Christian writings.

From the very beginning of the Byzantine Empire in the days of Constantine the emperors played a dominant role in the life of the Orthodox Church as well as in the education offered throughout the empire. In the middle of the fourth century the emperor Julian, in an effort to abolish Christianity, attempted to reform education by restricting the influence of Christian teachers. In his *Rescript on Christian Teachers* he advocated education in the classical Greek tradition and issued this command:

> I give the [Christian teachers] this choice; either not to teach what
> they do not think suitable, or, if they wish to teach, let them first really

persuade their pupils that neither Homer nor Hesiod nor any of these
writers whom they expound and have declared to be guilty of impiety,
folly and error in regards to the gods, is such as they declare . . . ,
[For] it seems to me absurd that they should teach what they do not
believe to be sound . . . . For religious and secular teachers, let there
be an ordinance to this effect. (In Bowen, 1972, p. 293)

Christian teachers and students left the schools but returned shortly
when Julian was killed in a military campaign.

Jovian who succeeded Julian as emperor restored Christianity
and established in 364 an institution of higher Christian education at
Constantinople, considered to be the first institution of higher Christian studies in Christendom. The institution attracted students from the
entire empire. The Capitol School, as it was called, prepared students
for civil service and teaching. The emperors controlled the curriculum,
the professors, and the students. There does not appear to have been a
separate faculty of theology at the school. The curriculum included
studies in grammar, rhetoric, philosophy, and law. During the time of
Emperor Justinian in the sixth century the school became prominent in
the teaching of law. In the tenth century the Capitol School was closed
and replaced by a school devoted mainly to religious studies and was
under the control of the patriarch of Constantinople.

A resurgence of outer learning took place in the east in the ninth
century under the emperor Theophilus and lasted through the twelfth
century. Scholars copied and studied the ancient manuscripts, which
became part of the basis for the Western Renaissance. Our knowledge
of the classical world is indebted to the efforts of scholars of this time.
There also emerged during this time many private school teachers who
gave instruction in the liberal arts. Some Church schools added to these
classical subjects an instruction in the patristic literature. These
schools found creative ways to combine Christian studies with the
classical learning, using the advice of early church fathers as a principle of interpretation and instruction in reading Greek literature. However, the humanism that sprung from this early Byzantine Renaissance
did not reach the levels of western Scholasticism and the western Renaissance. According to one scholar, it lacked their coherence and dy-
namism and "was not able to break the widespread conviction of many
Byzantines that Athens and Jerusalem were incompatible. The watch-
dogs in this respect were the leading representatives of a monasticism
which persisted in a staunch opposition to 'secular wisdom' " (Meyendorff, 1979, p. 55).

A noted scholar during this period of resurgence was the patriarch Photius (ca. 820–891), considered the father of Byzantine humanism, and a man learned both in the classical and Christian traditions of education. Though deeply involved in political conflicts with
Ignatius, the former patriarch, as well as with the pope in Rome,
Photius still managed to maintain scholarly interests in teaching, reading, and compiling summaries of Greek writings, including literature,
history, philosophy, and theology. In philosophy he was more a disciple of Aristotle than of Plato; he also remained committed to the theological positions of the early councils and fathers. Photius defended
Orthodox teaching on the controversial *filioque* issue, relating to an understanding of the Trinity. In matters of belief he sought to discover
through study the common faith and the past doctrinal decisions that
received the greatest support in the tradition of the church. Photius embodied an excellent example of a Christian scholar who in contrast to
some Orthodox monks that avoided secular learning made extensive
and effective use of the Greek classics in his writing and teaching.

The high point of this first revival of Byzantine learning took
place in the eleventh century when the Capitol School of Constantinople was reformed. The school was reorganized around the faculties of
law and philosophy. In philosophy Aristotle's logic was studied at the
lower level while Plato was imbibed in the curriculum of higher education. Many religious families, however, did not permit their sons to
study Plato and sent them to the monasteries at the age of eighteen.

Prominent in the faculty of philosophy at the school was the Platonic scholar and monk Constantine Psellus (1018–1078). Psellus, an
esteemed and popular teacher, was highly influential in strengthening
higher education in Constantinople. For him philosophy was the highest learning for it provided students with insights into ultimate matters.
In his words:

> There is nothing comparable to philosophy, which is drawn from all
> studies and contains a synthesis of them all. The man who attempted
> to make a comparison [between it and other studies] would be judging
> between it and itself; one cannot, upon that basis preserve it in its
> position as the art of all the arts and the knowledge of all forms of
> knowledge. (In Bowen, 1972, p. 309)

Psellus was eclectic in his philosophy, drawing on both Plato and Aristotle. Although in his theology he remained committed to the traditional teachings of the Orthodox Church, during his lifetime Psellus

had to face charges of heresy because of his attempt to bridge the gap between philosophy and theology. He defended himself against these charges in a written profession of faith in which he appealed to the Greek fathers of the fourth century, finding much to value in these ancient writings. Psellus made it clear that he always placed Christ before Plato.

While Psellus was never brought to trial for his teachings, Italus, his disciple, was brought to trial in 1076–1077 and in 1082. He was charged with using reason to explain the Incarnation and the nature of Jesus, and for declaring that philosophy was a valid source of religious knowledge. Hounded by his foes, Italus was eventually condemned and went into monastic life where he continued to pursue philosophy and theology (Hussey, 1986, p. 145). The condemnations of Italus had repercussions in the later history of Orthodox theology and education. These condemnations expressed a highly negative view toward Greek philosophy. In them "the Byzantine Church solemnly refused any new synthesis between the Greek mind and Christianity, remaining committed only to the synthesis reached in the patristic period" (Meyendorff, 1979, p. 64). Ironically, these condemnations came at the same time that the West was developing a creative synthesis between the Greek mind and Christian thought.

A second Byzantine Renaissance in learning and scholarship took place in the last three centuries of the Byzantine Empire, from the thirteenth to the fifteenth century. At a time of political decline and decadence, scholars emerged who again tried to unite the inner learning of Christianity with the outer learning of the ancient Greeks. While many monks still condemned the classical learning, other monks and most lay persons sought to pursue and promote both forms of education. It was believed by the former advocates that while philosophy taught persons *how* to think it was only theology, revealed by God in the Scriptures, councils, and fathers that could teach persons *what* to think. Beyond the knowledge revealed by these accepted sources of God's revelation lay the mystery about which, according to the Orthodox apophatic tradition, we know more about what this mystery is not than what it is.

The prosecutions of Psellus and Italus triggered a decline in the study of philosophy for a while. Then some Byzantine philosophers and teachers again began to test the outer limits of reason and revealed truth. They argued about the nature of the Trinity and Hesychasm. Some scholars even became interested in the work of Western theologians, notably Thomas Aquinas.

In the fourteenth century Byzantine philosophers entered into a most heated debate with the monks over the nature of mysticism and of our knowledge of God. The Greek philosopher Barlaam criticized the doctrines and practices of the Hesychasts, accusing these mystics of both philosophical error and useless navel gazing. The Hesychast mystical prayer and spiritual formation found its champion in Gregory Palamas, the fourteenth-century theologian (1296–1359). Though Gregory was well educated and wrote in the classical style, he assumed a negative attitude toward the classical writings. In defending the Hesychasts Gregory was also offering a defense of the inner learning of the Orthodox Church.

In his work *Triads in Defence of the Holy Hesychasts* Gregory refuted the views of philosophers like Barlaam who argued that humans could not know God directly. He did this by making a distinction between knowing God's essence, which is not possible for humans, and knowing God's energies or actions, which humans are capable of knowing. Gregory also based his defense of the Hesychasts on the doctrine of the Incarnation and the Scriptural description of human persons as consisting of body as well as spirit. He likened the mystical experience to the vision afforded the three apostles of Jesus when they saw him transfigured before their very eyes. Gregory thus affirmed and defended the hiddenness of God as well as God's nearness and accessibility. For philosophers like Barlaam who had been affected by Western scholasticism and who did not have a profound knowledge of the fathers, the mystical tradition and its spirituality bore little truth and was out of touch with reality. Hesychast mysticism, however, prevailed in the East even though it was opposed by many scholars and even denounced by the Roman Catholic Church (Runciman, 1970, pp. 47–48).

The most noted philosopher of the Late Byzantine Renaissance was George Gemistus, self-surnamed Plethon (1355). This Greek philosopher saw no difference between the outer learning of philosophy and the sciences and the inner learning of theology. He rejected the Orthodox apophatic theology contending that God gave us our reasoning abilities so that we could understand all of reality. His philosophical allegiance was to Plato. Unfortunately, little from his writings on theology has remained for the patriarch of Constantinople ordered his unpublished manuscripts to be burned. Though Plethon attended the Council of Florence that dealt with the reunion of the Orthodox and Roman Church, he spent most of his time lecturing in schools on his beloved Plato.

The Late Byzantine Renaissance made a modest contribution to the development of learning, but had little or no impact compared to what the Western Renaissance had. With regard to education, it clarified the meaning of inner learning as wrestling with eternal truths about which humans could know little except what God had chosen to reveal. Students of this learning could explain and comment on these truths but they could not substantially add to them. Mystics might penetrate a bit deeper into these truths but philosophers as such could add nothing to our knowledge of religious truths, since philosophy was restricted to earthly truths. Ironically, the most lasting philosophy from this Renaissance was the work of Gregory Palamas who viewed himself not as a philosopher but as an expositor of divine and eternal truths. His books on Hesychism are considered "the product of a formidable intellect expressed with lucidity rare amongst Byzantines and are of prime importance in the history of religious thought" (Runciman, 1970, p. 96).

Byzantium came to an effective end with the fall of Constantinople to the Turks in 1453. While there are negatives in the Byzantine legacy to modern Orthodoxy, its positive contribution has been defined as providing:

> An historical framework for a tradition which maintained the
> eschatological character of Christianity. . . . [T]he Orthodox settled
> for a ghetto life: the closed liturgical community, with its experience
> of the heavenly, served both as a refuge and as a school. It
> demonstrated a remarkable capacity for survival and also, as for
> example in the nineteenth and twentieth century Russia, for
> influencing intellectual development. (Runciman, 1970, p. 200)

Orthodox Education after Byzantium

Orthodox theology and education greatly suffered from the eleventh century onwards when Constantinople came under the control of the Turkish sultans. By the latter years of the empire, education had become the province of the aristocrats. The masses of people were educated only through the services of the church. Education in schools was directed more to the maintenance of a classical Hellenic culture than it was to preserve the Orthodox faith. By the nineteenth century a Russian traveler made this assessment of post-Byzantine education:

> The academic love of Hellenism, without systematic study of it,
> satisfied with excerpts, leads only to a limited, one-sided education

that is next door to ignorance. The consequence of it is pedantry and pomposity, resulting from a ridiculous desire to apply ancient Hellenic phrases in simple conversation, and, finally, scorn for ordinary but useful knowledge. The teachers prefer to explain something about the state of the country two thousand years ago than to acquaint people with its contemporary situation. Byzantine arrogance, which acknowledges that a man is of value only if he is a Greek, continues to sow the most nonhumanistic concepts among Christians. (In Schmemann, 1963, p. 282)

The Orthodox Church was not able to maintain its institutions of higher education. Consequently, the education of clergy and monks suffered greatly and young people traveled to the West to seek their education. By the seventeenth and eighteenth centuries Orthodox theology had become greatly "latinized." Even as late as 1937 Georg Florovsky, a Russian theologian, who spoke of the Western captivity of the Orthodox mind, could write that:

Until the present time the Orthodox theologian has been too dependent on Western support for his own constructive work. He received his primary sources from Western hands, read the Fathers and the acts of the councils in Western editions (which often were not accurate), and learned the techniques of dealing with the assembled material in a Western school. (In Schmemann, 1963, p. 286)

Understandably, the Orthodox Church during this period developed a defensive posture and an overly conservative spirit. Theological education did not resume until a seminary was established on the island of Chalcis in 1844. The Roman Church made special efforts to bring about the conversion of Eastern Orthodox Christians. Even Protestant churches attempted to win Orthodox Christians over to their view of Christianity. With the weakening of Greek Orthodoxy, leadership in the Orthodox movement shifted to Russia.

The definitive split that took place between the Eastern and Western parts of Christianity in the fifteenth century solidified some of the principal differences between Eastern and Western theology, spirituality, and education. It is not a total simplification to characterize Western Christianity as practical, juridical, and rational, and depict Eastern Christianity as speculative, mystical, and experiential. Theology in the East tended to stress the language and ideas of the Greek fathers while theology in the West developed a Scholasticism that depended to a great extent on the categories of Greek philosophy. This is not to ignore, however, the serious cultural, political, and theological disputes that were greatly responsible for the breakup or schism of Christianity into an Eastern or Orthodox version and a Western or Roman Catholic version.

The nineteenth century witnessed the rebirth of independent Orthodox nations in Greece, Serbia, and Bulgaria. It took many years to shake off the suffocating effects of living under Turkish control. The new states, however, did not give a prominent role to the Orthodox churches. In these national revivals monasticism was nearly extinguished, the clergy became civil servants, and theology became a professional field or a narrow specialization. A vibrant Orthodox faith did not immediately appear.

One event of theological and educational significance did take place during the period of Turkish control. It was the publication in 1782 of the *Philokalia* [Love of Beauty], edited by Macarius of Corinth and Nicodemus, a monk of Athos. The collection was intended both for monks and lay people as a resource for their life of inner prayer, especially the Hesychast variety. *Philokalia* is a collection of ascetical and mystical writings from the fourth to the fifteenth century. These writings helped spark the theological and spiritual renewal in Orthodoxy that took place in nineteenth-century Russia. The collection, now translated into many languages, is a rich resource for living the spiritual life

Renewal of Orthodoxy in Russian Orthodoxy

A significant event in the history of Orthodoxy occurred in the tenth century with the spread of Orthodoxy into Bulgaria, Serbia, and Russia, an event made possible because Orthodoxy allowed national churches to use the language of the people. The inroad of Orthodoxy into these countries was prepared for by the ninth-century missionary activity of the Greek brothers Cyril and Methodius. What Orthodoxy brought to the Slavic people was a hybrid system of Christian doctrine and an Eastern civilization.

The conversion of Russia to Orthodoxy took place in the later part of the tenth century when members of Russian royal families were baptized in the Orthodox faith. In the eleventh century monasteries were established in Russia. The Grand Vladimir was most influential in the spread of Christianity among the elite and intellectuals of Russia. For years Christianity existed in Russia as a foreign religion since it was embedded in the Greek culture of Byzantium. While intellectuals had access to the literature of Orthodoxy, the uneducated masses had become attached to its splendid ritual.

There is some evidence of the encouragement of learning and schooling from the earliest days of the Russian Orthodox Church (Fennel, 1995, p. 42). Most children were taught in homes but eventually some schools were established. Early leaders of the church in Russia complained about the lack of literate men to ordain to the priesthood. There is no evidence of how priests were recruited and trained in the Orthodox faith. Action was taken on this front in 1051when a meeting of church leaders decreed that schools should be established in the homes of priests for the education of young men to prepare for the priesthood. These homes were often open to other children. Instruction was given in basic literacy and in the doctrines of the church. It does not appear that a large number of schools were established outside the larger cities and the monasteries (Johnson, 1969, pp. 12–13).

The Russian religious spirit became manifest in the early centuries of Russian history. The centuries from the tenth to the thirteenth constitute the Kievan period of Russian history when the foundations were laid for Russian theology, spirituality, and education. Its religious spirit was rooted in nature and an appreciation for beauty. The influence of Byzantium is seen in the veneration of icons that marked the early Russian churches. Icons of Mary depicting her as the Mother of God were common. Book learning was esteemed within the culture as shown in a chronicle of the activities of Prince Iaroslav in the eleventh century:

> Great is the fruit of book learning; by books we are shown and taught the ways of repentance, we acquire wisdom and conscience from the words of books; they are rivers watering the universe, they are the fountainhead of wisdom, by them we are comforted in sorrow, they are the bridle of temperance. (In Fedotov, 1956, p. 277)

The lives of the early Russian saints reveal a respect for the learning that they received in the grammar schools. The possession and copying of books, even secular ones, were considered worthwhile activities, even for monks. This early period is rich in works that contributed to historical theology as well as to ascetical and mystical spirituality. Ethical writings highlight the importance given to social ethics and charity. Learning however was not extended to the area of scientific investigation, which came about only with the Westernization of Russian learning and education (Fedotov, 1956, p. 380).

While the beginnings of the Russian Orthodox Church were in Kiev, in the thirteenth century Moscow emerged as the political capital and the center for the Orthodox Church and its metropolitan bishop. The Russian Orthodox church lost some of its independence when it moved to Moscow and came more under the political control of the Russian state and less under the religious control of the patriarch of Constantinople.

The Russian Orthodox Church received a spiritual legacy from Byzantium. It attempted to maintain the doctrinal purity that characterized Byzantium. It also inherited the rich Byzantine liturgical tradition, notably its poetry and music. This tradition was shared in not only by the monks but also by the illiterate masses. The liturgical tradition gloried in the liturgy as heaven on earth. Over time the Russian Orthodox Church introduced some changes into the liturgy received from the Byzantines. In the opinion of the historian George Fedotov, the Russian Orthodox Church over the years acquired its own distinctive characteristic, less intellectual, more open to ethical issues, to social justice and service, and to human emotion (In Meyendoff, 1990, p. 8).

Early in the eighteenth century Peter the Great and Catherine II introduced radical reforms into the Orthodox Church. The church was made a department of the state. Monasteries were severely restricted in their social work and then closed. Through the efforts of these tsars the Orthodox Church became Westernized. The principles of the Western Enlightenment were propagated into Russia at the Kiev Academy. Western art, music, and theology made their appearance in Russia. Those rebelling against these reforms "turned not to the teachings of Byzantium and ancient Russia, but to religious or pseudo-religious movements in the contemporary west: Protestant mysticism, German pietism, Freemasonry" (Ware, 1990, 1993, p. 116). The true Orthodox spirit was not totally lost, however, for it was found in the writings of Bishop Tikhon of Zadonsk (1724–1783) and the Ukrainian Paissy Velichkovsky (1722–1794). The latter's disciples rejuvenated the monastic movement in Russia by immersion in the tradition of the Hesychasts. It was Velichkovsky who corrected the Slavonic texts in light of the original Greek texts of the fathers and whose work led to a renewed interest in Orthodox spirituality and theology.

One of the leaders of the nineteenth-century revival of Russian Orthodoxy was the monk Filaret of Moscow (1782–1867). His accomplishments in education include a catechism, biblical translations, textbooks, sermons, and additional writings on the basics of Orthodox faith. Filaret was a major figure in the nineteenth century "delatiniz-ing" of Russian theology through his return to the scriptural and pa-tristic sources for theology and education. Filaret's scholarly reach ex-tended to ecumenical activity and the reform of monastic life. He established a monastery, the Gethsemane skete or cloister, where he introduced patristic theology and ascetical practices. He promoted a distinctive Russian Orthodox spirituality, rooted in the spirituality of the early Christian monks (Nichols, 1990, pp. 81–91). A lay theologian largely responsible for moving Russian theology away from depen-dence on the West was Alexis Khomiakov (1804–60). His major in-terest was in the theology of the church.

Other theologians, classified as theological liberals by Valliere (1990), were involved in the renewal of Russian Orthodoxy, including Sergius Bulgakov (1871–1944) who utilized historical scholarship to recover the undogmatic spirit of primitive Christianity. Vladimir Soloviev and Sergei Trubetskoi made important connections between Christian doctrine and ethics. Soloviev introduced an experiential method into theology. He also struggled to establish an Orthodox Church free from dependence on the state, and advocated serious ecu-menical dialogue with Roman Catholicism. In the early part of the twentieth century Nicolas Berdyaev (1874–1948) was a major force in the development of Russian theology at a Russian center in France.

Orthodox Education in North America

In 1794 the first Orthodox Christians came as Russian missionaries to what was then Russian Alaska. These monks preached the gospel and converted almost the entire population of the island. The missionaries built on the foundation of beliefs and practices they found among the people (Oleksa, 1983). When Alaska became part of the United States in 1867 the property and rights of the Russian Orthodox Church were recognized.

A vast number of Orthodox Christians came into the United States during the immigration in the first part of the twentieth century. The principal groups that came were Greek Orthodox and Russian Or-thodox. By the end of the first decade of the twentieth century over fifty Greek Orthodox parishes were established. Neither group developed its own approach to religious education. At one time the Greek Ortho-dox Church even adapted an Episcopalian curriculum for its purposes (Nicozisin, 1977, p. 35).

In the first part of the twentieth century the principal educational efforts by Orthodox Christians in North American centered on the establishment of parish schools where instruction in religious education and in the respective foreign languages was given. Children attended these schools either on a Saturday or Sunday or on weekday afternoons usually for one to three hours. Bilingual catechisms were commonly used. The Greek Orthodox Diocese of New York issued the following in its report on education:

> The Committee on Education recommends that along with the Greek School, which teaches our language, traditions and customs, it is imperative that a Catechetical School for children be organized too. Furthermore, it is recommended that a Special Committee be appointed and study in detail the organization of a Catechetical School for Adults and render a report. (In Nicozisin, 1977, 21–22)

The report made it a high priority that a school for children be established in each parish, that it be under the supervision of the pastor, and that a uniform curriculum be drawn. There is little evidence that these programs were ever implemented on a wide-scale basis. Similar directives were issued from time to time.

After the Second World War the common practice of the Orthodox Church was to have English Sunday schools on the model of what was happening in the Protestant churches (Tarasar, 1994). Protestant curricula were also imitated in drawing up materials for Orthodox education. Adopting the Protestant Sunday school model also entailed that children were separated from parents during the Divine Liturgy.

Recent Orthodox religious education has benefited from three movements (Tarasar, 1990, p. 462). First, it was made possible by the flowering of Russian Orthodox theology after the Russian revolution of 1917 and was centered in the St. Sergius Theological Institute in Paris. Out of this intellectual movement came outstanding theologians and bishops. The second movement was the Orthodox youth movements in Western Europe and the Middle East. Young people participated in liturgies, education programs, mission activities, and the renewal of monastic life. Prominent leaders also emerged from this movement.

The beginnings of a distinctive approach to religious education among Orthodox Christians were in the foundation of the Orthodox Christian Education Commission (OCEC) in 1956. Founded by Sophie Koulomzin, an emigrant from France, this group of theologians and educators reflected on the Orthodox tradition and attempted to relate it to contemporary culture. At this time the commission had representatives from the Carpatho-Russian, Greek, Romanian, Russian (Metropolia), Serbian, Syrian (Antiochian), and Ukrainian jurisdictions. The specified aims of the commission were:

> -to seek an Orthodox approach to the readily-adopted Protestant pattern of Sunday schools which, in spite of its usefulness, was felt to be inadequate, and in some respects, inapplicable to Orthodox understanding of education,
>
> -to relate Orthodox life and teaching to the American situation and particularly to new contemporary approaches to education, and
>
> -to seek to create an inter-Orthodox forum for the exchange of ideas, problems, and practical solutions of the educational needs of the orthodox parishes and dioceses. (In Tarasar, 1994, p. 4)

OCEC has held international conferences and contacts among theologians and educators the world over. In 1961 it began to prepare a curriculum to be used by all Orthodox churches, which has been revised on a number of occasions. However, after a twenty-year effort Sophie Koulomzin, a leader in the OCEC, could write that "the Orthodox Church today faces a challenge to discover an approach to religious education that is rooted in the total church tradition (Koulomzin, 1975, p. 14). Catherine Tarasar succeeded Koulomzin as executive secretary of the OCEC. The commission has continued to develop educational materials to this day.

Theoretical Approaches to Orthodox Christian Education

A number of scholars and educators have attempted to develop theoretical approaches to Orthodox religious education. One of the first attempts centered Orthodox education around the concept of a distinctive Orthodox *phronema,* which is:

> [A]n attitude, a position and/or posture, which reflects a particular spirit, a theological sentiment of mind. An Orthodox Christian *Phronema* in Christian education then, is a program which postulates a scriptural, traditional, doctrinal, and historical spirit, a sentiment and frame of mind which is reflected and existentialized in the liturgical life of the individual both within and without the church. (Nicozisin, 1977, p. xiii)

For Nicozisin the four dimensions—scripture, tradition, doctrine, and history—converge, blend to become the foundation comprising the *phronema*. This *phronema,* which is passed down from one generation to the next, begins in the Christian home where children learn from parents. It is further enriched through active participation in the liturgy and informative instruction. Nicozisin exposed the limitations and weaknesses of relying solely on classroom instruction and contended that the Divine Liturgy is meant to help us live our theology, achieve our theosis, and manifest our Orthodox *phronema*. (p. 104)

The eminent liturgical scholar Alexander Schmemann enhanced the foundation of Orthodox education by unfolding the rich meaning of Orthodox liturgy. He presented as the goal of religious education building up the church by bringing members into its liturgical life. For Schmemann (1974) religious education:

> [I]s not merely the communication of religious knowledge, not training a human being to become a good person, but the edification—the building up of the Body of Christ, a member of that new chosen race and holy nation whose mysterious life in this world began on the day of Pentecost. (p. 11)

Undoubtedly, religious education has the task of explaining to new members of the church what is happening to them as they participate in the sacred rites. But for Schmemann liturgical experience comes before catechesis. Christians must first taste and then see or understand. Schmemann explained that:

> The Orthodox faith has its most adequate expression in worship and that truly Christian life is the fulfillment of the grace, vision, teaching, inspiration and power that we receive in worship. Therefore it is in the organic connection between the liturgical life of the Church and her educational effort that we find the uniquely Orthodox principle of religious education. (Schmemann, 1983, p. 5)

Religious education does not end with worship for "the understanding of worship must lead to the assimilation of Christian doctrines and to the practice of the faith" (pp. 23–24).

Schmemann's work in basing religious education on liturgy has impacted the work of Catherine Tarasar. She has considerably expanded his approach and brought into Orthodox education both contemporary social sciences and educational theory. Tarasar develops a curriculum theory out of the three elements specified by Schmemann: worship, teaching, and praxis. Her model for Orthodox curriculum broadens the context or aim for education by incorporating the fullness of church life in worship, instruction, and praxis in family and community. Its content is the telling of the story of the church's life through liturgy, scripture, doctrine, and spiritual life. Its focus is on personal and communal relationships with God and fellow humans. Its immediate context is an understanding of personal growth and development—physical, cognitive, social, and spiritual (Tarasar, n.d, ch. 2, pp. 6–7). The resources tapped for learning include the entire fund of tradition: scripture, patristics, liturgy, liturgical music, hymns, icons, and lives of the saints.

Tarasar (n. d.) has created a parish model for Orthodox education integrating education through worship, formal teaching, and praxis in personal and community life. The context for education through worship is the church. The focus is the celebration of the mystery of Jesus. The content of this education includes liturgy, revelation, and the manifestation of God. Education through worship makes use of a language that is mystical, experiential, spiritual, and affective. It welcomes nondiscursive forms of knowing and the use of poetry, music, and hymns. People are invited to learn through observation, immersion, participation integration, reception, commemoration, and communion. This multifaceted worship involves the entire worshipping community, including celebrants, acolytes, readers, and choir.

According to Tarasar's paradigm education through formal instruction takes place in classrooms, camps, and informal groupings of youth or adults. Education offers learners the opportunity to reflect on and understand the events celebrated and proclaimed in the worship. The content of this education is an exposition and explanation of doctrine. Its forms and language are rational, cognitive, conceptual, analytic, discursive, and theological. Methods comprise study, investigation, research, reflection, discussion, analysis, and synthesis. Participants involved in this education are teachers, students, peer groups, youth and adult leaders, special staff, painters, musicians, and iconographers.

Furthermore, education through praxis is the informed practice or application of one's faith in home or community life. The focus of praxis is the integration of the liturgical event and its extension into one's life by the application of these to real-life situations. The content of this education revolves around making real one's faith through ethical applications. Modes of learning are relational, social, communal, practical, functional, interactive, experiential, and personal. Praxis education takes place through action, rehearsal, modeling, service outreach, witness, and counseling. Personal relationships characterize this form of education: elder-disciple, parent-child, confessor-penitent, or coach-athlete.

Although Tarasar presents these three forms of education as distinct she is careful to note that Orthodox education should be holistic. She contends that "the reintegration of worship with teaching and praxis is essential if we are to recover the holistic vision and experience of life in the church" (Ch. 2, p. 12). Further, she offers this challenge to Orthodox educators: "we need to learn by celebrating together and by living and acting together in witness and service. All three contexts of worship, teaching and praxis are needed for the renewal of the church in today's society" (Ch. 2, p. 12).

John Boojamra (1989) has mapped out the intellectual foundations of Orthodox religious education that should guide church educators in total parish planing. These foundations are the church or community as the context for socialization, the family as the primary place for socialization, and the developing person as the subject of religious education. While he admits that there might be other foundations, Boojamra proposes these as providing "the matrix for discussion and integrating other aspects of Christian education that might arise" (p. 164). In this work he contends that "Christian education rests on a series of theoretical and practical foundations, on a series of assumptions about the Church, the family, the person, and their respective roles in the total education of the parish community" (p. 174).

Influenced by the writings of C. Ellis Nelson and John Westerhoff, Boojamra has made socialization the primary concept to provide foundations for planning Orthodox Christian education. The primary focus for him is not the liturgy or school; he explains that "the entire Church is the educator, that each member—the Christian person—is a learner, and that the Church's life in all its aspects is the matrix for the educational ministry" (p. 7). Boojamra is critical of Orthodox education for focusing only on classroom education of children. He advances the idea that Orthodox education should be a lifelong socialization or formation in Christian faith. He finds support for this approach in the common-sense experience of the church and in the practice of early church fathers.

Socialization for Boojamra bespeaks a process by which Christians are integrated into the church. People become Christians "not by learning about Christianity but by being integrated into an existing Church through experiencing the rites, symbols, and stories of the community" (p. 31). He contends that *theosis,* the divinization of the person takes place not through a single event like baptism but as a process occurring in a community. Boojamra makes clear that while liturgy is at the heart of the socialization process, he still believes that liturgy has been emphasized to the exclusion of other aspects of Christian life, service, and witness. For him persons become socialized into Orthodox Christianity by interacting both bodily and mentally with "the values, attitudes, behavioral expectations, and symbols of the Church" (p. 36). He especially stresses the importance of interacting with works of art such as icons.

Within his socialization approach Boojamra devotes special attention to the role of the family in Orthodox education. Making the judgment that Orthodox educators have not applied adequate analyses and guidelines for family religious education, he draws on the Orthodox tradition as well as on social science and psychological concepts in proposing a family-centered education. He makes the strong case that:

> If [the Orthodox] do not maintain the home as the primary, though not exclusive, responsibility for the nurture of its children, then we are violating the theology we are so fond of touting. We will have a faith in one space and a family in another with no meaningful interaction; there will be no flesh on our theology, and theology without flesh is dead and deadly to its practitioners. (Boojamra, 1989, p. 98)

Boojamra cites the insights of St. Basil on the spiritual advantages of community life over solitary living. Living with others fulfills not only our physical needs but also affords us opportunities to be charitable, recognize our weaknesses, observe the commandments, maintain our motivation, and share in the gifts of others. The task of Orthodox Christian educators is to aid families to nurture healthy persons. For Boojamra this task is best done not through a schooling or instructional approach but through family-centered religious education. For him family-centered does not necessarily imply child-centered, for children are not essential for the family life. Though Boojamra makes this critical point, most of his treatment of family presumes the presence of children. He also brings a systems approach to the understanding of families. Boojamra unites spiritual and social science traditions in presenting the family as a source of trust and love, personhood and identity, and community and intimacy.

In his description of the developing moral person as the third foundation for Orthodox education, Boojamra makes a synthesis of biblical-patristic writings and the research of psychologists. While he finds some insights in the behaviorist approach of Skinner and the psychoanalytic approach of Erikson, he clearly favors the work of the developmentalists Piaget and Kohlberg. Their value for him lies in the fact that rationality is central in their theories of moral development, something that he finds deeply rooted in the Christian tradition. Boojamra's main criticism of behaviorism from the perspective of Christian education is that it does not deal with discernment, which is essential to the moral life. He judges as unhealthy many of the ways that the Church has used in the past to control behavior. That is why Boojamra finds some value in the psychoanalytic approach since it deals with the important concept of modeling, strongly supported in the New Testament and the writings of the Fathers.

Moreover, Boojamra unearths evidence for a developmental perspective in the New Testament and the fathers. The letters of Paul stressed the importance of thinking, understanding, and reasoning. The fathers claimed that it is reason and not custom upon which people are to be judged. Further, patristic writers locate the image of God in human reason. Boojamra's reading of the tradition is that "personhood is based on awareness and self-understanding and no one is born with it fully developed. Personhood, image of God, and moral development are intimately tied together" (p. 117). For him the patristic anthropology is one "in which moral reasoning, as the ability to reason generally, develops slowly and in stages" (p. 121).

Lawrence Kohlberg's theory of moral development through specified stages receives extended treatment in Boojamra's foundations. Though aware of some of the criticisms leveled against Kohlberg, he still finds value in the theory because "it seems congenial to elements of patristic anthropology—process, personhood, self-knowledge, and the natural differences among people" (p. 131). Kohlberg's theory, according to Boojamra, is convenient for discussing moral development and education for Orthodox Christians. He does, however, note that moral education for Orthodox Christians should also have an affective dimension and thus is drawn back to the integration of Kohlberg's approach with behavioral and psychoanalytic considerations.

Boojamra concludes his work on foundations by drawing some

conclusions for the practice of Orthodox education. From the foundation of the church as socializer he states that "the Church's rituals, and stories—its traditions—must be vigorous, reasonable, alive, and obvious to all, and all must have a share in them. It is as simple as kissing an icon, making a procession, partaking of the eucharist" (p. 167). The church's rites should be carried into the home through icon centers, Bible readings, prayers, and Christian service to others. Likewise, the church should foster family life by encouraging an active family ministry by providing for support groups, family specialists, libraries, and parent or family meetings. Finally, Boojamra opines that educators and parents can respect the developing person by using methods that are suitable to the needs, interests, and abilities of learners.

Boojamra's approach to Orthodox education permeates the philosophy of the Orthodox Christian Education Commission. As the executive director of the commission he outlined the Total Parish Education program as one based on developmental foundations that is also true to the experience centeredness needed in Orthodox education (*Total Parish Education,* n.d.).

A noteworthy attempt to translate and embody Orthodox theology and spirituality into curriculum has been the *Living Our Orthodox Faith* textbook series of the Greek Orthodox Church. Under the direction of Ernest Villas this series has tried to combine orthodoxy (the content of Orthodox faith) and orthopraxis (the living of the Orthodox faith). These dimensions are sustained within the life of worship, community, discipleship, service, and witness. The series has articulated the purpose of Orthodox Christian education:

> The Purpose of Orthodox Christian Education is to help build up the Church, the Body of Christ, by nurturing every person in the life of personal communion with the Holy Trinity, and this, through this ministry, to bear joyful witness to God's living and redeeming work in the world. Being only one part of the total life of the Church, Christian education is effective in the context of living faith in the home and the local parish. Living faith is concretely expressed through all believers—bishops, priests, parents, teachers, parish leaders, youth leaders, and all Orthodox Christians seeking to know and to live the new life in Christ by the power of the Holy Spirit. (In Vrame, 1999, p. 11)

Anton Vrame (1996) has given a careful and thoughtful analysis of this comprehensive statement. He contends that it marks the beginning of an approach within Orthodox thought that stresses an integrated curriculum, narrative presentations, experience-based teaching, and involvement of learners.

The most recent attempt to present a full theory for Orthodox Christian education is found in Vrame's *The Educating Icon* (1999). In this work he has offered a profound and clearly written theology of Orthodox education that may well guide educators and curriculum planners for years to come. Vrame builds on the theoretical works of Schmemann, Tarasar, and Boojamra "through the exploration of the educational potential of the iconic aspect of our Tradition with respect to both its theory and its ability to direct our paths as educators" (p. 13). He argues that catechesis is the best term for Orthodox religious education, viewing it as a process of socialization, education, liturgical, sacramental, ethical, and moral cultivation, and devotional life within the context of the ecclesial community" (p. 20).

The purpose of his work is clearly stated. It develops "a series of principles that form the basis of catechetical endeavors in the Orthodox Church. These principles are suggested by the artistic style of the icons, the use of icons in the life of the church, the theology of icons, and the place of icons in the lives of the people who interact through them for spiritual nourishment" (p. 2). Drawing on the academic disciplines of church history, theology, liturgical studies, philosophical anthropology, philosophy of art, cultural anthropology, and educational theory, Vrame propounds a reasoned but passionate description and explanation of theological and educational principles for Orthodox catechesis.

In a careful manner Vrame has reviewed the iconoclastic controversy to clarify the theological and educational principles involved in the disputes. The resolution of the conflict in favor of the use of icons established important principles about Christ, human nature, the goodness of matter, and the nature of worship. Icons differ from ordinary paintings in that they derive their form from spiritual vision, understanding, and content. Educational implications of the controversy are that icons are "books equal to the Scriptures" in their catechetical value, that icons engage the entire person both cognitively and emotionally, and that they call persons to "iconic living" or a life of virtue in imitation of what is portrayed in the icon.

The aims of iconic catechesis for Vrame are summed up in iconic living and knowing. He identifies iconic living and knowing with *theosis,* the ultimate destiny of humans, their participation in or union with

God. Vrame establishes a philosophy of persons based on Orthodox theological anthropology. Persons are unique, free, and relational human beings that possess a potential to develop into creative and loving beings. Aware of the dangers of a preoccupation among educators with reason and rationality, Vrame sees icons as pushing individuals beyond the rational since they:

> Capture, portray, create and express a realm of human experience that extends beyond the rational and speak to all aspects of the person. Words and concepts cannot fully express on their own, what can be expressed in and through the icon. (p. 81–82)

In his treatment of iconic knowing or epistemology Vrame connects the Orthodox tradition not only with the philosophy of persons but also with a philosophy of art. Icons are presented as works of art that are expressive in their language. These sacred images have the potential of engaging persons at various levels. They convey knowledge; they fire the imagination; they activate memories; and they present a body experience. Icons invite persons into the *theosis,* communion or fellowship with God that Orthodox theologians have presented as the heart of Orthodox living and education. Thus icons offer and embody a vision of divine life by depicting what it means to be a holy or deified person. Vrame anticipates the objection that iconic catechesis may merely invite person to copy the holy lives of others and not develop their unique selves in freedom.

Vrame deals with the issue of the curriculum of iconic catechesis, that is, how icons might educate a person in faith, by probing the notions of sacred place, time, presence, and communion. While the visible curriculum in iconic catechesis is the icons, the invisible curriculum is the value system that guides the catechesis. Icons imaging the divine are found in sacred places, in homes, and in churches. Icons draw the beholders to the sacred time of sacred history, the sacred present in which Christians live, and the future time of eternal life. To be face to face with an icon is to be face to face with the sacred presence of the divine, including the presence of Christ and the saints.

From educational theory Vrame adopts the axiom that the processes involved in education are informing, forming, and transforming. He then explains how iconic catechesis is involved in these three processes, utilizing examples of particular icons that convey deep theological truths. Iconic catechesis gives information by telling in pictorial form the story of the community and by presenting "the values of the Church, and the Church's interpretation of the story which has been transmitted through texts, homilies, hymns and customs" (p. 141). Vrame recognizes that believers need the guidance of catechists in getting at the truth and proper interpretations of the icons.

Tapping into socialization theory Vrame explains how the icons form believers in the faith. Appealing to both John Dewey and Clifford Geertz, he demonstrates how icons speak to the heart and affect the perceptions of believers. He shows how through participation in the liturgies of the church believers develop the attitudes and values of what they perceive in the deeply symbolic rites and icons. For Vrame "liturgical services in an icon-filled environment can provide this intense ordering of experience, directing the heart to respond to its understanding of the event—a powerful formative experience" (p. 149).

Vrame makes a strong case that iconic catechesis can not only inform and form believers but also contributes to personal, social, and even cosmic transformation. Iconic catechesis invites believers to *metanoia* or personal transformation because, in the words of the educational philosopher Maxine Greene, "as works of art they move people to critical awareness, to a sense of moral agency, and to a conscious engagement with the world" (p. 161). Recognizing that Orthodoxy has been criticized for its lack of social teaching and social awareness, Vrame describes liturgy and iconic catechesis as actions for the life of world that have the potential for raising both social and political consciousness about forms of oppression in the world. Finally, he asserts that iconic catechesis is most suited to promote cosmic and ecological transformation because of the respect that it engenders for the created universe.

In concluding his work Vrame develops the notion that in Orthodoxy catechesis or education in faith can be viewed as a sacrament. For him the notion of sacrament, richly described, sums up what he has said about iconic catechesis. Iconic catechesis conveys the uncreated and invisible life of divine grace through the instrumentality of created and visible works of art. Vrame explains how this might be done in families, parishes, and classrooms. For him parents and catechists should view themselves as "icons for the Tradition for their learners" (p. 194). They do this by imitating the:

> Qualities of icons, their openness, their ability to engage believers, to speak to their hearts, patiently and silently awaiting the response of those who encounter them. Just as the aim of the icon is to lead the

viewer to the person depicted and not remain fixed on the icon, so the aim of teachers is not to draw attention to themselves but to point learners to Christ. (p. 195)

Summary

Orthodox Christian education has its deepest roots in the Scriptures, the writings of early church fathers, and the theology expressed in the first five ecumenical councils of the church. Education in the Byzantine Empire was comprised of an inner learning that was theological and mystical and an outer learning that revolved around Greek classical authors. With the fall of Byzantium, Orthodox churches adopted many Western ideas and practices. A far-reaching renewal in the nineteenth century took place first in Russian Orthodoxy and then in other Orthodox churches. Orthodox Christian education in the United States has in recent years received strong theoretical foundations in the writings of Orthodox Christians who have attempted to correlate the Orthodox tradition with contemporary modes of thought.

Epilogue

As the Christian church enters a new millennium it is appropriate to look both back and forward at Christian education. Reviewing the history of Christian education one can discern a pattern of dialogue and dialectic with emerging cultures and cultural changes. This dialogue and dialectic has been motivated by a desire to remain faithful to a living tradition as well as to adapt this tradition to changed situations. Out of this dialogue and dialectic there arose the different forms, theories, and movements in Christian education described in this book. From this historical perspective one can also project what forms Christian education might take in the beginning years of the new millennium as it confronts new situations.

Although Christian education emerged in a Jewish culture it soon had to dialogue with and enter into a dialectic with Greco-Roman culture. The beginnings of this confrontation between Christianity and culture are found in the canonical writings where the efforts of the Apostle Paul are described in some detail. Early church scholars such as Augustine, Origin, and Basil continued this task of refashioning Christian theology and education into the language and cultural forms of the Greco-Roman world. What came from this effort was a mode of Christian theology and education in which rational categories of philosophy played a prominent part.

With the establishment of Christianity as the religion of the Roman Empire, Christian education faced a major challenge: how to maintain the purity of faith and education in light of the changed social status and civic responsibility of many Christians. One form of Christian life that attempted to maintain this purity was monasticism, in which a decidedly spiritual form of education prevailed. Monasteries, which originated during the period of Christian persecution in the Roman Empire, spread throughout the lands and gave rise to a distinctive form of Christian education that concentrated on a spiritual and mystical approach to Christian life. While in some cases monastic education ignored the Greco-Roman culture, in other situations it developed careful and guarded approaches to the classical writings.

This tension between a rational and a mystical form of education is found throughout the medieval period. In the West, while scholastic philosophers and theologians attempted to deal with the new cultural situation occasioned by the introduction of Aristotle and the need for an education for a world of church involvement in trade and political life, spiritual educators attempted to maintain the purity of the tradition by stressing prayer and meditation on the principal writings of the Christian tradition. In the East an inner or mystical education at times supplemented and at other times replaced the outer education that was based on the classical writings. The presence of the same theological tension in both the East and the West may be a sign that the division in Christianity between East and West, between Eastern Orthodoxy and Western Christianity, might owe more to political and social factors than to theology and culture.

The rise of Renaissance humanism in the West, a broad cultural movement reflecting the values of a new class seeking a more worldly education than provided by the scholastics, occasioned another change in Christian education. Christian humanists used education in the classics to form Christian men and women who could assume leadership roles in church and society. The primary humanist goal was to educate persons who, rooted in Christian faith and piety, would take up responsible positions in society. All human learning and endeavors were encompassed in this education.

The tumultuous events surrounding what has come to be called the Protestant Reformation gave rise to multiple forms of education in the West. Protestant reformers, while basically true to humanist principles, stressed an education through biblical literacy, congregational singing in the vernacular, catechisms, and a minimum of ritual. Distinctive approaches to Christian education were developed by Puritans, Methodists, and Quakers. The humanist education that characterized the Catholic Counter Reformation manifested itself in the efforts of the Jesuits and other religious orders who placed paramount emphasis on the authoritative teaching of the Roman Catholic Church and its ritual celebrations. Both of these forms of Christianity grappled with the beginnings of the modern world of vernacular languages, the invention of printing, and increased political conflicts in the countries of Europe.

The greatest challenge to Christian education in the second millennium was undoubtedly the various strains of the Enlightenment. Both Protestant and Catholic educators were challenged by thinkers who dethroned authority and tradition in order to extol the virtues of reason and experience. Rationalism, romanticism, and empiricism offered multiple challenges to theologians and educators who appealed to the authority of the Bible or the tradition of the church as decisive in matters of faith and morality. Those Enlightenment figures who did not totally reject religion fashioned a reasonable faith that they felt adequately reconciled the demands of the tradition with the demands of reason and experience. In the nineteenth and twentieth centuries Christian theologians and educators took up the challenges of Enlightenment thought.

The Orthodox churches in the East for the most part remained unaffected at this time by Reformation struggles and Enlightenment thought. Attempting to maintain their Orthodox tradition these churches remained committed to liturgical and mystical forms of education. Eastern Orthodoxy changed greatly as its central focus moved from Constantinople to Russia. Education in the monasteries and the influence of spiritual ascetics preserved a rich tradition of theology, spirituality, and education.

Religious educators in the newly formed United States of America were heirs to the theological and educational battles of Europe. Early education in this country was fashioned out of the humanist Reformation education. Renaissance and Reformation humanism as well as Enlightenment thought made up the educational legacy out of which the various strands of education in the New World were formed. Colonial education, however, was largely controlled by sectarian groups such as the Puritans, Quakers, and Methodists, rather than the dominant religious groups in Europe, namely, Roman Catholicism, Anglicanism, and Lutheranism. While these groups replicated many of the religious forms of education of the old country they also utilized religious revivals and a transformed Sunday school. Furthermore, these churches were instrumental in fostering the common school movement, which in its early days provided a nondenominational Protestant religious education for children.

In the United States in the nineteenth century dramatic changes in the culture brought about by industrialization, immigration, and urbanization spawned additional forms of religious education for Protestants as well as for the increasing number of immigrant Catholics. While periodic evangelical revivals characterized Protestantism and led often to the establishment of Sunday schools and denominational colleges and seminaries, Catholics put much effort into creating an entire system of education from parish primary schools up to universities and seminaries.

Influenced by the progressive movement in politics and education and the liberal theologies developing in Europe and the United States, Protestant educators in the twentieth century mounted a powerful movement to make religious education both a profession and an academic discipline. Professional organizations and journals marked the coming of age of Protestant religious education, a development that would take place among Catholics and Orthodox Christians in the latter half of the century. Vatican II constituted a watershed for the development of Catholic theology and religious education, giving rise to movements in liturgy, ecumenism, and catechetics. Orthodox developments were inspired by the revival of Orthodox theology and spirituality among scholars and educators in Europe and the United States.

A knowledge of history certainly helps us understand the past and how the past has shaped the present. It may enable us to understand present challenges and move toward a more hopeful future. Looking back over the history of Christian education affords us some perspectives or principles for conducting Christian education in the future. By examining the educational thought and forms of past centuries we gain a wisdom that fortifies us for present-day and future challenges, for as one prominent historian noted history teaches everything including the future.

Christian educators need to be rooted in a knowledge of the Christian tradition found in the biblical writings and the thought of myriad witnesses to the Christian tradition. But a rootedness in the past should not prevent an openness to a transformation of or improvement on this tradition. A knowledge of past developments in Christian education shows convincingly that there is always the possibility for new approaches for dealing with the tradition. Among those in previous centuries who transformed Christian education one can point out Origin, Augustine, Basil, Abelard, Thomas Aquinas, Luther, Calvin, Erasmus, and Ignatius. Closer to our own times we have the example of Newman, Coe, Fahs, Miller, Moran, Groome, and Vrame. The contemporary scene is replete with the thought of Christian educators who explore the implications for religious education of ecumenism, multi-culturalism, feminism, and postmodernism.

Christian education in our time needs to deal seriously with the continuing divisions that exist among the Christian churches. The ecumenical movement among Christian churches has been a dominant event in the second half of the twentieth century. As we move into the next millennium one can question the continuance of centuries-old theological differences among Christian churches. Fortunately there have been mergers, doctrinal agreements, and fruitful dialogue among churches that have softened past theological positions. While Christian unity still remains a distant ideal, Christian educators can foster its achievement through a religious education that focuses on common beliefs and deals respectfully with beliefs and practices about which there are still differences.

As the United States increasingly becomes a multicultural society that includes both Christian and non-Christian faiths, religious educators face even greater challenges. In recent years a fruitful dialogue among Christian and Jewish religious leaders and educators has led to greater and mutual understanding of both religious traditions and the potential for cooperation in social and community causes. Christian educators have become aware that the Christian tradition includes many teachings and events that have portrayed the Jewish faith in a negative light. Although greater sensitivity toward this history has been manifested in curricular materials developed in recent years, much still needs to be done in Christian education to present in an honest and authentic manner both Judaism and the often sad history of Christian-Jewish relations.

Additional challenges face Christian educators in dealing with the various forms of Islam as well as with Buddhism, Hinduism, and Confucianism. Many of the more recent immigrants to this country profess one of these faiths. Even though Christian educators in this country have even less familiarity with these world religions, a place must be found in the curriculum of Christian education for a fair presentation of the principal tenets and practices of these faiths. Educators can be guided in this endeavor by an examination of materials in use for the past thirty years in the United Kingdom, where studies in world religions have been included in school curriculum.

At a more theoretical level Christian educators have begun to take up the challenge of postmodernist thought as it affects religious education. Postmodernism is a broad cultural movement that questions many Enlightenment ideas that have formed the basis of modern culture. Postmodern ideas have had influence in art, architecture, science, philosophy, and theology. Postmodernists challenge the guiding assumptions and primary projects of the cultural leaders of the Western world in the past three centuries. These thinkers question many of our cherished beliefs about how we arrive a knowledge, our view of nature, and our interpretation of the society in which we live.

The task for Christian educators is to take up the challenge of these ideas as Christian educators in the past dealt with other influential movements. While some forms of postmodernism are destructive and even bordering on pessimism and nihilism, there also are forms that can be termed constructive and emancipatory. Some theologians see a convergence between postmodernism and forms of liberation theology as well as process theology. Educators in the Christian churches who see their task not only as conserving a tradition but also in enriching it will not fear grappling with new cultural movements.

References

Abbott, Walter. (Ed.). (1966). *The documents of Vatican II. Declaration on religious liberty.* New York: America Press.

Adamson, J. W. (1971, 1905). *Pioneers of modern education in the seventeenth century.* New York: Teachers College Press.

Alexander, M. Van Cleave. (1980). *The growth of English education, 1348–1648: A social and cultural history.* University Park, PA: The Pennsylvania State University Press.

Anderson, R. D. (1975). *Education in France, 1848–1970.* Oxford: Clarendon Press.

Apostolic Fathers. (1952). Volume I (Kirsopp Lake, Trans.). Cambridge, MA: Harvard University Press.

Augustine, A. (1926). *De catechizandis rudibus* (J. Christopher, Trans.). Washington, DC: Catholic University Press.

Augustine, A., Bishop of Hippo. (1996). *Teaching Christianity: De doctrina Christiana* (Edmund Hill, Trans.). Hyde Park, New York: New City Press.

Axtell, J. (1976). *The school upon the hill: Education and society in colonial New England.* New York: Norton.

Barclay, W. (1959). *Training a child: Educational ideals in the ancient world.* Philadelphia: Westminster Press.

Barnard, H. C. (1969). *Education and the French revolution.* Cambridge: Cambridge University Press.

Beck, George. (1964). Aims in education: Neo Thomism. In T. H. B. Hollins (Ed.), *Aims in education: The philosophic approach.* Manchester: University of Manchester Press.

Becker, Carl, L. (1959). *The heavenly city of eighteenth century philosophers.* New Haven, CT: Yale University Press.

Bellah, Robert N. (1970). *Beyond belief: Essays on religion in a post-traditional world.* New York: Harper and Row.

Bellah, Robert N., & Hammond, Philip E. (Eds.). (1982). *Varieties of civil religion*. San Francisco: Harper and Row.

Boethius. (1969). *The consolation of philosophy*. (V. E. Watts, Trans.). London: Penguin Classics.

Bonaventure, Saint (1956). *The journey of the mind to God*. Edited with Introduction and Notes by Stephen F. Brown. Indianapolis, IN: Hackett Publishing Co.

Boojamra, John. (1989). *Foundations for orthodox Christian education*. Crestwood, NY: St. Vladimir's Seminary Press.

Bowen, James. (1972). *A history of western education, Volume 1: The ancient world*. New York: St. Martin's Press.

Bowen, James. (1975). *A history of western education: Volume 2: Civilization of Europe: Sixth to the sixteenth century*. New York: St. Martin's Press, 1975.

Bowen, James. (1981). *A history of western education. Volume 3: The modern world*. New York: St. Martin's Press.

Bower, William Clayton. (1925). *The curriculum of religious education*. New York: Scribner.

Boys, Mary C. (1979). Access to traditions and transformation. In Padraic O'Hare (Ed.), T*radition and transformation in religious education*. Birmingham, AL: Religious Education Press.

Boys, Mary C. (1980). *Biblical interpretation in religious education: A study of the kerygmatic era*. Birmingham, AL: Religious Education Press.

Boys, Mary C. (1989). *Educating in faith: Maps and visions*. San Francisco: Harper and Row.

Brinton, H. H. (1958). *Quaker education in theory and practice*. Wallingford, PA: Pendle Hill.

Broudy, Harry, & Palmer, Robert. (1965). *Exemplars of teaching method*. Chicago: Rand McNally.

Brown, D. (1978). *Understanding Pietism*. Grand Rapids, MI.: Eerdsmans Publishing Co.

Brown, G. (1990). Reformed education. In Iris V. Cully & Kendig Brubaker Cully (Eds.), *Harper's encyclopedia of religious education* (pp. 542–543). San Francisco: Harper and Row.

Brueggemann, W. (1982). *The creative word: Canon as a model for biblical education*. Philadelphia: Fortress Press.

Bruni, L. (1987). *The humanism of Leonard Bruni*. Binghamton, NY: Medieval and Renaissance Texts and Studies.

Bryk, Anthony S., Lee, Valerie E., & Holland, Peter B. (1993). *Catholic schools and the common good*. Cambridge MA: Harvard University Press.

Burgess, Harold William. (1975). *An invitation to religious education*. Birmingham, AL: Religious Education Press.

Burtchaell, James. (1998). *The dying of the light: The disengagement of col-*

leges and universities from their Christian churches. Grand Rapids, MI: Eerdsmans Publishing Co.

Bushnell, Horace. (1967, 1847). *Christian nurture.* New Haven, CT: Yale University Press.

Cantor, Nicholas. (1993). *The civilization of the Middle Ages.* New York: Harper Collins.

Carlson, Robert. (1975). *The quest for conformity: Americanization through education.* New York: John Wiley.

Castle, E. B. (1958). *Educating the good man.* New York: Collier Books.

Channing, William. (1838). *The Sunday school.* Boston: James Munroe.

Charlton, K. (1965). *Education in renaissance England.* London: Routledge and Kegan Paul.

Chisick, H. (1981), *The limits of reform in the enlightenment: Attitudes toward the education of the lower classes in eighteenth-century France.* Princeton, NJ: Princeton University Press,

Clarke, Norris. (1979). *The philosophical approach to God: Neo Thomistic perspective.* Winston-Salem, NC: Wake Forest University Press.

Coates, Wilson H., White, Hayden V., & Schapiro, J. Salwyn. (1966). *The emergence of liberal humanism, an intellectual history of Western Europe.* New York: McGraw Hill.,

Coe, George Albert. (1917). *A social theory of religious education.* New York: Scribner.

Coe, George Albert (1929). *What is Christian education?* New York: Scribner.

Copleston, Frederick. (1960). *A history of philosophy: Vol. VI: Wolff to Kant.* Westminster, MD: Newman Press.

Cremin, Lawrence A. (1970). *American education: The colonial experience, 1607–1783.* New York: Harper and Row.

Cremin, Lawrence A. (1980). *American education: The national experience, 1783–1876.* New York: Harper and Row.

Cully, Kendig Brubaker. (Ed.). (1960). *Basic writings in Christian education.* Philadelphia: Westminster Press.

Cully, Kendig Brubaker. (1965). *The search for a Christian education-since 1940.* Philadelphia: Westminster Press.

Cully, Iris V., & Cully, Kendig Brubaker. (Eds.). (1990). *Harper's encyclopedia of religious education.* San Francisco: Harper and Row.

Donohoe, J. (1958) *St. Thomas and education.* New York: Random House.

Donohoe, John. (1973). *Catholicism and education.* New York: Harper and Row

Dulles, Avery. (1997). Theological education in the Catholic tradition. In Patrick W. Carey & Earl C. Muller (Eds.). *Theological education in the Catholic tradition: Contemporary challenges.* New York: Crossroad.

Dunning, James B. (1979). The rite of Christian initiation of adults: Model of adult growth. *Worship,* 52/3, 142–156.

Durka, Gloria. (1984). Women, power, and the work of religious education. In Marvin Taylor (Ed.), *Changing patterns of religious education.* Nashville, TN: Abingdon Press.

Durka, Gloria. (1990). Aesthetics. In Iris V. Cully & Kendig Brubaker Cully (Eds.). *Harper's encyclopedia of religious education* (pp. 18–20). San Francisco: Harper and Row.

Dykstra, Craig, & Parks, Sharon. (Eds.). (1986). *Faith development and Fowler.* Birmingham, AL: Religious Education Press.

Edwards, Jonathan. (1959, 1743). *A treatise concerning religious affections.* (John E. Smith, Ed.). New Haven, CT: Yale University Press.

Elias, John L. (1999). Whatever happened to Catholic philosophy of education? *Religious Education,* 94, 1, 92–110.

Elliot, Harrison. (1940). *Can religious education be Christian?* New York: Macmillan.

Ellis, John Tracy. (1955). American Catholics and the intellectual life. *Thought* 30, 351–399.

Erasmus, D. (1965). *Christian humanism and the reformation: Selected writings of Erasmus* (John C. Olin, Ed.). New York: Harper and Row.

Fahs, Sophie L. (1952). *Today's children and yesterday's heritage.* Boston: Beacon.

Fedotov, George P. (1956). *The Russian religious mind.* Cambridge: MA: Harvard University Press.

Fennell, John. (1995). *A history of the Russian church to 1448.* London: Longman.

Fichte, Johann. (1979, 1808) *Address to the German nation.* (R. F. Jones & G. H. Turnbull, Trans.). New York: Greenwood Press.

Fitzpatrick, John. (Ed) (1933). *St. Ignatius and the Ratio Studiorum.* New York: McGraw Hill.

Foster, Charles, R. (1982). The faith community as a guiding image for Christian education. In Jack Seymour & Donald Miller et al., *Contemporary approaches: Christian education.* Nashville, TN: Abingdon Press.

Foster, Charles R. (1994). *Educating Christians: The future of Christian education.* Nashville, TN: Abingdon Press.

Fowler, James. (1982). *Stages of faith.* San Francisco: Harper and Row.

Freire, Paulo. (1970). *Pedagogy of the oppressed.* New York: Seabury.

Freire, Paulo. (1973). *Education for critical consciousness.* New York: Seabury.

Fuller, E. (Ed.). (1957). *The Christian idea of education.* New Haven, CT: Yale University Press.

Gaebelein, Frank E. (1967a). *A varied harvest,* Grand Rapids, MI: Eerdsmans Publishing Co.

Gaebelein, Frank E. (1967b, 1951). *Christian education in a democracy.* New York: Oxford University Press.

Gallin, Alice. (Ed.). (1992). *American Catholic higher education: Essential documents, 1967–1990.* Notre Dame, IN: Notre Dame.

Gangel, Kenneth O. (1978). Christian higher education at the end of the twentieth century. *Bibliotheca Sacra,* 100–105.

Gay, P. (1966). *The enlightenment: An interpretation: The rise of modern paganism.* New York: Random House.

General catechetical directory. (1971). Washington, DC: United States Catholic Conference.

General education in a free society: Report of the Harvard committee. (1945). Cambridge, MA: Harvard University Press.

Gilson, Etienne. (1991,1936). *The spirit of medieval philosophy.* Notre Dame, IN: Notre Dame University Press.

Gilson, Etienne. (1952). *The breakdown of morals and Christian education.* Toronto: St. Michael's College.

Gleason, Philip. (1992). American Catholic higher education, 1940–1990: The ideological context. In George M. Marsden & Bradley J. Longfield (Eds.), *The secularization of the academy.* New York: Oxford University Press.

Gleason, Philip. (1995). *Contending with modernity: Catholic education in the twentieth century.* New York: Oxford University Press.

Good, H. G., & Teller, J. D. (1969). *A history of western education* (3rd ed.). New York: Macmillan.

Goodman, Anthony, & McKay, Angus. (1990) *The impact of humanism on western Europe.* New York: Longman.

Grafton, Anthony, & Jardine, Louise. (1986). *From humanism to the humanities.* Cambridge, MA: Harvard University Press.

Grattan, C. Harley. (Ed.). (1959). *American ideas about adult education, 1710–1951.* New York: Teachers College Press.

Greaves, R. L. (1972). *The puritan revolution and educational thought.* New Brunswick, NJ: Rutgers University Press.

Groome, Thomas H. (1980). *Christian religious education*: *Sharing our story and vision.* San Francisco: Harper and Row.

Groome, Thomas H. (1993). *Sharing the faith.* San Francisco: Harper and Row.

Halsey, M. (1980). *The survival of American innocence: Catholicism in an era of disillusionment, 1920–1940.* Notre Dame, IN: Notre Dame Press.

Harris, Maria. (1987). *Teaching and the religious imagination.* San Francisco: Harper and Row.

Harris, Maria. (1988). *Women and teaching: Themes for a spirituality of teaching.* New York: Paulist Press.

Harris, Maria. (1989). *Fashion me a people.* Louisville, KY: Westminster/John Knox.

Haskins, C. H. (1955, 1927). *The renaissance of the 12th century.* New York: World Publishing Co.

Haskins, C. H. (1957, 1923). *The rise of universities.* Ithaca, NY: Cornell University Press.

Hellwig, Monika K. (1997). Theological education in the undergraduate core curriculum. In Patrick Carey & Earl C. Muller (Eds.), *Theological education in the Catholic tradition: Contemporary challenges.* New York: Crossroad.

Hofinger, Johannes. (1957). *The art of teaching Christian doctrine.* Notre Dame, IN: Notre Dame Press.

Hole, Helen G. (1978). *Things civil and useful: A personal view of Quaker education.* Richmond, IN: Friends United Press.

Howie, G. (1969). *Educational theory and practice in St. Augustine.* New York: Teachers College Press.

Hugh of St. Victor. (1961). *The didascalicon of Hugh of St. Victor: A medieval guide to the arts* (Jerome Taylor, Trans.). New York: Columbia University Press.

Hussey, J. M. (1986). *The Orthodox church in the Byzantine empire.* Oxford: Clarendon Press.

Hutchins, Robert. (1999, 1936). *The higher learning in America.* Piscataway, NJ.

Jaeger, C. Stephen. (1994). *The envy of angels: Cathedral schools and social ideals in medieval Europe, 950–1200.* Philadelphia: University of Pennsylvania Press.

Jaeger, Werner. (1961). *Early Christianity and Greek paideia.* Cambridge, MA: Harvard University Press.

John of Salisbury. (1962). *The metalogicon of John of Salisbury: A twelfth-century defense of the logical and verbal arts of the trivium* (Daniel D. McGarry, Trans.). Berkeley: University of California Press.

John Paul II. (1980). *Catechesi tradendae.* Washington, DC: United States Catholic Conference.

John Paul II. (1991). Ex corde Ecclesiae. *Current Issues in Catholic Higher Education,* 31–42.

Johnson, William H. E. (1969). *Russia's educational heritage.* New York: Octagon Books.

Jungmann, Josef. (1962, 1936). *The good news yesterday and today.* New York: Sadlier.

Kaestle, Carl F. (1983). *Pillars of the republic: Common schools and American society, 1788–1860.* New York: Hill and Wang.

Kant, Immanuel. (1960). *Education.* Ann Arbor, MI: University of Michigan Press.

Keely, Barbara Anne. (Ed.) (1997). *Faith of our foremothers: Women changing religious education.* Louisville, KY: Westminster/John Knox.

Kelley, Donald R. (1991). *Renaissance humanism.* Boston: G. K. Hall and Co.

Kelty, Brian. (1999). Toward a theology of Catholic education. *Religious Education,* 94, 1, 6–23.

Kennedy, William. (1986). Ideology and education: A fresh approach for religious education. *Religious Education,* 80, 3, 331–344.

Kimball, Bruce. (1995). *Orators and philosophers: A history of the idea of liberal education.* Expanded Edition. New York: The College Board.

Knowles, David. (1962). *The evolution of medieval thought.* New York: Random House.

Koulomzin, Sophie. (1975). *Our church and our children.* Crestwood, NY: Saint Vladimir's Seminary Press.

Kramer, R. (1978). *Maria Montessori.* Oxford: Blackwell.

Kristeller, Paul. (1961). *Renaissance thought: The classic, scholastic, and humanistic strains.* New York: Macmillan.

Kristeller, Paul. (1962). Studies on renaissance humanism during the past twenty years. *Studies in the Renaissance* 9.

Kung, Hans. (1968). *On being a Christian.* New York: Doubleday.

Langemann, Ellen Condliffe. (1983). *Private power for public good: A history of the Carnegie foundation for the advancement of teaching.* Middletown, CT: Wesleyan University.

Laurie, S. S. (1969, 1903). *Studies in the history of educational opinion from the renaissance.* New York: Augustus M. Kelley.

LeClerq, Jacques. (1959). *The love of God and desire for learning: A study of monastic culture.* New York: Fordham University Press.

Lee, James Michael. (1971). *The shape of religious education.* Birmingham, AL: Religious Education Press.

Lee, James Michael. (1973). *The flow of religious education.* Birmingham, AL: Religious Education Press.

Lee, James Michael. (1985). *The content of religious education.* Birmingham, AL: Religious Education Press.

LeGoff, Jacques. (1993, 1957). *Intellectuals in the middle ages.* Cambridge, MA: Blackwell.

Littell, Franklin. (1971). *From state church to pluralism.* New York: Doubleday.

Little, Sara. (1993). The clue to religious education. *Union Seminary Quarterly Review* 47, 7–21.

Locke, John. (1968). *The educational writings of John Locke.* (J. L. Axtell, Ed.). Cambridge, MA: Cambridge University Press.

Luther, Martin. (1962). *Luther's works,* 45, In W. I. Brandt (Ed.), *The Christian in society,* vol. 2 (p. 45). Philadelphia: Fortress Press.

Lynn, Robert Wood, & Wright, Elliot. (1971). *The big little school.* New York: Harper and Row.

Machiavelli, Niccolò. (1964, 1505). *The prince.* (Mark Musa, Trans.). New York: St. Martin's Press.

Mackenzie, M. (1908). *Hegel's educational theory and practice.* London: Longman.

Maloney, Edward F. (1973). A study of the religious orientation of the Catholic colleges and universities in New York State from 1962 to 1972. Ph.D. diss., New York University.

Maritain, Jacques. (1943). *Education at the crossroads.* New Haven, CT: Yale University Press.

Maritain, Jacques. (1955). Thomist views on education. In Nelson B. Henry (Ed.), *Modern philosophies of education.* Chicago: University of Chicago Press.

Marrou, H. I. (1956). *A history of education in antiquity.* New York: Sheed and Ward.

Marsden, George M. (1994). *The soul of the American university: From Protestant establishment to established nonbelief.* New York: Oxford University Press.

Marthaler, Berard L. (1978). Socialization as a model for catechesis. In Padraic O'Hare, (Ed.), *Foundations of religious education.* New York: Paulist Press.

Marthaler, Berard L. (1997). Catechesis isn't just for children anymore. In Patrick W. Carey & Earl C. Muller (Eds.), *Theological education in the Catholic tradition.* New York: Crossroad.

McBrien, Richard. (1981). *Catholicism.* Minneapolis, MN: Winston Press.

McCool, Gerald A. (1977). *Catholic theology in the nineteenth century: The quest for unitary method.* New York: Seabury/Crossroad.

McCool, Gerald. (1981). Education and the Catholic mind: Past and present. *Catholic Mind,* 27–38.

McGutchen, William J. (1942). The philosophy of Catholic education. In *Philosophies of education, forty-first yearbook of the National Society for the Study of Education. Part I.* Chicago: University of Chicago Press.

McLoughlin, William G. (1978). *Revivals, awakenings and reform: An essay on religion and social change in America, 1607–1977.* Chicago: University of Chicago Press.

Messerli, Jonathan. (1972). *Horace Mann: A biography.* New York: Knopf.

Metzger, Walter. (Ed.). (1977). *The American concept of academic freedom: A collection of essays and reports.* New York: Arno Press.

Meyendorff, John. (1979). *Byzantine theology: Historical themes and doctrinal trends.* New York: Fordham University Press.

Meyendorff, John. (1990). From Byzantium to the new world. In John Meyendorff (Ed.). *The legacy of St. Vladimir.* Crestwood, New York: St. Vladimir's Seminary Press.

Miller, Randolph Crump. (1950). *The clue to religious education.* New York: Scribner.

Miller, Randolph Crump. (1956). *Biblical theology and Christian education.* New York: Scribner.

Miller, Randolph Crump. (1961). *Christian nurture and the church.* New York: Scribner.

Moore, Allan. (1982). Liberation and the future of Christian education. In Jack Seymour & Donald Miller et al., *Contemporary approaches: Christian education.* Nashville, TN: Abingdon Press.

Moore, Allan. (1990). Methodist education. In Iris V. Cully and Kendig Brubaker Cully (Eds.), *Harper's encyclopedia of religious education* (pp. 408–411). San Francisco: Harper and Row.

Moore, Mary Elizabeth. (1983*). Education for continuity and change: A new model for Christian religious education.* Nashville, TN: Abingdon Press.

Moore, Mary Elizabeth Mullino. (1998). *Teaching from the heart: Theology and educational method.* Harrisburg, PA: Trinity Press International.

Moran, Gabriel. (1966a). *Catechesis of revelation.* New York: Herder and Herder.

Moran, Gabriel. (1966b). *Theology of revelation.* New York: Herder and Herder.

Moran, Gabriel. (1970). *Design for religion.* New York: Herder and Herder.

Moran, Gabriel. (1979). *Education toward adulthood.* New York: Paulist Press.

Moran, Gabriel. (1993). *Religious education as a second language.* Birmingham, AL: Religious Education Press.

More, Thomas. (1965, 1516). *The complete works of Thomas More.* Volume 4: *Utopia.* (E. Sturtz & J. M. Hextal, Eds. and Trans.). New Haven, CT: Yale University Press.

Morgan, Edmund S. (1966). *The puritan family: Religion and domestic relations in seventeenth century New England.* New York: Harper and Row.

Morgan, James. (1990). A work in progress. Catechumenate. *The Living Light.*

Morgan, John. (1986). *Godly learning: Puritan attitudes towards reason, learning, and education, 1560–1640.* Cambridge, MA: Cambridge University Press.

Murray, John Courtney. (1957). The Christian idea of education. In Edmund Fuller (Ed.), *The Christian idea of education.* New Haven, CT: Yale University Press.

Nelson, C. Ellis. (1967). *Where faith begins.* Richmond, VA: John Knox Press.

Newman, John. (1982, 1852). *The idea of a university.* Introduction and notes by Martin J. Svaglic. Notre Dame, IN: Notre Dame Press.

Nichols, Robert L. (1990). Filaret of Moscow as an ascetic. In John Meyendorff (Ed.), *The legacy of St. Vladimir.* Cresswood, NY: St. Vladimir's Seminary Press.

Nicozisin, George. (1977). *The road to Orthodox phronema: Christian education in the Greek Orthodox archdiocese of North and South America.* Brookline, MA: Greek Orthodox Archdiocese of North and South America, Department of Religious Education.

Niebuhr, H. Richard. (1991). *Christ and culture.* New York: Harper and Row.

Nord, Warren A. (1995). *Religion and American education: Rethinking a national dilemma.* Chapel Hill, NC: University of North Carolina Press.

O'Brien, David J. (1994). *From the heart of the American church: Catholic higher education and American culture.* Maryknoll, NY: Orbis Press.

O'Gorman, Robert T. (1997). The faith community. In Jack L. Seymour, *Mapping Christian education: Approaches to congregational learning.* Nashville, TN: Abingdon Press.

O'Hare, Padraic. (Ed.). (1983). *Education for peace and justice.* New York: Paulist.

Oleksa, Michael. (1983). The confluence of church and culture. In Constance J. Tarasar (Ed.), *Perspectives on Orthodox education.* Synosset, NY: Department of Religious Education of the Orthodox Church in America.

Olson, Paul A. (1995). *The journey to wisdom: Self-education in patristic and medieval literature.* Lincoln, NE: University of Nebraska Press.

O'Malley, John. (1993). *The first Jesuits.* Cambridge, MA: Harvard University Press.

Osmer, Richard Robert. (1990). *A teachable spirit: Recovering the teaching office of the church.* Louisville, KY: Westminster/John Knox.

Panofsky, Erwin. (1962). *Studies in iconology: Humanistic themes in the art of the Renaissance.* New York: Harper and Row.

Paul VI. (1974). *Evangelii nuntiandi.* Washington, DC: United States Catholic Conference.

Pius XI. (1929) *Divini illius magistri [On the Christian education of youth].* Washington, DC: National Catholic Educational Association.

Prince, John. (1926). *Wesley on religious education.* New York: The Methodist Book Concern.

Quasten, Johannes. (1992, 1950). *Patrology: Vol. I: The beginnings of patristic literature.* Westminster, MD: Christian Classics, Inc.

Richards, Lawrence. (1975). *Theology of Christian education.* Grand Rapids, MI: Zondervan.

Riche, Pierre. (1976, 1962). *Education and culture in the barbarian west: Sixth through eighth centuries.* (John J. Contreni, Trans.). Columbia, SC: University of South Carolina Press.

Rousseau, Jean Jacques. (1961). *Emile.* (Barbara Foxley, Trans.). New York: Everyman's Library.

Rudolph, Frederick. (Ed.). (1965). *Essays on education in the early republic.* Cambridge, MA: Harvard University Press.

Rummel, Erika. (Ed.). (1990). *Collected works of Erasmus: Literary and educational writings.* Toronto: University of Toronto Press.

Runciman, Steven. (1970). *The last Byzantine empire.* Cambridge, MA: Cambridge University Press.

Russell, Letty. (1984). Changing my mind about religious education. *Religious Education* 79, 5–10.

Sawicki, Marianne. (1988). *The gospel in history: Portrait of a teaching church: The origins of Christian education.* New York: Paulist Press.

Schaeffer, James. (1972). *Program planning for Christian adult education.* New York: Paulist Press.

Schipani, Daniel S. (1988). *Religious education encounters liberation theology.* Birmingham, AL: Religious Education Press.

Schmemann, Alexander. (1963). *The historical road of eastern Orthodoxy.* New York: Holt, Rinehart and Winston.

Schmemann, Alexander. (1974). *Liturgy and life: Christian education through liturgical experience.* Synosset, NY: Orthodox Church in America Department of Religious Education.

Schmidt, Stephen. (1983). *A history of the religious education association.* Birmingham, AL: Religious Education Press.

Schouls, Peter A. (1992). *Reasoned freedom: John Locke and enlightenment.* Ithaca, NY: Cornell University Press.

Schultz, Delbert. (1990). Lutheran education. In Iris V. Cully and Kendig Brubaker Cully (Eds.), *Encyclopedia of religious education.* San Francisco: Harper and Row.

Seymour, Jack L. (1997). *Mapping Christian education: Approaches to congregational learning.* Nashville, TN: Abingdon Press.

Seymour, Jack L., & Miller, Donald E. et al. (1982). *Contemporary approaches: Christian education.* Nashville, TN: Abingdon Press.

Seymour, Jack L., & Miller, Donald E. (Eds.). (1990). *Theological approaches to Christian education.* Nashville, TN: Abingdon Press.

Sloan, Doughlas. (1971). *The Scottish enlightenment and the American college ideal.* New York: Teachers College Press.

Sloan, Doughlas. (1994). *Faith and knowledge: Mainline Protestantism and American higher education.* Louisville, KY: Westminster/John Knox.

Sloyan, Gerard S. (Ed.). (1958). *Shaping the Christian messages: Essays in religious education.* New York: Macmillan.

Sloyan, Gerard S. (1960). *Modern catechetics: Essays in religious education.* New York: Macmillan.

Smart, James D. (1954). *The teaching ministry of the church.* Philadelphia: Westminster.

Smith, Gregory A. (1990). Quaker education. In Iris V. Cully and Kendig Brubaker Cully (Eds.), *Harper's encyclopedia of religious education* (pp. 529–530). San Francisco: Harper and Row.

Smith, H. Shelton. (1940). *Faith and nurture.* New York: Scribner.

Spitz, Lewis W. (1990). Humanism in Germany. In Anthony Goodman & Angus McKay, *The impact of humanism on western Europe.* New York: Longman.

Spring, Joel. (1986). *The American school, 1642–1985.* New York: Longmann.

Tarasar, Constance J. (1990). Orthodox education. In Iris V. Cully and Kendig Brubaker Cully (Eds.), *Harper's encyclopedia of religious education* (pp. 461–463). San Francisco: Harper and Row.

Tarasar, Constance J. (1994). The North American experience in Orthodox

Christian religious education. A paper presented at the Consultation on Orthodox Christian Education, held at Kykko Monastery in Cyprus.

Tarasar, Constance J. (n. d.) *Orthodox Christian education: A vision of life and way of life: Lectures and guidelines for priests and educators.* Unpublished manuscript.

Tierney, Brian. (1992). *The Middle Ages: Volume I: Sources of medieval history* (5th ed.). New York: McGraw Hill.

Total parish education: The curriculum of the Orthodox Christian Education Commission. (n. d.). Orthodox Christian Education Commission.

Toton, Suzanne C. (1982). *World hunger: The responsibility of the Christian educator.* Maryknoll, NY: Orbis.

Towns, Elmer L. (1970). John Wesley and religious education. *Religious Education* 64, 4, July-August.

Turner, Frank M. (Ed.). (1996). *John Henry Newman: The idea of a university.* New Haven, CT: Yale University Press.

Ulich, Robert. (Ed.). (1947). *Three thousand years of educational wisdom.* Cambridge, MA: Harvard University Press.

Ulich, Robert. (1968a). *History of educational thought.* New York: Van Nostrand.

Ulich, Robert. (1968b). *A history of religious education: Documents and interpretations from the Judaeo-Christian tradition.* New York: New York University Press.

United States Catholic Conference. (1976). *A vision of youth ministry.* Washington, DC: United States Catholic Conference.

Valliere, Paul, (1990). The liberal tradition in Russian Orthodox theology. In John Meyendorff (Ed.), *The legacy of St. Vladimir.* Cresswood, NY: St. Vladimir's Seminary Press.

Vernon, Walter. (1993). The Methodist church. In Iris V. Cully & Kendig Brubaker Cully (Eds.), *Westminster dictionary of Christian education* (pp.421–424). Philadelphia: Westminster Press.

Vieth, Paul. (1947). *The church and Christian education.* St. Louis, MO: Bethany Press.

Vives, Juan. (1908, 1531). *De tradendis disciplinis [The transmission of the arts].* (Foster Watson, Trans.). London: Dent.

Vrame, C. Anton. (1996). Forming Orthodox identity in the curriculum of the Greek Orthodox church. In John T. Chirban (Ed.), *Personhood: Orthodox Christianity and the connection between body, mind, and soul* (pp. 173–184). Westport, CT: Bergin and Garvey.

Vrame, C. Anton. (1999). *The educating icon: Teaching wisdom and holiness in the Orthodox way.* Brookline, MA: Holy Cross Orthodox Press.

Wallace, Ronald S. (1988). *Calvin, Geneva and the reformation.* Edinburgh, Scotland: Scottish Academic Press.

Ware, Timothy. (1990). Eastern Christendom. In John McManners (Ed.), *The Oxford history of Christianity.* New York: Oxford University Press.

Ware, Timothy. (1993). *The Orthodox church.* London: Penguin Books.

Warford, Malcolm. (1976). *The necessary illusion: Church culture and educational change.* Philadelphia: Pilgrim Press.

Warren, Michael. (1982). *Youth and the future of the church.* New York: Seabury Press.

Warren, Michael. (1997). *Seeing through the media: A religious view of communication and cultural analysis.* Philadelphia: Trinity Press International.

Welter, Rush. (1962). *Popular education and democratic thought in America.* New York: Columbia University Press.

Westerhoff, John. (1976). *Will our children have faith?* New York: Seabury.

Wollstonecraft, Mary. (1992, 1792). *A vindication of the rights of woman.* Edited with an Introduction by Miriam Brody. New York: Penguin Books.

INDEX OF PRINCIPAL NAMES

INDEX OF PRINCIPAL SUBJECTS